GET OUTTA HERE!

Travel Experiences, Adventures and Destinations from Around the Globe

Edited by
The Associated Press

The Associated Press
200 Liberty Street
New York, NY 10281
www.ap.org

Edited by Beth J. Harpaz
Project Management by Peter Costanzo
Design and Production by BNGO Books
Cover Design by Mike Bowser
Visit AP Books: www.ap.org/books
All photographs provided by AP Images: www.apimages.com

Brought to you by

CARNIVAL
CORPORATION & PLC.

CONTENTS

Part II
Destinations and Insider Guides   **165**

Contents

Appendix

INTRODUCTION

This collection of favorite travel stories from The Associated Press will take you around the world in 80 ways.

Share in unique experiences as we forage for supper in the English countryside, stay with a Peruvian family en route to Machu Picchu and ride the Trans-Siberian Railroad.

Join challenging adventures as we go mountain biking in North Dakota, trekking in Nepal and walking the highlands of Scotland.

And get the essentials, in a mere 800 words, for visiting a destination, whether it's highlights for an entire country like Ethiopia, a rock like Gibraltar, the state of Wisconsin or the city of Buenos Aires.

We'll also give you insider tips for enjoying favorite seasons and holidays, from fall foliage in New England to Mardi Gras in New Orleans.

We've got itineraries for themed trips, like a pilgrimage to Minneapolis in honor of Prince, or the hidden historic sites connected to "Hamilton," the hit Broadway musical.

In some cases, we've chosen to showcase less familiar destinations in the hopes of piquing your interest—like Guangzhou and Shenzhen in China, rather than Beijing and Shanghai.

In other cases, we feature well-known places like New York

and Tokyo, but we concentrate on demystifying these complicated cities with insider guides.

We've also thrown in two bonus sections, one about cruises and the other offering advice on saving time and money when you're planning trips or flying. The cruises section has tips for first-time cruisers, a look at small ships and insights from three experts on what's new in cruising and more. How-to travel topics include a guide to TSA Precheck and using credit cards to accumulate travel rewards.

Whether you're an armchair traveler or a globetrotter, we know you'll enjoy reading these dispatches, each written for The Associated Press by journalists who share destinations worthy of your time. And all were selected without any outside influence and represent the places we feel you just might want to know about.

One word of caution: Prices go up, attractions change, restaurants and other businesses move and sometimes even close over time. So be sure to check online for the places we recommend before you plan a trip.

We hope you'll find the stories inspiring and useful for planning your own travels. Now . . .

GET OUTTA HERE!

—*The Associated Press*

Listen to our podcast "Get Outta Here!" on iTunes at
http://apple.co/2s2ruHY

Follow us on Twitter at
@AP_Travel

**A MESSAGE FROM CARNIVAL CORPORATION,
A GLOBAL CRUISE COMPANY.**

Hitting the road, finding inspiration

When we pack our bags and hit the road, whether for pleasure or business, we are not always certain what we'll encounter. But from experience, we have learned that the journey and our destinations can have a lasting impact. If we allow ourselves, we open our eyes, our minds and our hearts to discovering new places, new adventures, new cultures and new people.

Whether our trip takes us into the mountains or onto the oceans, we make meaningful and sometimes unforgettable connections, often with family members and friends but also with complete strangers. And it is through our travel experiences that we learn to celebrate both our differences and our common ground, and often we learn we are much more alike than we ever realized.

This is only a small part of why travel is powerful, and so popular. Travel helps us look at the world in a new way, and can help make our own dreams and aspirations become clearer. We return home refreshed, inspired and rejuvenated, ready to more fully embrace our family, friends, passions and professions with new vigor while already contemplating our next great adventure.

PART I

EXPERIENCES, ADVENTURES AND THEMED TRIPS

EN ROUTE TO MACHU PICCHU:
A HOMESTAY IN PERU

By Fritz Faerber

OLLANTAYTAMBO, Peru—The nearly bare room had unadorned white walls and twin beds with thick, alpaca wool blankets beneath polyester covers. A shower curtain hung from a mop handle to screen off a small bathroom, but there was no hot water or heat.

On a small table with a single chair was something that turned these Spartan accommodations into a warm home for a night: four fresh red roses in a jar.

Luz Marina Bejar Romero cut them for me, her guest.

LIVING LIKE A LOCAL

I met Luz Marina in her hometown in the Sacred Valley of Peru, a place that tourists heading to Machu Picchu pass through. She and her son Rajoo lived down a dusty street in a small home surrounded by a high wall. They kept chickens, guinea pigs, ducks and a noisy turkey.

I was there for a homestay. At about $20 for a night with three meals included, it was a bargain. But for me, the real attraction was an opportunity to live like a local for a night and get to know my host family.

I chatted haltingly in Spanish with Rajoo about international soccer and his favorite player, Brazil's Neymar. I found similarities between him and my own son, separated by language, a few years and several thousand miles. They both loved soccer and sports, were budding naturalists and enjoyed math. We talked about the animals that live in the region and he asked about my home. Luz Marina chimed in from the kitchen where she was making a simple, tasty dinner of rice and fried chicken. She'd killed the chicken just for me, prompting a twinge of guilt on my part.

THE TOWN

Ollantaytambo—sometimes shortened to Ollanta—is filled with all types of lodging for the waves of tourists who come through en route to Machu Picchu: B&Bs, hippie hangouts, hotels. The small Andean town is located about 90 minutes by train from Machu Picchu. Many hiking treks also depart from Ollantaytambo for those walking the Inca Trail. At one end of town, sweeping terraces ascend dramatic cliffs where a temple fortress marks the last site of an indigenous victory over invading Spaniards. Temples, storehouses and other ancient structures dot the steep mountainsides surrounding the town.

As impressive as the old stone is, I was more interested in contemporary local culture. It's why I connected with Awamaki, an organization in Ollantaytambo that works to preserve traditions while building economic opportunities like the homestays.

Awamaki offers homestays and other immersive experiences in the nearby communities of Huilloc and Patacancha. The accommodations are rustic but allow visitors to learn what life is like there.

WEAVING WORKSHOPS

The group started in 2009 to help a weaving cooperative in Patacancha, a small Quechua village. Volunteers also run a storefront to help the women sell their vibrant textiles directly to visitors.

In addition local women lead weaving workshops where visitors can try their hand at spinning and dyeing yarn and weaving bracelets. A weaving class that I attended drew an eclectic group of expats living in Peru. For a few hours we struggled to hold a consistent pattern as a colorfully-clad local cheerfully helped us.

"The best thing about it is you get an entire experience from beginning to end of all to do with weaving, which is a great part of their lives. And, it's just a little bit more than hopping in, doing something quick and going away," said Chrissie Ellison, a British expat teaching in Peru.

Spaniard Jose Manuel Rabanal brought his wife and two children for the tour. The kids made friends with village children and dove into making bracelets.

Rabanal had a bit more trouble with the loops of yarn tied to his waist. At last, his "professor" completed his bracelet, eliciting a cheer and warm hug from Rabanal.

"It's been an amazing experience and these ladies, they deserve a recommendation, they do very professional work. I've seen some of their (weaving) patterns and I was amazed by them," said Rabanal, showing off his new bracelet.

THE IMPACT

Income from tourists have helped improve the lives of villagers. Some families have been able to replace thatch roofs with tin. Others can afford to send their children to better schools in bigger towns and have added more fruits and vegetables to their diets.

"I'm happy. I'm an artisan, and when visitors come, I sell my textiles, crafts. I sell them my artisanal goods. If there were no visitors, I would not sell. I'm pleased," said weaver Cristina Sullcapuma, speaking in Quechua.

Not far from the town and the weavers, Machu Picchu's stunning views and awe-inspiring engineering offer a window into ancient Incan culture. But a visit to that world wonder is all the more meaningful with a glimpse of contemporary daily life, offered by the Incas' descendants.

If You Go . . .

AWAMAKI: http://awamaki.org/. Non-profit based in Ollantaytambo, Peru, en route to Machu Picchu, offering homestays ranging from B&Bs to bare-bones dirt-floor lodging.

MEXICO ROAD TRIP: CANCUN AND BEYOND

By Amir Bibawy

CANCUN, Mexico—The police didn't ask for bribes. The roads were safe and fast. The food was particular, yet delicious.

A road trip across southeast Mexico offered the perfect antidote to winter: sun, beaches, yummy food, great drinks and amazing sights, from a colonial old town to ancient Mayan structures.

Best of all, the longest stretch of driving was just five hours from Playa del Carmen on the Caribbean to Campeche on Mexico's Gulf Coast.

The roughly 1,000-mile (1,600-km) loop also traversed three remarkably different states. Quintana Roo, home to resort-laden Cancun and Playa del Carmen, has more of an American feel than most places in Mexico. Campeche's laidback and colorful atmosphere is a nice contrast to Yucatan's earthy cuisine and cultural significance.

Car rental rates are low (though locally obtained insurance, which is essential, will up the cost). Major highways in the region are split into freeways and toll roads, called cuotas. The tolls are relatively inexpensive and the cuotas are often empty. At times you can travel almost alone for miles. And round-trip flights from the U.S. are usually affordable, while the dollar typically offers good value against the Mexican peso.

HISTORY AND IGUANAS

This trip started at Petit Lafitte, a small locally-owned resort situated just far enough outside of Playa del Carmen to avoid the town's boozy vibe. Petit Lafitte has drawn a faithful clientele of Americans for decades. Returning guests greet staff with hugs and everyone is on first-name basis.

After a week of lazy beach days and ceviche feasts, the road beckoned. First stop, Campeche's capital city, also called Campeche, which has a small town feel and a colorful grid of streets. The old town, which dates to the mid-17th century, is surrounded by a hexagonal wall with seven intact bulwarks, each unique in design and significance. Right outside the Puerta del Mar bulwark is a long, beautiful seaside walkway where joggers, strollers and tourists congregate.

An hour from Campeche lies the pristine Mayan site of Edzna, which dates to the seventh century B.C. Perfectly manicured lawns separate the Mayan structures, the most impressive of which is the Edificio de los Cincos Pisos (which means building of five floors). Kids will love running around spotting iguanas.

Driving from Campeche to Yucatan's capital, Merida, consider a stop at the beautiful Hacienda Santa Rosa, a luxury Starwood property. The restaurant serves delicious Yucatan fare at reasonable prices in a serene atmosphere. The spa was once a small church.

MERIDA, FLAMINGOS AND UXMAL

Merida is everything Campeche isn't. It's big, busy, noisy and dusty. But this cultural hub has many interesting sights to lure tourists and, increasingly, American and Canadian retirees. The town's cathedral is an austere and intimidating structure whose once-ornate decorations were stripped away by secular Mexicans during the revolution. Churches dot the town's historic center. Caleche (horse-drawn carriage) rides through the old town are an entertaining way to spend an hour. Open bus tours visit Merida's modern neighborhoods, which have some stunning mansions, especially along Paseo de Montejo. The local Starbucks looks like something from a belle epoque flick.

Merida is also a good jumping-off point for the trip's most stunning sites: the biosphere reserve at Celestun, and Uxmal, a Mayan mecca.

Celestun will draw shrieks of wonder from even the most bored teenager with its year-round colony of thousands of pink flamingos. Small motor boats take you 100 yards or so from the colorful flocks, which look like a haze of pink from far away. You won't need binoculars to watch them gracefully fly, then land on water.

The sprawling Uxmal complex boasts many unique structures including the Governor's Palace, the Nuns' Quadrangle (take note of the intact colorful decorations on its walls), and the amazing Pyramid of the Magician, with curved outlines unique among Mayan pyramids. Uxmal provides a solid impression of what Mayan life was like without the crowds of the more-touristy Chichen Itza.

FOOD

If beaches, colonial cities and Mayan sites aren't enticing enough, the region's cuisine will do the trick. Mexican ceviche (different from Peruvian, without potatoes or corn, just seafood) and fresh fish cooked in garlic and chili sauce are amazing. The region's ubiquitous main dish, cochinita pibil, is pork marinated in citrus and spices, then wrapped in banana leaves and slow-roasted for a unique, delicate yet earthy flavor. Relleno negro is another specialty of turkey stuffed with chopped pork, cooked in a rich dark sauce. In Merida, evening food carts sell hot crepes filled with Nutella or cheese for about a dollar. For breakfast, feast on huevos motulenos (fried eggs topped with beans, peas, ham, cheese and chili on a tortilla).

Best meals: La Pigua, an upscale fish restaurant outside the walls of Campeche, and Portico del Peregrino in Merida, with distinctive mole dishes.

Mexican chocolate is all the rage in hipster joints across America. Merida and Campeche offer a chance to try the real thing (Chocolateria de la Mora in Campeche is excellent). Opt for less milk and less sugar to truly savor the chocolate.

BRAZIL'S AMAZON FOREST: DOLPHINS, ALLIGATORS AND TRIBES

By Peter Prengaman

MANAUS, Brazil—The warning from our guide made clear that this "forest walk" would be anything but a leisurely stroll.

"Look before grabbing any branches because the ants bite. You will be in pain for 24 hours," said Jackson Edirley da Silva, wearing a bright yellow shirt and rubber boots. "And watch where you step. You don't want to get bitten by a snake."

Our group, about a dozen tourists, got quiet.

"Don't worry," I whispered to our sons, ages 6 and 7. "We will be careful where we step."

CABIN IN THE RAINFOREST

My wife and I had flown with our kids from Rio de Janeiro to Manaus, a major jumping-off point for Brazil's Amazon rainforest. From there, we took a boat for an hour ride up a tributary of the Rio Negro, or Black River, and then walked 15 minutes to an "eco lodge" in the middle of a forest.

Even at the edge of the forest, the sounds made a strong impression. Monkeys screeched, birds bellowed and bugs buzzed, a cacophony that felt both terrifying and calming. Ironically, we would learn that it's rare to actually see most of the animals. You are in their house, and they know how to hide.

Our cabin was sparse but had some essentials: a small refrigerator for bottled water, mosquito screens on the windows and an air-conditioning unit that combated the oppressive humidity that would cling to us upon walking outside.

TOURISM IN THE AMAZON

Despite its worldwide fame, not to mention increasing importance as climate change becomes a global issue, the Amazon is not visited in great numbers. Amazonas, Brazil's largest and heavily forested state, which includes Manaus, was visited by just under 1.2 million foreign and Brazilian tourists in 2014, the most recent year for available statistics. By comparison, the Eiffel Tower in Paris gets roughly 7 million visitors a year.

For those who get here, it's hard to imagine disappointment. Over the course of a week, we swam with fresh water dolphins, gawked at alligators wrestled from river banks by scrappy guides, fished for piranhas and stood in awe at "the meeting" of the Negro and Solimoes Rivers (called the Amazon River in Manaus and eastward), where a difference in density and temperature means that for miles black and yellow waters flow side by side.

FOOD

The food also has unique tastes. Massive tucunare fish get chopped into fillets that taste like chicken with an extra dose of zest, potato-like manioc roots are prepared with forest spices that most people have never heard of and acai berries are ubiquitous. The kids particularly enjoyed sucking on acai popsicles during the afternoon heat.

CONSERVATION

The Amazon basin, which spans several countries in South America and is nearly as large as the continental United States, has always been central to Brazilian identity, even if most Brazilians will never visit. Conspiracy theories periodically erupt about other countries' alleged attempts to take the territory or plunder its myriad resources, and pressure from international organizations to stop deforestation often draws the ire of politicians.

Luiz Inacio "Lula" da Silva, president between 2003 and 2010, once famously said: "I don't want any gringo coming here asking us to let an Amazon dweller die of hunger under a tree."

Te Batista, a boat operator who we hired two days to take us to several areas of the Rio Negro, told me tourists always ask him about conservation. "Foreigners are afraid about the future of the forest," said Batista, who added flatly that he was not. "They worry that the cutting here will mean they die in their countries" because of global warming.

THE INDIGENOUS PEOPLE

At the heart of conservation discussions are indigenous tribes, who provide windows into life in the Amazon both before the arrival of Portuguese colonists in the 16th century and today. While there are still scores of "uncontacted" tribes in the Amazon, most are at least partially connected to Brazilian society and live in ways that combine their traditions with aspects of modern-day life.

One day we visited a small village of about 100 people belonging to the Dessana tribe.

As they have for centuries, the women wore hay skirts and were topless. The men wore small woven cloths on their hips, though noticeably with tight black briefs underneath. They all had red face paint and many wore feathers on their heads and necklaces made with alligator and jaguar teeth. Recently caught fish cooked over a fire and a pottery bowl of large baked black ants were available to snack on.

Speaking limited Portuguese, a young man named Bohoka told me the tribe lived as they always had — in little huts without electricity, running water or cellphones — but with a few modern twists that included allowing tourists to visit.

"Tourism allows us to maintain our way of life," said Bohoka, 24, who showed us necklaces and other handcrafts for sale.

The village was only about a 90-minute boat trip from Manaus but worlds away. The gritty port city of over 2 million people is an eclectic mix of a colonial architecture, urban sprawl and hustle from hardscrabble touts trying to eke out a living. It reached its splendor in the 19th century when growing global demand for rubber brought throngs to the area to cut and gather sap from rubber trees. A beautiful opera house built during that time, which today hosts several shows each year, is the city's main tourist attraction.

As I chatted with Bohoka, a small boat pulled up on the riverbank. About a dozen members of the tribe, all dressed in slacks and T-shirts, got off carrying plastic bags. They disappeared into their huts and re-emerged a few minutes later wearing traditional clothes.

Bohoka explained they had gone to "the city," or Manaus, to buy sewing materials.

"Why couldn't they just wear traditional clothing there?" I asked, somewhat jokingly.

Bohoka laughed. "Impossible," he said. "Indians' home is the forest."

SARAJEVO:
A HOSTEL OFFERS A TASTE OF WAR

By Aida Cerkez

SARAJEVO, Bosnia-Herzegovina—A hostel in Bosnia is offering visitors a unique experience: the opportunity to live like civilians in a war zone.

But at the Sarajevo War Hostel, guests have the luxury of knowing they won't be killed, starved or lose family or friends. And unlike the Sarajevans who actually endured the 1992-95 war, the visitors can leave any time.

HELMETS, FLAK JACKETS AND CANDLES

Those who check in to the War Hostel are greeted by the owner wearing a helmet and a flak jacket. They get to sleep in rooms with just one bulb on the ceiling, running on a car battery. The plastic sheets on the windows are just like the ones the United Nations High Commissioner for Refugees handed out to Sarajevans so they could replace window glass shattered by bombs.

At night, they use candles to move around the hostel and to read by. The walls are plastered with wartime newspaper articles—most of them from The Associated Press—depicting the daily struggle in besieged Sarajevo.

At the War Hostel, visitors quickly discover it is one thing to watch people surviving wars on TV. But it is really something else to spend the night on a sponge mattress on the floor, covered with military blankets, and in the darkness listen to the sound of exploding bombs outside. A tape of the bombs plays all night long.

ZERO ONE

In a makeshift bunker and by candlelight, the hostel owner, Zero One, now in his 20s, shares with guests his childhood memories of wartime and the postwar era, and tells them how wars can influence people's lives forever. His birth name is Arijan Kurbasic, but he calls himself Zero One, the wartime code name used by his father, who was a soldier in the Bosnian Army. The code name conceals his ethnic background.

"I just want to be identified as a human being as this was the most important thing to be during the war. Either you are one or you are not," he explained. "Zero One I chose to honor my father."

THE HISTORY

The war unfolded after Yugoslavia fell apart and its republics declared independence one after the other. Nationalist politicians were determined to divide the new country of Bosnia and Herzegovina along ethnic lines and pitted the country's Muslim Bosnians, Roman Catholic Croats and Christian Orthodox Serbs against each other.

However, Sarajevo, as well as other parts of Bosnia, were ethnically diverse and many locals rejected the nationalist plans—for which they paid a high price.

The Serb siege of Sarajevo went on for 46 months—precisely 1,425 days—longer than the siege of Leningrad, now St. Petersburg, during World War II. Sarajevo's 380,000 people were left without food, electricity, water or heating, as they hid from snipers and the average 330 shells a day that smashed into the city.

Over 100,000 people were killed during the Bosnian war, 11,541 of them in Sarajevo.

THE GUESTS

Guests appreciate the intensity of the hostel simulation. "The best way to learn about something is usually experience," said Andrew Burns, a hostel guest from the U.S. "It provides emotions behind events. I can read a textbook all I want, but most of that information escapes from the mind immediately. But when I come here and I see people who talk about their experiences, that makes it real, that makes me want to learn about it, to try to help, try to love."

Zero One also offers guests a chance to watch documentaries about the siege, and can organize tours of the city's war sites, like the front lines and a tunnel Sarajevans dug under the airport runway to connect the city with the outside world.

"They come here, they experience this and it changes their perspectives," Zero One says of his guests. "For one or two nights, to live like this, it changes their views and then they appreciate their own life, they appreciate water, they appreciate comfort, they appreciate a bed, they appreciate everything else. It really gives them a different perspective and that is the whole point of this."

Guests agree that the War Hostel is "unique," as Eren Bastaymaz, from Turkey, put it. "You can find better hostels anywhere in the world, but this atmosphere, I've never seen anything like this before."

Associated Press Sabina Niksic contributed to this story from Sarajevo.

If You Go . . .
SARAJEVO WAR HOSTEL: https://warhostel.com/. Rates, depending on room or dorm, 10 to 30 euros nightly.

A TOURISM BOOM
IN MELANIA'S SLOVENIA

By Dusan Stojanovic

LJUBLJANA, Slovenia—When Melanija Knavs drove around Ljubljana in a fluffy skirt on a metallic blue Vespa with her boyfriend in the late 1980s, the Slovenian capital was a sleepy town that offered little excitement to the rare visitor.

But in the two decades since she left her native Slovenia, became a model known as Melania Knauss and married American billionaire Donald Trump, Ljubljana has turned from a gray and drab place into a lively city filled with restaurants, cafes and nightclubs packed with foreigners.

Slovenia has become one of Europe's hottest destinations since splitting from Yugoslavia in 1991. Only 2 million people live here, but nearly 4 million foreigners visited in 2016.

Tourism officials say the Slovenian-born American first lady has created even more interest in the country. The number of U.S. visitors rose 15 percent in the months after Donald Trump took office.

Slovenian tourist agencies have even organized tours in "the footsteps of Melania Trump," showing the places where she lived, studied and worked. Websites promoting the nation say: "Welcome to the homeland of the new First Lady of the United States of America!"

But she would hardly recognize the place since she last visited.

The heart of the city has also been closed to traffic, so Mrs. Trump would no longer be able to ride by scooter to her favorite cafe, then called the Horse's Tail, near Tromostovje, a charming stone triple bridge in the heart of the city decorated with small dragon-like statues.

The city is dominated by a majestic castle on a hill by the river Ljubljana that splits the town into two. At night, the castle is lit bright green, the city's traditional color. A boat cruise along the river reveals spectacular architecture while street artists play music and perform for visitors.

The city's center on the banks of the river offers romantic dining and other excellent culinary offerings, including an open kitchen on Fridays when chefs prepare international dishes on makeshift stands that serve as an open-air market the other days of the week.

Slovenia is blessed with stunning natural scenery that includes both a coastline on the Adriatic Sea and a chunk of the Alps. It is also known for tasty wines and food specialties such as Kranjska klobasa, a juicy pork sausage, or struklji, a traditional Slovene pastry with various fillings.

Slovenia has sometimes been confused in the past with another small central European state, Slovakia. But a Slovenian-born U.S. first lady has helped distinguish the country's identity.

"Whatever you think of Melania, she put Slovenia on the map of the world," said Janez Bosnjak, a Ljubljana resident.

Born in the hilly industrial town of Sevnica in 1970 when Slovenia was part of Communist Yugoslavia, Mrs. Trump's early life has come under media scrutiny—especially after her official biography had her graduating from the Ljubljana university.

Rok Bogataj, who knew her when they studied at the Faculty of Architecture, said she regularly attended lectures but did not graduate.

"I had an impression that she had serious ambitions to finish her studies, but one day she simply disappeared. We heard that she decided to become a fashion model and that she went to Milano," Bogataj said.

For tourists, Ljubljana is the perfect jumping-off point for daily trips to other attractions. The country offers an abundance of contrasting landscapes and cultures and is proud of being the only country in the world with the word "love" in its name.

One must-see destination northwest of Ljubljana is Lake Bled where emerald-green waters create a spectacular landscape, with a lush, tiny island and a church tower peeking out of evergreens surrounded by the rocky Julian Alps.

It was at lakeside Grand Hotel Toplice in Bled where Mrs. Trump introduced Donald Trump to her parents during their brief visit to Slovenia in July 2002, two years before they engaged. It is believed that it was the last time that the former model visited her native country.

Not far from Bled are the seaside towns of Piran, called the Venice of Slovenia because of the colorful Venetian gothic mansions, and Portoroz, a French-Riviera style resort with luxurious hotels lining along a sandy beach.

It was in Portoroz in 1992 where Mrs. Trump got a big break in her modeling career when Slovenia's women magazine Jana staged its "Look of the Year" contest. She took the second place that gave her the invitation to cast for an international modeling agency in Milan.

"Melania was one of the girls who participated at the event," said Jana's editor Bernarda Jeklin. "I wouldn't say that Melania was outstanding. She was quiet, introverted. But what I remember were her dangerous, tiger-like green eyes."

IN FLANDERS FIELDS, THE POPPIES STILL BLOW

By Raf Casert

YPRES, Belgium—Crimson poppies still dance in the breeze as if nothing horrific happened in Flanders Fields. But a century after World War I, the flowers endure as a symbol of war dead, in part because of a celebrated poem:

"In Flanders fields the poppies blow—Between the crosses, row on row."

The famous flowers are among many reminders of the region's connection to the Great War. Amid monuments and headstones in this western corner of Belgium, Flanders' eerie landscapes, trenches and bunkers continue to evoke the soldiers who died here by the hundreds of thousands. As carefree 21st century travel goes, a tour of Flanders Fields packs a punch that can long stay with you.

The haunting poem, "In Flanders Fields," was written by Lt. Col. John McCrae, a doctor from Canada who ran a field hospital during the war.

One stunning aspect of a visit here is the region's beauty and serenity. A spectacular springtime can turn the once barren, muddy battlegrounds lush with ripening wheat fields and pastures where cows graze.

Walk through Ypres, which has four battles named for it, and you'd be forgiven for thinking you're in a splendidly preserved medieval town with a Gothic hall, gabled houses and spires. But what was left of the town on Nov. 11, 1918 when the war ended were stumps, rubble and vague memories where homes once stood. Ypres' second battle saw the first use of chemical arms in warfare, and its third, named for the tiny village of Passchendaele, saw 150,000 men die in 100 days.

Some wanted Ypres to stay in ruins as remembrance. The people immediately decided otherwise and started rebuilding, "as if there never had been a war. It was very much a psychological reaction," said Piet Chielens, coordinator of the In Flanders Fields museum, which is housed in the rebuilt neo-Gothic hall on the marketplace. "Ypres immediately became a centre of remembrance. The first tourists and pilgrims arrived in early spring of 1919."

And they're still coming 100 years later, with hundreds, sometimes thousands, at the 8 p.m. playing of the Last Post, the daily salute at Ypres' Menin Gate, where walls list 54,000 soldiers who perished but were never found.

The deafening silence once the bugle stops playing is a must in remembrance tourism, as is the In Flanders Fields Museum.

But visitors should also take time away from the ceremonies and crowds to wander across the flat fields dotted with low-flung ridges where so many fought and died.

"The real museum is still out there," said Chielens. "The traces, the scars in the landscape, the numerous monuments and cemeteries that will give you that sense of loss and tragedy."

It might be a tiny cemetery where only dozens of soldiers lie, a rain-sodden trench, or a derelict German bunker.

The city of Diksmuide has the Ijzertoren memorial with sweeping views of battlefields from atop its 275-foot (84-meter) tower. Nearby, the warren of Dodengang trenches brings the claustrophobia of war home, even if it no longer has the rats, stench and enemy within shouting distance.

Yet tourists should not limit their trip to pondering war. "You learn to understand what the importance of living and enjoying life is after you have been confronted with the experience," Chielens said.

For kids, that might mean a visit to the Bellewaerde theme park. For grown-ups, local gastronomy stands out. And there's nothing like a summer's evening with a Hommelbier or St. Bernardus tripel beer on a terrace to let the day sink in.

While the memory of those fluttering poppies may fade, the sense of what happened here will likely grow stronger. As McCrae wrote:

"If ye break faith with us who die—We shall not sleep, though poppies grow—In Flanders fields."

AP photographer Virginia Mayo contributed to this story.

FINDING AFRICAN-AMERICAN HISTORY IN PARIS

By Russell Contreras

PARIS—The great African-American writers James Baldwin and Richard Wright began their feud over Wright's novel "Native Son," at Cafe Les Deux Magots. Jazz trumpeter Miles Davis held hands with his white girlfriend, French actress Juliette Greco, while strolling along the Seine after hanging out with Picasso. Entertainer Josephine Baker became a megastar at the Theatre des Champs-Elysees.

Some travelers to Paris seek selfies with the Eiffel Tower, go to see the "Mona Lisa" at the Louvre or stroll to the Arc de Triomphe. But you can create a different type of itinerary exploring African-American connections to the City of Light. Some of the United States' greatest black intellectuals and performers sought an escape here from the racism of 20th century America, and with a little homework, you can follow their footsteps.

"Paris. ... There you can be whatever you want to be. Totally yourself," poet Langston Hughes wrote, as writer Paule Marshall recounted in her memoir "Triangular Road."

"I've never felt a moment of sorrow," Wright said about leaving the U.S. for France.

How and why these black expats felt more at home in Paris than in their own country is the theme of Black Paris Tours, founded and led by Ricki Stevenson.

In the U.S., African-Americans contended with segregation, racial terror and little support for their art. But in Paris, they drank wine with surrealists, frequented bars that aided the French Resistance during World War II, and enjoyed accolades for their work, Stevenson said. The French showered them with admiration and opportunity—ironic given France's treatment of its African colonies. Paris today is a multiethnic city, but immigrants from its former colonies, especially North Africans, often face racism and discrimination.

Yet decades ago, African-Americans felt welcomed here. St. Louis-born Freda Josephine McDonald, for example, came to Paris as a dancer after a life of cleaning houses and babysitting for wealthy white families. In the U.S., she was criticized for being "too dark." The New York Times once called her a "Negro wench." But in Paris, she drew immediate fame for her

1925 performance in La Revue Negre at the Theatre des Champs-Elysees. As Josephine Baker, she became one of the era's most popular performers.

"The opportunity to live a rich, full life is something that she could have in Paris," Stevenson said. "She could not have this in the United States."

When Baker died in 1975, she was buried in a French military uniform with her medals for her role in the French Resistance during World War II.

Today, you can catch a show at the Art Deco-style Theatre des Champs-Elysees, visit Baker's favorite restaurant La Coupole and take photos at Place Josephine Baker, a square. Her image, rarely seen in the U.S., is widespread in Paris. There's a swimming pool named for her too, in a barge floating on the Seine.

And while the Lenox Lounge, a famed Harlem jazz club where Billie Holiday sang, has closed, Paris jazz clubs such as Caveau de la Huchette in the city's Latin Quarter still serve up energetic evenings of live swing and bebop.

Founded in 1947, Caveau de la Huchette was one of many clubs where African-American performers sought to make a living amid changing music tastes in the U.S. It played host to the likes of Lionel Hampton and Art Blakey and his Jazz Messengers. Last year, the club got a cameo appearance in the movie "La La Land." One evening last summer, a trio of saxophonists drew a diverse crowd of swing dancers enjoying 1940s-era jazz.

Around the corner from Caveau de la Huchette, vintage shops sell posters of African-American jazz artists and hard-to-find vinyl albums like "The Hawk in Paris" by Coleman Hawkins.

In Saint Germain des Pres, Cafe de Flore is known as a favorite hangout of Ernest Hemingway's. But it's also where James

Baldwin, a son of Harlem who came to Paris with only $40, crafted his novel "Go Tell It on the Mountain." There's a small photo of Hemingway upstairs but no image of Baldwin.

At Le Select cafe, a gathering place for intellectuals before World War II, Baldwin finished "Giovanni's Room," a novel about an American in Paris and his affair with an Italian man.

The famed English-language bookstore Shakespeare and Company served as a meeting place for African-Americans and other expats throughout the 20th century and still does. On a recent afternoon, the African-American writer Colson Whitehead talked to a crowd outside the store about his Pulitzer Prize-winning novel "The Underground Railroad." He answered questions about slavery in the U.S., police shootings and the state of African-Americans in a post-President Barack Obama nation. Inside, books on display included "They Can't Kill Us All: The Story of the Struggle for Black Lives" and "Why I'm No Longer Talking to White People About Race."

Looking back on his time in Paris, Miles Davis once wrote: "I loved being in Paris and loved the way I was treated."

Stevenson said visitors can learn about that chapter of the African-American experience today. "All you need to know is the history," she said. "And know where to visit. It's all here."

If You Go . . .
BLACK PARIS TOURS: http://www.blackparistour.com/

CAFE LES DEUX MAGOTS: 6 Place Saint-Germain des Pres

CAFE DE FLORE: 172 Boulevard Saint-Germain

CAVEAU DE LA HUCHETTE: 5 Rue de la Huchette

SHAKESPEARE AND COMPANY: 37 Rue de la Bucherie

FORAGING FOR FOOD IN THE
ENGLISH COUNTRYSIDE

By Jerry Harmer

TOLLER PORCORUM, England—"This," said our guide James Feaver, "is our main course."

We were standing in front of a dung heap in a high meadow in the English countryside. Pushing up out of the ooze was a low-growing weed. He bent down, plucked a sprig and held it up.

"Fat hen. Humans have eaten it for thousands of years. We're going to need a lot of it."

After a glance among us, my family and I set about picking

with an approximation of gusto. When you are foraging for your food you can't be too squeamish about little things like cow dung beneath your fingers.

I have long been fascinated with the idea of living off the land, finding sustenance among the wild plants that teem in hedges and fields. So a week's holiday in Dorset, in southwest England—a county bursting with picture-book countryside—gave me the chance to see how abundant nature's larder really is.

THE TEACHER AND THE PLACE

Foraging is increasingly popular in the U.K. and there are many teachers to choose from.

On a recommendation, I contacted Hedgerow Harvest and booked a half-day course for me, my partner Fon and our young son Jimmy.

On a classic English summer's day—meaning we experienced all weather conditions in one afternoon—we met up with James Feaver, who gave up office work for professional foraging eight years ago. He now runs courses in south and southwest England, but mostly in Dorset, his adopted home.

We met him in the village of Toller Porcorum, donned rubber boots and light waterproof jackets, and set off in search of wild provender.

We spent the next few hours walking through lanes hedged in with soaring banks, down tracks drenched in birdsong, beside clear streams and across uncut meadows in search of ingredients for a three-course meal.

FINDING THE EDIBLES

If like me you can't tell wild sorrel from a blade of grass, this quickly becomes daunting. But Feaver has gimlet eyes and an encyclopedic knowledge of the edible.

High in a hedgerow, a spray of tiny white flowers stood proud of the foliage. He hooked it with his hazel stick, pulled it down to picking height, and inhaled.

"The smell of summer," he said.

For centuries, country-folk have used the fragrant elderflower to add a zesty flavor to food and drink. Now it would bring its zing to our dessert. We plucked head after head. I lifted up Jimmy so he could join the harvest.

In quick order we found red currants, wild mint and tiny, sweet, wild strawberries. The wicker basket James provided, a nice touch, began to fill.

So far so idyllic, but this arcadia comes with thorns.

THE RULES AND THE BEACH

Of the many rules of foraging the most important is this: Don't eat anything unless you are 100 percent certain you know what it is. Some edible plants look uncannily like ones that are deadly. For example, cow parsley goes well in salads but is easily mistaken for something you wouldn't want near your dinner plate: hemlock.

Other rules include don't uproot anything (it's illegal), only take sustainably and don't pick from ground-hugging plants near footpaths "where dogs can wee on them." That was Jimmy's favorite rule.

Time was getting on. From Toller Porcorum we drove down steep, narrow lanes to a nearby beach. Here you can see the stunning coastline sweep in an arc from Portland in Dorset right into neighboring east Devon. A trove of fossils has earned it the name

Jurassic Coast and UNESCO World Heritage status.

But we weren't there for beauty or geology. We were there for sea beet leaves, a close relative of garden spinach that grows in low belts along the pebbly foreshore. More free food, right at our feet.

THE FEAST

But don't go thinking you can kiss goodbye to supermarkets just because your eyes have been opened. That's not the idea of the course.

"Foraging isn't really about survival," Feaver had said at the start. "It's about taking the best of the wild and adding it to conventional ingredients to make great-tasting food."

Great tasting? We'd be the judges of that.

Back at our holiday cottage, Feaver supervised the preparation of the feast. For starters, sea beet soup. For main course, fat hen pesto bake, with more fat hen as a side dish, washed down with sparkling elderflower wine. To finish, elderflower and gooseberry fool, garnished with wild strawberries.

It was a revelation, especially the sea beet soup which was one of the most delicious soups I have ever had: rich, velvety and homey, like swallowing a big bowl of contentment.

It had been a long day. We'd started at 1:30 p.m. and the last spoon didn't scrape its empty bowl till 9 p.m.

As he packed away his stick, basket and scissors, Feaver said that after doing the course, "people look at the countryside with different eyes."

Yes, I thought. With eyes like dinner plates.

If You Go...

HEDGEROW HARVEST: http://www.hedgerow-harvest.com. Full day summer foraging, 70 pounds a person.

ASSOCIATION OF FORAGERS: List by region, http://www.foragers-association.org.uk

LONDON:
THE PUNK ROCK SCENE, FOUR DECADES LATER

By Jonathan Elderfield

LONDON—The Sex Pistols and The Clash led the British punk rock revolution in the steamy summer of 1976.

Four decades later, I set out on a pilgrimage to find and explore the places where the music began, from the Pistols' rehearsal and living space, to Notting Hill, where the Clash witnessed riots, to the pubs and clubs that hosted their first shows.

In some spots, I found the opposite of the angry energy that inspired anthems like the Pistols' "Anarchy in the UK" and The

Clash's "London's Burning." But I also found some venues still going strong.

First stop: Portobello Road to see a mural of Clash frontman Joe Strummer, which was painted after this death. Sadly the mural was covered up. I looked in vain for signs of Strummer's anti-establishment vibe, but all I found was a bustling market selling knickknacks, clothing and antiques while passers-by peered at their iPhones. From there I headed to Tavistock Road, the street that inspired Strummer's "White Riot," his call to arms after a West Indian carnival ended in riots in Notting Hill in the summer of '76. But I failed to find any sign of punk's past on the quiet thoroughfare, so I settled in the Metropolitan Pub on Great Western Road for a hand-pulled pint.

The Rough Trade record shop opened in 1976 on Kensington Park Road. Today it's on Talbot Road, filled with vinyl and CDs, its walls and ceiling adorned with posters featuring The Clash, Sex Pistols and others.

In Central London, I marveled at the fine instruments at NO.TOM, a small guitar shop on Denmark Street, near the Tottenham Court Road tube. The short street, once known as London's Tin Pan Alley, was home to many music publishers and studios. Behind NO.TOM there's a tiny 19th century cottage where the Sex Pistols once lived. It's covered with graffiti created by the Pistols' John Lydon (Johnny Rotten), including a drawing of the Pistols' manager Malcolm McLaren, and another of Nancy Spungen, Sid Vicious' girlfriend.

At 100 Oxford St., the 100 Club is marked with a sign and poster for upcoming shows. The Sex Pistols played here in May 1976 and the venue hosted a punk festival in the fall of '76. In January 2016, '70s bands including 999, The Members, UK Subs and Discharge played here as part of a punk series.

In Chelsea, at 430 King's Road, a giant "SEX" sign once hung outside a shop of the same name shared by McLaren, the Pistols' manager, and designer Vivienne Westwood. Westwood still runs a boutique here called Worlds End.

Next stop: Camden Market. Today this thriving collection of bars, restaurants, shops and stalls is overrun with shoppers perusing food and fashion, from espresso to T-shirts bearing the Union Jack. I was here to find the spot where The Clash posed for a photograph that became an iconic image adorning their first album. The photo was taken on a ramp that's since been converted to steps. I took a selfie standing there but couldn't help feeling a pang of regret. My favorite band, often called "the only band that matters," once stood here on the cusp of fame, but today the spot seems to embody the opposite of punk's anti-materialistic message. And I had become part of the iPhone-toting tribe intent on the next purchase and picture.

Where was the Pistols' "Anarchy in the UK"? Where were "All The Young Punks" from The Clash song?

Maybe they were up the road at the Roundhouse. This fine music venue, originally a 19th century railway repair facility, has hosted performers since 1966. The Clash played their fifth-ever show here in September 1976. The Pistols, The Damned, The Ramones and Patti Smith all played here too.

My final destination was London's Islington neighborhood, home to the Hope and Anchor pub, 207 Upper St., and Screen on the Green, 83 Upper St. Hope and Anchor has a lovely ground-floor pub with a small theater space upstairs and music venue in the basement. The basement's roster has included The Jam, The Ramones, The Police, The Stranglers, XTC, U2, The Cure, Joy

Division and The Pogues. Hope and Anchor also hosted pre-punk bands playing what was called pub rock, including a group led by Joe Strummer, the 101ers. The pub's Facebook page lists upcoming shows, and today's audiences aren't likely to be hit by flying sheets of spit ("gob" as the Brits call it) the way they were in the early punk era, with fans gobbing at performers and musicians spitting right back.

Screen on the Green, with a fabulous neon facade, hosts movies and live events. It's one of the oldest cinemas in the UK. The Clash, Sex Pistols and Buzzcocks played together there on the night Aug. 29, 1976. It was the end of the long, hot summer when punk was born.

THE MYSTERIOUS HOLLOWAYS OF DORSET

By Jerry Harmer

SYMONDSBURY, England—Dorset is one of England's often overlooked gems: rolling countryside, ancient thatched-roof villages, the birthplace of 19th century novelist Thomas Hardy and a sea that breaks on a World Heritage Site coastline.

But if you ask me, the county's most startling treasure is its least-known: holloways.

Holloways are paths sunk deep below ground level by centuries, perhaps millennia, of passing feet, cartwheels and livestock.

Dorset conceals many within its bucolic folds. Long since abandoned as thoroughfares, and overgrown with brambles and bushes, they are often unknown to all but the very local. When I asked the tourist office in the market town of Bridport how to find one, no one there knew what I was talking about.

But I kept looking and asking. Finally, one recent sunny Saturday afternoon, after getting directions from a bearded countryman who pointed up a lane with a stick, my family and I strode northwest out of the village of Symondsbury.

For some way our path was just an ordinary country lane but then the greenery thickened, the path twisted and everything changed.

Parallel walls of soft brown rock suddenly climbed above us forming a narrow gorge 20 feet high (6 meters high) in places. It was if a giant finger had gouged the earth then left it to settle back as it may. Trees clung to the sides at astonishing angles as if frozen in the act of falling, their roots exposed like giant snakes, their branches intertwined high above to form a roof that filtered the sunlight.

We stood stupefied in a green underworld. It was like being in a mythical landscape, utterly detached from reality. It was awe-inspiring and incredibly serene. I was sure the spell would break but nothing moved and no one else came. The only sounds were birdsong and the occasional whoop of delight from my 6-year-old son.

But there was also an ambivalence. As we explored we noticed faces and giant eyes expertly carved into the rock. For all its tranquility in daylight it is probably an unnerving walk at dusk or later. It was then I remembered the name my guide had used for the path: Hell Lane. I kept that information to myself.

Later I looked for the holloway on a satellite map. All that's there is a line of greenery like any other, among a patchwork of fields; an astonishing slice of England hiding in plain sight.

IN IRELAND, A PILGRIMAGE FOR ST. PATRICK

By Helen O'Neill

WESTPORT, Ireland—Shrouded in mist, the sacred mountain rises above the countryside, majestic, mysterious and a little foreboding.

Here, on this rocky west coast promontory overlooking the Atlantic, St. Patrick is said to have fasted for 40 days and nights as he wrestled with demons and banished snakes from Ireland.

Every March 17, the world throws a lavish celebration for the fifth-century preacher who tramped around Ireland converting its people and spinning endless miracles along the way. Revelers around the globe slurp green beer, host parades and wear silly hats.

But those who truly want to honour the patron saint come to Croagh Patrick, a remote, rugged mountain in County Mayo, which draws over a million pilgrims and tourists each year.

Elders and children, believers and hikers, tourists and locals. They come with walking sticks and hiking boots, guide books and rosary beads. They come for the sweeping views of Clew Bay, for the fresh air and camaraderie, for a day of fun—and penance.

Trekking to the summit in the saint's footsteps, some climb in their bare feet, pausing at three "stations" along the way to recite a series of prayers. There is a small oratory on the summit where Mass is celebrated on certain feast days and on the last Sunday in July—"Reek Sunday"—traditionally the holiest day to climb, when up to 30,000 visitors flock to the slopes.

"I do it for the graces it gives me all year," said Patrick Breen, as he began his descent on a summer day, his bare feet bruised and swollen after several hours on the mountain. "It's a gift, a beautiful gift."

All around, thick Irish brogues mingled with languages and accents from around the world. A family of four from Colorado huffed up the final leg, the father celebrating his 55th birthday, his teenage daughter dreaming of the spa that awaited when they got back to their hotel. They passed a trio from County Cavan, hiking barefoot in honor of two toddlers from their community who had drowned in a lake earlier in the summer. A German tourist with a backpack helped his mother scale the rocks. A young Englishwoman wiggled her pink toenails and boasted about climbing barefoot just to prove to her boyfriend that "fancy toes" could do it. An older Polish couple picnicked at the summit with ham sandwiches and flasks of hot tea.

Although the mountain is just 2,500 feet high (764 meters), even seasoned hikers are surprised by its steepness and difficulty. Over the years, climbers have eroded the original trail, so what remains is rocky, unforgiving and often slippery terrain. The last leg, before the summit, is a formidable cliff of rolling rocks and shale known as "the scree." Casualties are common and every year local rescue squads airlift numerous injured climbers from the slopes.

But that doesn't deter pilgrims who have been flocking to the site since ancient times. Long before Patrick, the Celts celebrated the harvest festival of Lughnasa here, beginning in early August. The sacred mountain was considered especially important for woman who would sleep on the summit during Lughnasa to encourage fertility.

Today St. Patrick is big business in the area with dozens of Patrician statues, holy wells and shrines. Westport, a pretty port town about 6 miles (10 km) from the mountain, is filled with stores selling Patrick memorabilia and the wooden staffs that are ubiquitous on the mountain. (Westport was also home to 16th century pirate queen, Grace O'Malley, who vies with Patrick for local attention and lore.)

Twelve miles (19 km) from Westport is Ballintubber Abbey, where Patrick founded a church and baptized his earliest converts. The present abbey has been in daily use as a church for nearly 800 years. Ballintubber also marks the beginning of an ancient pilgrimage route (now called Tochar Phadraig) that winds for 22 miles (35 km) over hills and fields, ending at Croagh Patrick. Along the way, pilgrims pass a round tower, a holy well and a raised stone carved with Neolithic circles called St. Patrick's Chair.

But it is the mountain that remains the big draw for pilgrims and tourists alike. At almost any time of the day, any time of the year, it is possible to make out a steady stream of climbers in the distance, inching their way toward the summit, hunched over their wooden crooks, little specks of humanity disappearing into the mist.

If You Go...

WESTPORT, COUNTY MAYO: http://www.westporttourism.com/westport-facts.html

CROAGH PATRICK VISITOR CENTER: http://www.croagh-patrick.com/visitorcentre/croagh-patrick .The visitor centre at the base of the mountain has a cafe, craft shop and information about guided tours in the area.

BALLINTUBBER ABBEY: http://www.ballintubberabbey.ie/. Open daily 9 a.m.-midnight

SCOTLAND: A WEEK OF WALKING THE WEST HIGHLAND WAY

By Lynn Dombek

GLASGOW, Scotland—Scotland has more than two dozen official long-distance trails through moors, peat bogs and forests. We chose one of the most popular, the West Highland Way.

As first-time walkers in Scotland, my companion and I used a travel company to plan our route, book accommodations and arrange baggage transfers. But we met others who used baggage services and booked their own lodging, along with folks who camped out.

Like the wildly variable Scotland landscape, there's no end of ways to enjoy the walks.

Walkers we met were a disparate bunch: young Swiss backpackers; mountaineers from Virginia; a Swedish mother with teenage daughters; a Scottish couple, world travelers but out to see more of their own country; an extended family from England ages 16 to 50; and a Louisiana couple celebrating their 50th wedding anniversary. We were mid-50s professionals out for adventure.

We took lots of walks at home to get ready. Knowing June could be rainy and cold, we tested gear beforehand. Our essentials were good boots, breathable rain jackets, rain pants or shorts, and wool or suitable base layers (no cotton!).

A runner recently set a record walking the West Highland way in under 14 hours. We did the standard itinerary: 95 miles (150 km) in seven days.

THE DAILY ITINERARY

DAY ONE: *Milngavie to Drymen, 12 miles (19 km)*
Our first, lovely day transitions from Milngavie, a small town north of Glasgow, into a pastoral landscape dotted with sheep and cows, mossy stone walls and livestock gates. The peaceful walking is on mostly well-worn trails and roads. We stop into Glengoyne distillery for a wee dram, then on to Drymen. We eat that night at the Clachan Inn, licensed in 1734, seated next to a couple who reappear on Day Three to save us in an uncertain moment. We're soundly asleep by 8 p.m.

DAY TWO: *Drymen to Rowardennan, 14 miles (22.5 km)*
It's pouring rain through moors and forests, then up and steeply

down Conic Hill on the boundary fault separating lowland Scotland from the highlands. In good weather it has glorious views of Loch Lomond (loch means lake). We lunch in Balmaha, a popular resort town, and continue on the rocky lakeshore path toward the Rowardennan Hotel, a rustic lodge. The pub, with its corner fireplace, serves as both restaurant and meeting place for walkers. We exchange stories, and stumble off to bed.

DAY THREE: *Rowardennan to Inverarnan, 14 miles (22.5 km)*
It's overcast but no rain. We're now firmly in Rob Roy country (he's an 18th century highlands folk hero). We're still on the loch's shore where the path is a challenging mix of roots and boulders. Guidebooks describe it as "torturous," despite extraordinary ferns, waterfalls and forests. Six hours in, we convince ourselves a turn was missed and wearily head back. Then the Day One couple appears. The man pulls out his GPS to show we're on track. I sheepishly pocket my map and we're on our way. We share dinner with our new Scottish friends, Stephen and Jane McNaughton, at the Drovers Inn, established in 1705.

DAY FOUR: *Inverarnan to Tyndrum, 13.25 miles (21.25 km)*
We hit old military trails as yesterday's rigors are forgotten. The rain is back, as are the sheep. We move from farmlands to a thickly wooded conifer plantation, and happily eat lunch on a hillside, the mountaintops shrouded in mist. Nearing Tyndrum we walk through heather, bog myrtle and pinewoods. It's a peaceful end to the day, despite having trekked in earshot of busy route A82.

DAY FIVE: *Tyndrum to Kings House, 18.75 miles (29.75 km)*
Our longest, favorite day. The path starts on the glen floor, zigzags up through woods and descends through spectacular

moorland toward Loch Tulla. A few more miles and we're out on Rannoch Moor, a landscape of peat bogs and small lakes and sky, surrounded by heather and mountains. We're smitten. The wind is fierce but rain holds off. For most of the day we see no one else, save our Scottish friends. Guidebooks say this point is as far from civilization as any place on the Way. It feels like it.

DAY SIX: *Kings House to Kinlochleven, 9 miles (14.5 km)*
We start in sunshine near Glencoe, feeling like tiny blips on the massive glen floor surrounded by towering peaks. Soon we're cloaked in heavy mist on the Devil's Staircase, a zigzag ascent to the Way's highest point at 1,800 feet (550 meters). We again miss views of high peaks as clouds dip lower, but there's a soggy beauty. We sense the enormous presence of the surrounding mountains.

DAY SEVEN: *Kinlochleven to Fort William, 15 miles (24 km)*
Our last day brings excitement, along with torrential rain and wind. By the time we cross the gorgeous but unforgiving expanse of the valley Lairig Mor, we're soaked. Walkers in ponchos and rain gear flutter in the distance as we splash through mud. The peak of Ben Nevis, the United Kingdom's tallest mountain, is obscured by clouds as we make our final descent into Fort William. We feel elated nonetheless, and lucky to have experienced a week of such awesome beauty.

If You Go . . .
LONG-DISTANCE WALKS IN SCOTLAND: https://www.walkhighlands. co.uk/long-distance-routes.shtml
OUTFITTERS AND BAGGAGE TRANSPORT: https://www.wildernessscotland.com/, https://www.contours.co.uk/index.php or http:// travel-lite-uk.com/

BIKING THE PYRENEES: HAUTE ROUTE

By Santiago Lyon

ANGLET, France—For many people, vacation means lying poolside or beachside, reading and relaxing. But for me, it meant biking through the French Pyrenees in a week-long race, taking in the famous climbs of the Tour de France with 400 others.

It was agonizingly difficult, one steep, grueling mountain road after another. But it was also wonderful.

The event was part of the Haute Route series, billed as "the highest, toughest and most prestigious amateur cycling events in the world." The events take place annually in the French

Pyrenees, French Alps, Italian Dolomites and a new route, the Rocky Mountains.

THE FIT FACTOR

Haute Route events attract cycling-crazy folks from around the world of all ages and abilities. At the sharp end of the stick are aspiring or retired professionals, in the middle are fit cycling enthusiasts like me and at the bottom are people who signed up on a whim and may be regretting it. Some brave souls do all three European events, back to back, the so-called "triple crown."

My August trip to southwestern France was a 50th birthday present from my wife. I met up for the race with a friend, Paul O'Donnell, also turning 50. Both of us race bikes regularly in the New York area and are, for our ages, very fit. This was to be a stiff test of our abilities: 500 miles (800 km) with 65,000-plus feet (20,000-plus meters) of climbing. Each day we'd burn 4,000 to 5,000 calories.

DAY ONE: RAIN AND COWBELLS

The event began in Anglet in rainy weather. Then we hit the first major uphill of the day, the Col d'Ahusquy, a steep 8-mile (13-km) ascent. I'd never been on a climb this long and difficult before and found myself breathless and exhausted halfway up, wondering what I'd gotten myself into.

A quick pause and it was down the other side toward the day's second and final climb, the Pierre St. Martin, a 10-mile (16-km) climb through heavy fog, with visibility dropping to about 20 meters (65 feet), a blessing because you couldn't see the long series of switchbacks coming.

It was quiet for long stretches but for the whirring of bikes and the riders' breathing, with cowbells softly tinkling in the distance. A car or motorcycle engine would come and go and then you could focus on your own engine again—heart, lungs, legs.

DAY TWO: HARD CLIMBS AND THE MIND

Day two saw four climbs, all hard and long, with the Col D'Aubisque the killer, on and on (and then on some more) for 10 miles (16 km). Exhausted, rationing water, stuffing down energy gels, controlling the breathing, I tried to focus. Sweat dripped into my eyes, stinging me onto another pedal stroke, and then another.

Some might call it suffering, but for me it was cleansing, liberating, nothing but effort and the road ahead. The mind? Circling the wheel, wondering what was to come. And then I passed a one-legged, one-handed man on his bike, also making his way up. He's Christian Haettich, a regular, who lost his leg and hand in a traffic accident as an adolescent and yet he's chugging away on some of the toughest climbs in Europe.

SCENERY, SWEAT AND SWITCHBACKS

At the top, the landscape was astonishing: massive mountains upholstered in green grass and trees like giant sleeping ogres and the Pyrenees, where Iberia smashes slowly into France.

Dropping down like a marble, through tunnels bored through the rock, we descended into the valley. Cows lay nonchalantly by the roadside, big metal bells around their necks, a few pigs too and some sheep, guarded by large mountain dogs. We were warned not to approach the sheep lest the dogs mistake us for wolves and attack, as had apparently happened in previous years.

And then to the base of the day's final climb, the Col de Spandelles, just 6 miles (10 km) long but with steeply graded ramps. Small groups of curious bystanders would form by the road, some clapping, some cheering us on.

We went through the legendary Tourmalet climb, scene of epic battles in Tour de France races. Drink, drink, sweat, sweat and drink some more. More switchbacks, focus, OK, half a mile (1 km) to go, pushing a bit harder and onwards, up and then down through majestic scenery, but always keeping an eye on the clock.

MISERY AND TRIUMPH

Each day had a time cut off and if you didn't make it, you'd be eliminated from the timed event and escorted to the "broom wagon" for a ride to the finish. The next day you could continue at your own pace, no longer timed.

The final day was a mere 105 miles (169 km), just one major climb and then mostly downhill through rolling farmland into Toulouse. And then it was over. We got our participant medals, then celebrated with pizza, soft drinks and later in Toulouse, a beer or two.

Reflecting on the week, each day had seemed as punishing as the next, my whole body a slippery sinew of muscle turning and turning. But I'd gradually adjusted to the effort, the fitness kicking in. What seemed like misery in the moment felt like triumph looking back.

But would I trade a beach vacation for a week of pushing uphill again?

Absolutely.

If You Go . . .

HAUTE ROUTE: http://www.hauteroute.org. Event organizers can handle hotels, meals and other logistics for participants. Punto Tours offers a more upscale experience with personalized support, https://puntotours.com/.

COOKING IN BARCELONA:
WHAT COLOR IS PAELLA?

By Marjorie Miller

BARCELONA, Spain—Of course we are familiar with the Spanish rice dish paella, we say. It is the color of a Mediterranean sunrise, a coral red or saffron yellow.

Chef Rosa Camprodon shakes her head. Or maybe that's a shudder. She is our instructor at a Barcelona cooking school that caters to tourists, and she is teaching us to make paella Catalonia-style: a rich coppery brown.

Camprodon tosses finely diced onion into a pan of hot olive oil and has one student stir it. Add the tomato, and stir. Never let it sit on the flame, she says. Never let it burn. Add rice and stir 15 minutes in all, or until the mixture is a deep brown, ready for other ingredients.

"There are as many paellas as there are cooks," Camprodon says. "But paella is not red or yellow. It is brown. The darkness depends on how long you caramelize the onions in their own natural sugar."

A LITTLE HISTORY

Chefs are nothing if not opinionated about food. And food, like art or history, is a great gateway into a new place. So on our first trip to Barcelona, my husband and I signed up for a half-day class with the Cook and Taste school. But before we tackled the paella, we spent a few hours on the history, gathering food for thought on a group walking tour about the Spanish Civil War.

Our guide, Nick Lloyd, met us in the morning near La Rambla and La Boqueria market as tourists and foodies began to pour in. But he took us back to a time when the city was draped in red and black flags, with workers armed for battle. Here in the 1930s, he explained, followers of "Karl Marx, Adam Smith and the anarchists" joined forces in a revolutionary government in Catalonia, to fight against the fascists led by Gen. Francisco Franco—before turning on each other.

Lloyd pointed out a building once occupied by anarchists, across the plaza from another occupied by communists, and down La Rambla to the hotel where George Orwell stayed when he joined other volunteers who came to Spain from around the world to fight Franco. Lloyd recited passages from Orwell's

"Homage to Catalonia" by heart, and explained that the war was a prelude to World War II.

Franco crushed Barcelona's revolutionary government when his forces took the city in 1939, and he ruled the country with an iron fist until his death in 1975. It took decades for Barcelona to recover, but today the city is a bustling cosmopolitan center, known not so much for its bloody past and revolutionary struggles as for, among other things, Gaudi, soccer and of course, food.

LOCAL CUISINE

The city's cuisine gained international fame in part thanks to the innovative chef Ferran Adria. His El Bulli restaurant closed in 2011 but his influence remains. And maybe that's why we even thought to take a cooking class.

The menu at Cook and Taste was gazpacho, roasted vegetables and cod over flatbread, seafood paella and, for dessert, crema Catalana. Our diverse group of 12 from the U.S., Singapore and Australia had much to learn and eat in four hours: The ham must be room temperature so the fat melts over the meat to bring out the flavor. The cockles for the paella should be cleaned in cold water with salt "so it feels like home," Camprodon said. The mussels, well, "they are very sociable, you know," so you must remove the thin beard-like membrane they use to cling to each other and to rocks.

We prepared dessert first so it would have time to chill. One group whisked egg yolks and milk infused with lemon peel and cinnamon. The scented mixture was poured into terracotta dishes and refrigerated.

Another group diced and blended gazpacho, using the traditional tomato, cucumber, green pepper and garlic along with unusual ingredients: watermelon and beets.

Camprodon prepared flatbread dough ahead, so it could rise before baking. We roasted eggplant, onions and red pepper, peeled the peppers and cut the vegetables into strips before boiling the cod in hot olive oil with garlic and cayenne. The bread was cut into squares and layered with vegetables and fish.

THE PAELLA

Finally, the paella. "This is a social event. We make it on Sundays with kids everywhere and sometime people fight, 'No, I make the best paella, I do it better...' but there is plenty for everyone to do. This is hard work," Camprodon explained.

We took turns stirring onions, added vegetables, rice and a saffron-garlic paste, then spread it evenly in a pan. "No empty spaces, please," Camprodon said. She added plenty of salt but not as much as locals seem to like.

Cockles, mussels and shrimp were laid on top, then fish stock was poured into the pan and brought to a boil. "Another rule of paella: Never, ever stir after the stock has been added," she said. "Ideally, the rice is a little al dente."

We ate gazpacho and flatbread as the paella cooked. At last, it was ready, as delicious as it looked. We savored the flavors but left room for the finale: our Catalan dessert, topped by sugar caramelized with a kitchen blow torch.

We left sated, educated and ready for a siesta.

If You Go ...

SPANISH CIVIL WAR TOURS IN BARCELONA: 25 euros, http://iberia-nature.com/barcelona/history-of-barcelona/spanish-civil-war-tour-in-barcelona/

COOK AND TASTE: 65 euros (children, half-price), http://www.cookandtaste.net/

CAMINO DE SANTIAGO: ENDURANCE, CONTEMPLATION, CAMARADERIE

By Giovanna Dell'Orto

EL ACEBO, Spain—About three hours into the day's hike, having just cleared the highest mountain point of the Camino de Santiago, I looked down into the valleys pockmarked with yellow and purple spring blossoms, and froze.

Surely that faraway black office tower, seemingly no bigger

than the trail stones making my scarred feet scream, could not be where I was planning to arrive that same night. Guidebook check: It was.

Dejected, I struggled downhill into the next hamlet, El Acebo. I was barely past the first of its slate-roofed stone houses when my name—"Giovanna!"—was called out by a fellow pilgrim.

And that was my camino experience: 31 days of physical endurance through awe-inspiring landscapes, of contemplation punctuated by deep connections. It was a combination that reset my Type-A internal clock so that stopping to pick a poppy or a bunch of grapes, or to compare blisters with hikers from Seoul or Hawaii or Naples, became not only permissible but also imperative.

THE ROUTE AND THE CROWDS

The "camino frances," or French way, is an 800-kilometer (500 miles) medieval pilgrimage route that crosses Spain from the Pyrenees at the French border to the purported burial site of the Apostle James in the cathedral of Santiago de Compostela.

Of several historical routes to Santiago, this is the most popular.

It's no wilderness hike: The longest stretch without crossing a village is 10 miles (17 km) through farmland. How much solitude you get depends on when and where you start.

More than 180,000 people arrived in Santiago via the camino frances in 2017, walking at least the last 62 miles (100 km) from Sarria, by far the most crowded stretch, or biking 124 miles (200 km). The busiest months are May-September, and the least busy is January. Over the last decade, yearly numbers have mostly risen, but 2010 saw the most pilgrims, likely because it was a Catholic "holy year."

I've walked the camino three times, in 2014, 2015 and 2017,

averaging 16 miles (26 km) daily, often for hours without seeing another pilgrim—though I got stuck for a day among hundreds of yellow-hatted German confirmation students.

With the universal greeting of "buen camino," I met bikers from Taiwan, retirees from New Zealand, school groups from Minnesota and southern Spain, couples who started at 4 a.m. to ensure solitude and singles who got a lively party scene going most nights. The only kind of person I did not meet was one not deeply affected by the experience.

SHORTER STRETCHES

For those who cannot devote four to five weeks to go the full way, there are shorter stretches.

Roncesvalles to Estella: After the first pilgrims' blessing in half-a-dozen languages at the ancient stone church in Roncesvalles, a two-day downhill trek through mountain woods where Charlemagne fought and Hemingway fished takes you to Pamplona, one of four major cities the camino crosses. Refueled with Basque txistorra sausage, you're off through rolling hills carpeted in wheat and vines, topped by castles and crisscrossed by Roman roads and medieval bridges until Estella, whose fortress-like medieval churches and palaces huddle in a gorge.

Burgos to Carrion de Los Condes: Burgos is the kind of city where, after plodding for half a day through suburbs, you still take 1.5-hour walking tours of the 13th-century cathedral or the main monastery, then limber along the river promenade to restaurants specializing in lechazo, roasted lamb. Beyond is the emptiness of the meseta (plains). Its shades of green and gold are interrupted by jewels like Castrojeriz, Fromista and Carrion de los Condes, with intact Romanesque churches.

Astorga to O Cebreiro: The camino's longest climbs start just past the Gaudi-designed bishop's palace and buzzing main square of Astorga. Through fragrant brush and below snow-covered peaks, you clamber up hamlets like Rabanal, with its mesmerizing chanted vesper prayers, then down into vineyards around pretty, riverside Villafranca del Bierzo. From there it's uphill to O Cebreiro's thatched-roof stone houses and Galicia's moss-draped, cow-clogged paths.

After two more bucolic days, the last 62 miles (100 km) are crowded with the "clean-shod," as we pilgrims hobbling on muddy boots called those who start here.

ARRIVAL IN SANTIAGO

That takes nothing away, however, from arriving in Santiago, with its incense-filled cathedral covered with stern medieval statues and swirling Baroque cherubs standing tall among homes, monasteries and student pubs.

Before going back to email and schedules, there's a stairway to climb to embrace the statue of St. James at the cathedral's altar, and one last chance to hug fellow pilgrims.

Perhaps you exchange Facebook connections, perhaps nothing but a whispered "good luck," because you both know that the real tough "camino" starts now.

If You Go . . .

GETTING THERE: From Madrid, take trains to any larger city along the camino; buses and taxis connect smaller ones.

LODGING: Buy a "credencial," which gets you in most public hostels. The credencial, stamped and dated along the way, earns you the compostela when you turn it in at Santiago's Pilgrims' Office, https://oficinadelperegrino.com. Hostels (albergues) charge 5 or more euros for a bed, first come, first served. Most towns also have hotels. Services transport backpacks for several euros daily. Most restaurants have three-course pilgrims' menus with wine, 8-10 euros.

TIPS: Train before you go; it's strenuous. The camino frances is so well-marked with yellow arrows and its shell symbol that you never need maps. If you read Spanish, the best guide is free at http://caminodesantiago.consumer.es/los-caminos-de-santiago/frances/. Take precautions, especially for female solo travelers. An American woman walking the trail was murdered in 2015.

EUROPE BY MOTORCYCLE:
JE SUIS UNE MOTO

By Erik Schelzig

BOLOGNA, Italy—Motorbikes are everywhere in Europe. They are easy to squeeze through traffic and park at busy tourist sites. Their fuel efficiency gives some relief from gas prices that seem high to Americans.

And you even get a discount on French motorways, though I was forced to resort to my patchy language skills when an error message flashed as I arrived at an automated tollbooth.

"Je suis une moto?" I offered uncertainly over the intercom.

I could have sworn I heard faint laughter before the gate swung open and sent me on my way.

10 DAYS ON A MOTORCYCLE

I was on a 10-day European motorcycling excursion. The bulk of my trip took place on a big BMW touring bike through 3,000 miles (4,800 km) of spectacular scenery and serpentine mountain passes in the Spanish Pyrenees and Austrian Alps, down the bustling streets of the glitzy French Riviera and to legal speeds of more than 135 mph (218 kph) on the German autobahn.

Stops along the way included visits to the factories of Ducati in Bologna and MV Agusta on the outskirts of Milan, the annual BMW Motorrad Days gathering in a Bavarian winter resort town and to Tavullia, hometown of Italian motorcycle racing legend Valentino Rossi, where church bells ring when the town's favorite son takes another win.

At pit stops for coffee and gas, a glance at the map beckoned detours to an isolated country road, Alpine pass or to check a previously unvisited country off my list. Andorra, Monaco, San Marino? Why not?

THE BASICS

All you need to rent a motorcycle in Europe is an unrestricted motorcycle endorsement (usually added to a regular driver's license) and an international driver's license, which you can get in the U.S. for about $15 from AAA. Note that most U.S. auto insurance providers and credit cards don't cover motorcycle rentals. At IMTBike, the standard deductible for damage or theft was 2,000 euros when I took my trip, but I chose to pay an extra 20 euros per day for the peace of mind of a 350-euro deductible if someone made off with the bike, or if a tip-over in a gravel parking lot did expensive cosmetic damage.

RENTING

Numerous options throughout Spain like IMTBike and Hispania Tours offer both guided tours and individual rentals. Keep an eye out for BMW Official Partner status that seeks to ensure German bikes are kept to top maintenance and servicing standards. BMW also offers bikes through the rental car giant Sixt in Germany during riding season.

Ducati supplies bikes and instructors on several road or track courses through its Ducati Riding Experience program in Italy.

Generally, daily rates decrease the longer you rent the bike. At the time of my trip, IMTBike charged 174 euros daily for BMW R1200 RT rentals of three days or less. For a week or more, the rate drops to 129 euros daily. The daily mileage cap was 300 kilometers on shorter rentals, with a 30-cent charge for every kilometer after that. There is no distance limit for rentals over a week. Most bikes come with built-in luggage, and extra travel bags can usually be left at rental offices.

FACTORY TOURS

BMW motorcycles are made in Spandau in western Berlin. You can tour the sprawling factory, which makes up to 700 bikes a day. Tours are also available at the Ducati plant and museum on the outskirts of Bologna. Both require reservations.

MIND THE LIMITS

The low police profile on roads may suggest little enforcement of speed limits. But traffic cameras are everywhere, as I was reminded several weeks after my trip when I got a ticket in the mail for going 109 kph in a 90 kph zone in northern Spain. One bright spot: As a non-resident, my fine was discounted to half of the 100-euro ticket.

FAIRY CHIMNEYS AND BALLOONS
IN CAPPADOCIA, TURKEY

By Courtney Bonnell

GOREME, Turkey—A few whooshing breaths of fire and up we went, a yellow orb rising in a sea of hot-air balloons like the sun brightening the morning sky.

Others followed close behind, climbing over craggy canyons, pink mountains and mushroom-shaped rock formations called fairy chimneys. Suddenly, our basket, packed with tourists angling for a perfect picture, bounced as it got bumped by an ascending balloon.

"Don't worry! It's OK," our young pilot hollered out, smiling behind his Ray-Bans and turning up the flame on the balloon's burner to climb faster.

We chuckled nervously, but it got our blood pumping in the thinning atmosphere. So did what we saw next.

We slowly spanned up a hillside and hundreds of balloons exploded into view, a colorful melange hovering above the valleys cut like lightning into the Turkish region of Cappadocia.

BOOKINGS

But before the breathtaking views comes the preparation. Online travel searches are good ways to scope out top-rated balloon companies in a region renowned for the rides. You will pay more for reputable operators and to share the experience with fewer people—something you will value as you try to shoot photos that don't include an errant hand or head.

Almost all offer a continental breakfast before the ride, transportation to the launch site and a "Champagne toast"—usually sparkling cider—and certificate after landing.

The region is a UNESCO World Heritage site whose economy survives on tourists flocking to see the fairy chimneys, cave dwellings, vast underground cities and ancient Christian churches carved into the mountainsides. Because of its popularity, hundreds of hotels are poised to handle balloon bookings.

The cave hotels, hundreds of which are packed onto a hillside in the small tourist town of Goreme, are a must-do. Pick one with windows to avoid feeling claustrophobic. I booked my balloon ride through the hotel, which allowed me to put the ride on my credit card and pay at checkout instead of needing cash.

My hotel contracted with three balloon companies of different price levels. I went with the midrange after looking up the operators on TripAdvisor. I saved 50 euros by skipping the top-rated balloon company, but I still had an unbelievable experience taking in the alien-like landscape from the sky.

ON THE GROUND AND UNDERGROUND

The formations and hillsides served as year-round homes, and the caves also provided safety for persecuted Christians in the 10th to 13th centuries. Visitors can climb through some of the houses of worship, decorated inside with elaborate murals, at the famed Goreme Open Air Museum. The museum is walkable from Goreme's town center.

The Christians also built extensive underground cities where they hid from attackers, sometimes for months at a time. Two are open to visitors.

At Kaymakli Underground City, you duck through narrow entryways into family rooms, living quarters, kitchens and even chambers where they buried their dead. They also brought down their livestock and made wine in buckets carved into the soft stone walls.

Above ground, you can hike through valleys with names like Love, Red and Rose; climb up cave castles, which are natural fortresses pitted with tunnels; and scramble through fairy chimneys at Pasabag.

The fairy chimneys have been created over eons by erosion. The soft, white rock at the bottom of the formation erodes more quickly than the sturdier rock at the top, leaving the mushroom shape.

Soaring over this otherworldly landscape is the ride of a lifetime. Getting up at 4 a.m., wrapping up against the chill and cramming into a bucket next to other tourists is not for the unadventurous or those on a tight budget. But as you dip low into the valleys and fly high above the mountains, even those afraid of heights will want to look down.

If You Go . . .

BALLOON RIDES IN CAPPADOCIA, TURKEY: The area is an hour by car from Kayseri airport and a bit closer to Nevsehir airport. Most visitors arrive the day before and stay overnight in a hotel because the balloons typically take off shortly after dawn. Multiple flights leave Istanbul daily for Kayseri and Nevsehir

TRANSCONTINENTAL RAILWAY: ACROSS MONGOLIA AND SIBERIA

By Jeremy Hainsworth

ST. PETERSBURG, Russia—It was the realization of a dream from a childhood obsessed with trains: taking one of the world's longest train rides, on the Trans Mongolian and Trans Siberian railways.

The trip went from Beijing, China, via Ulaanbaatar, Mongolia, and across Russia to Moscow and St. Petersburg with whistle stops in between. It spanned two continents, seven time zones, many cultures and some 5,000 miles (7,900 km).

The logistics are hard to organize on your own, so I travelled with G Adventures. Arriving several days early in Beijing to sample the city, I munched on deep-fried scorpion in a market, climbed ancient drum and bell towers, explored the sprawling Forbidden City and saw the preserved body of Mao Zedong in a mausoleum more resembling the shrine of a deity.

THE RIGHT MINDSET

Then our tour group—six in all—met for our three-week adventure, led by guide Aleksandr Paramanov. A week was spent in close quarters aboard trains. Each car had a hot water boiler, but you had to bring your own food, water and tea and get into the right mindset: Relax, chat with new friends or just gaze at the ever-changing landscape. Or befriend the carriage attendant, buy a few things from her and get on her good side.

The Trans Siberian is not a special train with specific runs. It's a regularly scheduled train; you book sections and get on and off as you wish.

Our first run, departing the madness of Beijing's main station for Ulaanbaatar, was filled with Chinese and Mongolian travelers heading home. After Chinese officials searched the train and stamped passports in the late evening, the train was taken apart. Carriages were moved into sheds, giant jacks raised them up and wheel chassis were replaced to handle Mongolia's gauge rail system.

MONGOLIA

We awoke to see the sandy-brown, scrub-dotted wastes Gobi Desert. Ulaanbaatar, the world's most remote capital city, comes into view as the train rounds a bend. Yurt tents dot the hills around the city of 1.1 million where more than 100,000 nomads still live under canvas.

We explored the Black Market, a massive jumble of stalls containing everything from horse blankets to antique Nazi bayonets. Beware of pickpockets not only in the market but throughout the city. I lost my credit cards in a brief bump with someone.

We stood amid Buddhist ceremonies with monks chanting and sampled horse cooked on flat metal grills. Later, we slept in a yurt on the steppes (Mongolian plains). A stove for heating needed stoking in the middle of the night. Cows meandered through the camp, the twilight on the distant hills making it seem like a scene from Middle Earth.

RUSSIA

Boarding the train again, we readied ourselves for Russian border officials. Passports were taken, bags searched and sniffer dogs led through the train.

On to Yekaterinburg, a city on the dividing line between two continents, a two-day ride through forests and rolling hills on rails that once carried Soviet exiles heading the other way to the gulag. In another compartment, strangers fed my travel-mate caviar, crabmeat, eggs and vodka.

Yekaterinburg's highlight is the Church of the Spilled Blood, the golden-domed sanctuary built on the site where the last tsar, Nicholas II, and his family were massacred by the Bolsheviks. A chapel marks the execution spot.

On May 9, we chanced to see the parade marking the anniversary of the end of World War II. Tanks and missiles rolled through the streets as fighter jets roared overhead.

Back aboard bound for Moscow, we were split between compartments, attempting communication with friendly but frustrated Russians.

In the Russian capital we explored Red Square, the Kremlin as well as Soviet monuments and art galleries.

Then, more than two weeks after departing Beijing, we boarded a night train for St. Petersburg. Leaving that final train was hard. We'd all lived a dream.

If You Go...

TRANS MONGOLIAN AND TRANS SIBERIAN RAILWAYS: It's complicated to organize this trip on your own. One option is to book through https://www.gadventures.com/trips/trans-mongolian-express/ ACTM/.

TRANS SIBERIAN RAILWAY: https://www.transsiberianexpress.net/ trans-siberian-express.html

VISAS: Requirements vary by country. Consult the Chinese, Mongolian and Russian consular sites. Letters of invitation may be needed for visas. Tour companies can assist.

TIPS: Beware of pickpockets. Money belts are a must. Don't carry all your credit and debit cards together. Pack efficiently—you carry everything you bring. Bring an e-reader for long stretches on the train.

FOOD: Some trains have dining cars but don't count on it. Pack tea or instant coffee to share with fellow travellers. Buy fruit, instant noodles, vegetables, dried meats and bread for days you'll be on the train.

ARCTIC CIRCLE SUMMER: REINDEER AND NORTHERN LIGHTS

By Cara Anna

ABISKO, Sweden—Few people outside Nordic countries know about the Kungsleden, or the King's Path, the most famous trail in Sweden. But it's considered one of the world's great hikes, and for good reason.

Northern lights? Yes. Reindeer? Yes, and at close range.

Icebergs and polar bears? No. But the views are clear and gorgeous. And while a good dose of self-sufficiency is required to tackle the multi-day hike, what's at first a challenge eventually becomes a point of pride.

The mountain huts are open between the end of June and mid-September, when there's rarely snow. This is when the far north shows itself in spare landscapes and unusual light. It's not the Himalaya, though hills lining the wide valley are the weathered nubs of mountains that were once just as high. Few trees obstruct the view. The path is dotted with bushes bearing edible, bright red lingonberries. The wind can be strong and cold.

Reindeer and the indigenous Sami people help break the open landscape. In summer, the semi-nomadic Sami round up and identify young reindeer. In fall, hunting and slaughtering season begins.

ABISKO

The most popular part of the Kungsleden is its northernmost stretch, easily reached by a brief Scandinavian Airlines flight and bus ride, or an overnight train from Stockholm. The train stops across from one of the biggest and busiest mountain lodges along the trail, in Abisko.

The tiny village is world-renowned for its view of the northern lights, and Japanese tour groups there were no surprise, since the lights are revered in Japanese culture. But I almost wished that someone would sound an alarm when the lights appear. I spent the evening in the lodge's one-room library, hopping up from time to time to glance outside. Eventually, I returned to the dormitory to sleep, then I happened to glance up and there they were, glowing green and slowly moving across the sky.

PATHS AND PROVISIONS

From Abisko, the Kungsleden offers what we need more of in the United States: a multi-day hike, accessible by public transport, with huts along the way. On the trail, you can also camp pretty much wherever you like. During hiking season, shelters are open with gas stoves, bunk beds, wood stoves for heat and candles for light. Water comes from nearby streams.

You're expected to fend for yourself. I quickly learned how to saw wood and light fires.

Custodians welcome you with a glass of juice, take payments and show you around. Bring your own food for the entire week-long hike in case the small shops in some shelters run low on staples like pasta and canned protein. Try the fish balls.

Between shelters, hikes run 8 to 14 miles (13 to 22 km). From Abisko to the bustling mountain lodge at Kebnekaise, near the foot of Sweden's tallest mountain, the walk is generally level or rolling. Marshy areas are crossed with two-plank walkways, and streams have bridges or stepping stones.

That almost relentlessly stony path is challenging, especially while carrying a backpack with a week's worth of food. But a good number of Kungsleden hikers were middle-aged, including a lanky 70-year-old man from Denmark and a pair of Swedish women in their 60s.

Near the shelter at Salka, located in a vast bowl formed where valleys meet, I stood still for several minutes as a small herd of reindeer wandered across the trail. Their leader snuffed in seeming impatience, and the younger ones butted and played.

The Kungsleden's simple pleasures shift back to civilization from the village of Nikkaluokta, a day's hike from Kebnekaise, where a couple of buses a day during hiking season go to the regional center of Kiruna less than an hour away. The small mining city offers good local food at the Safari Cafe, a well-resourced tourist bureau, a striking old wooden church, a bookstore with a modest English section and the local branch of the Swedish chain H&M. Good Swedish coffee is easily found. Kiruna also has several hostels and hotels, and a shared taxi to the airport a few miles away can be arranged.

From Kiruna, I flew back to Stockholm and spent my final day exploring neighborhoods with the city's bike-hire system and taking a ferry to one of thousands of islands in the Stockholm Archipelago on the edge of the Baltic Sea. In about 90 minutes I was on the tiny island of Grinda, following seaside paths, picking apples and contemplating a restaurant splurge at the sole hotel. It was a simple, beautiful day, a perfect end to the trip.

If You Go . . .

KUNGSLEDEN: Hiking trail in Sweden's Arctic Circle. Abisko, Kebnekaise and Kiruna accommodations can be booked via Svenska Turistforeningen, http://www.svenskaturistforeningen. se/en/.

TREKKING IN NEPAL: A FAMILY ADVENTURE

By Malcolm Foster

POKHARA, Nepal—If you're looking for a family adventure that immerses you in nature, beauty and a fascinating culture—and you're willing to rough it some—consider trekking in Nepal.

Our two boys, 12 and 10, loved our six-day trek in Nepal, an adventure that took us through lush forests, terraced fields and traditional villages nestled amid forbidding, yet starkly beautiful, peaks.

Sometimes the going was tough—like hiking two hours up steep, stone steps. Other times, we walked along gently undulating woodland paths.

We hiked four to six hours daily, depending on difficulty, usually reaching our destination by 3 p.m., allowing time to relax before supper.

Along the way, there were rewards: local children who ran to greet us (sometimes asking for money or candy), wildflowers beside the path, breathtaking views and cups of hot masala tea at little rest stops.

One of my older son's favorite parts was the camaraderie with other trekkers from around the world in common rooms at the "tea houses," or simple lodges where we stayed.

GHANDRUK-GHOREPANI-POON HILL LOOP

Children as young as 8 or 9 could handle the popular 40-mile (64 km) Ghandruk-Ghorepani-Poon Hill loop we hiked, just south of the Annapurna Range. Small children can be carried on the backs of porters.

With good weather, this route will give you stunning views of a string of mountains, including Annapurna I, the 10th tallest in the world; Machapuchre, or "Fishtail," with its distinctively shaped peak; and the towering Dhaulagiri, the world's seventh-tallest. Mount Everest, the world's tallest, is 190 miles (300 km) to the east and not visible on this loop.

HIRING A GUIDE

The circuit starts and ends near the lakeside town of Pokhara, central Nepal's trekking hub. We used 3 Sisters Adventure Trekking, which specializes in training and employing women, to hire our guide, Mana Kunwar, an experienced, flexible and fun Nepali woman who spoke good English. Her knowledge of the trail, culture and language, including contacts at tea houses where she booked our rooms, enhanced our experience immensely.

We also hired a male porter to carry one backpack while I carried another. My wife and kids hiked with smaller knapsacks. Hiring guides is not only a way to get to know locals, it also offers them a valuable source of income.

SEASONS AND WEATHER

Peak trekking season is October and November, when skies are clearest and temperatures hover between the 60s and 70s F (15 to 20 C). We mostly hiked in T-shirts and shorts (women's shorts should be knee-length out of respect for the local culture). But early mornings and evenings, when it got as cold as 40 degrees F (4 C), we needed fleeces and long pants.

We encountered no snow, but a week before our October visit, a freak blizzard and avalanche hit a pass at a higher elevation. April and May, also a good time to go, can be cloudier, but the rhododendron trees are in bloom. June, July and August are rainy.

PROVISIONS AND GEAR

Be prepared to rough it. Some tea houses offer hot showers, but water supplies are often limited. Rooms run $3-$5 a night, and are basic but clean. Blankets are available, but most trekkers bring sleeping bags, which can be rented or bought in Pokhara or Kathmandu at shops that sell everything you need, including knock-off brand fleeces and backpacks.

Trekking poles, about $5 apiece, are recommended, especially when descending. Don't buy hiking shoes when you arrive; break those in at home.

The food is rather monotonous: Lots of dal bhat, or lentil stew with rice, plus curries, pastas and soups, and not much meat or fruit. Deep-fried "gurung bread" is quite good. You may want to bring canned tuna or meat.

Some experiences require a lot of effort, like seeing a sunrise from Poon Hill. For that we woke at 5 a.m. and hiked 45 minutes from the village of Ghorepani, and we shared the experience with 300 to 400 other trekkers. We got a panoramic view of both the Annapurna and Dhaulagiri ranges in all their majesty, and like the rest of the trip, the effort was worth it.

If You Go...

GETTING THERE: From Kathmandu, head to Pokhara via Yeti Airlines or Buddha Air, or take a six-hour bus.

TREKKING AGENCIES: Trekking agencies can arrange everything, including domestic travel in Nepal, lodging in Kathmandu and Pokhara, and packages that include trail lodging, food, guides, trekking permits. However, it's usually cheaper to make your own domestic hotel and travel reservations online. For the trek portion, you can pay a package price, or pay for lodging and meals as you go, and a guide by the day.

3 SISTERS ADVENTURE TREKKING: Based in Pokhara, specializes in female guides, 3sistersadventuretrek.com

MOONLIGHT NEPAL TREKKING AND ADVENTURE TOURS: In Kathmandu, this company allocates some profits to health care and education, moonlightnepaladventuretours.com

TIGERS IN INDIA:
A PHOTO SAFARI

By Dean Fosdick

INDIA—Going on safari to India to photograph tigers in the wild is an unrivaled experience. These are the world's largest cats. They are stealthy, solitary, spectacular and scarce.

But sighting one in its natural habitat is never a sure thing. "All wildlife viewing is opportunistic and needs a certain amount of luck," said Toby Sinclair, an expedition leader with Natural Habitat Adventures in Delhi.

WHEN TO GO

Tilt the odds in your favor by arriving when the escalating heat of late spring drives tigers from the thick jungle scrub to more visible waterholes. Some national parks and wildlife sanctuaries are especially rewarding for visitors during the hot months of April to mid-June, Sinclair said.

"This is when the water is limited to a few pools and the animals, both prey and predator, have to come to drink water at least twice a day," he said. "It is also the time when much of the grass and undergrowth has died back so the areas of view are generally better."

There's a trade-off, though. In India, wildlife photographers generally travel in open safari vehicles. That makes it easier to spot bird and animal life high in the tree canopy. But it also exposes you to the punishing sun, making dehydration a possibility with temperatures reaching 115 to 120 degrees F (46 to 48 C). Dehydration can shut you down, causing vomiting, diarrhea, fainting and muscle cramps. Reduce the risk by eating right and frequently hydrating.

How about other times of the year? "Because of its size and the varied landscapes, there are parts of India that are closed during the monsoon (late June to late September) and a few (parks) that don't open until November," Sinclair said.

Weather is cooler in late fall and early winter but it can be harder to see the tigers because the landscape is lush. "You want to go there when it's warm but it's not too late into the summer so you don't bake to death," said Joseph Van Os, owner of Joseph Van Os Photo Safaris.

VIEW FROM AN ELEPHANT

Five of India's national parks (Bandhavgarh, Kanha, Kaziranga, Periyar and Corbett) offer visitors a unique option: searching for tigers from the back of an elephant. It's a popular way for photographers to access remote park corners.

But be selective about vendors. Some have been known to crowd the cats once discovered in remote scrub. Go with an operator recommended by your travel agent or tour operator.

"Getting on elephants in these parks is critical in getting close to tigers," Van Os said. "You can go right up to the caves where the tigers are sheltering from the heat rather than waiting for them to show up at the waterholes.

"Elephants," he said, "are the ultimate four-wheel drive vehicle."

PROTECTING TIGERS

India was home to some 40,000 tigers a century ago but habitat loss, poaching and population pressure reduced that to fewer than 2,000 by 1970. To reverse the decline, India established wildlife sanctuaries that now include more than 600 protected areas along with 50 tiger reserves.

That conservation effort has seen India's tiger population grow slightly. But numbers remain fragile: a government-estimated 2,226 tigers in 2014 representing 70 percent of the world's total.

India must also balance tourism growth against protecting wildlife species, diversity and watersheds, Natural Habitat's Sinclair said.

"Most of the larger parks have caps on the number of vehicles that can enter at any one time," he said.

SAFARI DESTINATION: INDIA OR AFRICA?

Africa and India are both rich in wildlife. But they're worlds apart in what's available for viewing and how that viewing is managed.

Africa offers "big concentrations of wildlife. It's not like any other place in the world," Van Os said. "A lot of species and in big numbers. But in India, it's specialized. The parks are smaller and the diversity is not there. You go for one or two main species."

That means tigers, which don't live in the wild in Africa.

HEALTH

My warnings about heat come from a hard-earned lesson. I became severely dehydrated going too long without water while walking around Old Delhi. I suffered extreme headaches, weakness and nausea. I spent the final day of my trip in bed downing prescribed rehydration salts and meds. It took two weeks to fully recover.

But I did return with the prize of a shooter's lifetime: scores of photos taken of these rare, elusive and exceedingly beautiful animals.

If You Go...

GETTING THERE: I took my tiger safari in late May with Natural Habitat Adventures, a Colorado-based company. From Delhi, our group of six photographers traveled with the expedition leader by train five hours to Sawai Madhopur, where a safari truck drove us another 6 miles (10 km) to the outskirts of Ranthambore National Park and on to our hotel. We took two-a-day safaris for four consecutive days via open truck within the park and saw 15 tigers in various settings, most around waterholes. Prices run about $7,000 for the seven-day tour (plus airfare and insurance, $1,375 more for single supplement).

THE ART ISLAND OF NAOSHIMA, JAPAN

By Donna Bryson

NAOSHIMA, Japan—Because I had just emerged from the gloom of a tree-lined approach, the white stones that paved the courtyard seemed impossibly bright.

Then, my eyes caught something unexpected: a flight of chunky glass steps, a very modern touch on a renovated shrine.

Encountering surprising and beautiful juxtapositions defined my visit to Japan's Naoshima, a small island that Pritzker Prize-winning architect Tadao Ando has helped transform into a destination for lovers of contemporary art and design.

My trip to Naoshima was something of an Ando pilgrimage. I'd admired the work of the Japanese-born, internationally known Ando at the Art Institute of Chicago, where he created a powerfully contemplative gallery for Japanese screens using simple pillars and lines of light and shadow. My daughter came up with the phrase "art-itecture" during our visit to Naoshima because we focused so much of our attention on Ando's buildings, and less on the artworks they house.

For a 1989 festival, Ando designed a campground where the public could contemplate art and Naoshima's natural beauty. In 1992, an Ando-designed hotel-and-art complex opened, Benesse House. It's a dream come true for those of us who have always wanted to spend the night in a museum. I got a thrill passing one of Hiroshi Sugimoto's extraordinary photographs of theaters on my way to breakfast the two mornings I spent at Benesse House.

The hotel complex, which includes a seaside sculpture park, also is home to work by, among others, Jennifer Bartlett, Jonathan Borofsky, David Hockney, Bruce Nauman, Niki de Saint Phalle, Frank Stella and Andy Warhol. A giant spotted pumpkin by Yayoi Kusama that sits on a pier jutting into the Seto Inland Sea has become a mascot for the enterprise. Anyone can view the art, but hotel guests get after-hours access.

Over the next decades, Ando designed several more buildings for Naoshima, including additional suites of rooms for Benesse House, with the most exclusive connected to the main galleries by monorail.

Perhaps the most stunning of Ando's structures is the Chichu Art Museum, which opened in 2004. Chichu means underground, and the galleries are buried into a hillside so that they become part of the island's dramatic landscape. Yet the spaces are filled with natural light. A Claude Monet painting of water lilies hangs in a room over a floor of white stone cubes that reminded me of the bright stones in the shrine courtyard elsewhere on the island. Chichu also houses installations by James Turrell and Walter De Maria.

In another Ando museum on Naoshima, dark hallways lead like journeys to the revelations contained in the precise paintings and bold stone and steel sculptures of Lee Ufan, who was born in Korea and established himself as a leading figure in Japanese contemporary art.

Ando got a museum of his own on Naoshima in 2013. The architect set a concrete box inside a century-old house in Naoshima's Honmura area. The house literally and figuratively embraces exhibitions on Ando's work, which is rooted in the simplicity of traditional design and casts an admiring glance at ancient craftsmanship. The museum is a short bus or bike ride from Benesse House.

The Honmura neighborhood also is home to another Benesse initiative, the Art House Project launched in 1998. Artists have made galleries and installations out of abandoned homes, temples, a dentist's office and a hangout for players of the board game Go.

Benesse House is named for Japan's Benesse Corp., whose holdings include Berlitz, the language education company. Benesse founder Tetsuhiko Fukutake bought land on Naoshima as a base to explore ideas about nurturing children and worked with locals on projects linking economic and cultural development. He died in 1985, but his son, Soichiro, a collector of contemporary art, took his father's vision further, saying in an online welcome message that the island is "a place where art is not experienced by studying set attitudes but appreciated on your own terms."

Naoshima is craggily scenic, and so densely forested that the trees and ferns compete with sand for footholds along the shore. Before it became an arts destination, its economy centered on salt, fishing and manufacturing.

The glass steps that caught my eye are part of an Art House Project renovation of an Edo period shrine by Sugimoto. The steps link the hilltop shrine to an underground stone chamber. The glass stairs echoed timber risers I occasionally saw dug into the surrounding hills to ease the way for pedestrians. More than occasionally, I spotted humble roadside Shinto shrines at which the faithful had left flowers and other offerings. Seeing them, it was easy to imagine the island and its art-itecture teeming with spirits.

If You Go . . .

NAOSHIMA, JAPAN: http://www.naoshima.net/en . Benesse Art Site Naoshima: http://www.benesse-artsite.jp/en.

GETTING THERE: Fly or take a high-speed bullet train to Okayama; then 45 minutes by bus, taxi or train to Uno Port for a 20-minute ferry to Naoshima.

GETTING AROUND: Benesse House guests can take a hop-on, hop-off courtesy bus from art site to art site, and from the ferry port to the hotel. A walking map available at the Naoshima ferry port shows bus routes. Bike rentals available in town.

ACCOMMODATIONS: Benesse House is pricey, $350 to $500 depending on room and season. Cheaper inns (minshuku) are available.

NEW ZEALAND:
HIKING THE GREAT WALKS

By Carey J. Williams

FIORDLAND NATIONAL PARK, New Zealand—Several items are essential for exploring the magical Southern Alps mountains that run across New Zealand's South Island: insect repellent, rain gear and ear plugs.

The repellent is to ward off sand flies, those annoying black bugs that are the itchy scourge of hikers in Fiordland National Park. The park, which is bigger than Yosemite and Yellowstone national parks combined, is one of the wettest places on Earth. It gets an average 280 inches of rainfall a year, compared to Seattle's 38.6 inches.

And while there's plenty of peace and quiet to enjoy while hiking the region, you may want ear plugs to block the sound of snoring from exhausted hikers in the huts that offer lodging along the Great Walks.

THE GREAT WALKS

The Great Walks are routes featured by the country's Department of Conservation (DOC) for their "diverse and spectacular scenery." Five of the nine Great Walks are on the South Island (a 10th Great Walk is scheduled to open in 2019).

The Great Walks are highly regulated by the DOC, which maintains the trails, checks for hiking passes and staffs the huts with nightly educational talks. The huts on the most popular Great Walks are large, clean cabins with bunk rooms.

They're a great way to be social with like-minded tourists and hear languages from around the world. I had fun teaching my bunkmates how to play an old-fashioned card-and-board game, cribbage.

MILFORD TRACK, MILFORD SOUND

One of the Fiordland Great Walks, the Milford Track, is a world-famous four-day route. Hiking it requires planning as much as a year in advance if you're planning on visiting during peak Great Walks season, October to April.

For other South Island adventures, though, it's good to have some flexibility in your schedule as you'll pick up tips on things to do from other hikers and from the knowledgeable staff in DOC offices throughout the country.

One excursion that's popular with hikers is an overnight cruise from Milford Sound. The boat's all-you-can-eat buffet is a nice change from ramen noodles and other backpacker fare.

The crystal-clear waters along the Milford Track make it relatively easy to spot the freshwater longfin eel, featured on an episode of Animal Planet's "River Monsters." Elsewhere, watch out for backpack-eating alpine parrots called keas. They are ever-present in high-altitude regions and they're not afraid to peck at human gear in search of food.

You'll also want to pack a headlamp, both to navigate the huts at night, and for taking nighttime walks to look for glow worms, which are what they sound like.

Farther north, the rock scramble for a night's stay at the Mueller Hut is a must-do for its close-up view of Aoraki Mount Cook, New Zealand's largest peak at 12,218 feet (3,724 meters).

STEWART ISLAND AND ABEL TASMAN

On Stewart Island, a small island that's a ferry ride or short plane trip south of the South Island, you'll find another Great Walk, the Rakiura Track. Rakiura's 20-mile (32 km) loop has huts as well as campsites.

Stewart Island is popular with wildlife watchers hoping to glimpse kiwi, the national symbol of New Zealand. The flightless birds are famous for having among the largest eggs in relation to body size of any other bird species. But they're nocturnal and can be hard to see in the wild. A number of guided kiwi-spotting tours are offered on the island.

And keep in mind when planning a trip to New Zealand that it's in the Southern Hemisphere, with winter weather June-August, spring weather September-November and summer December-February.

At some point, you'll want to ditch the rancid hiking boots and exchange them for some sandals to walk the beautiful beaches in the Abel Tasman National Park—home to another Great Walk, the Abel Tasman Coast Track—on the northern tip of the South Island.

Finally, pick up a bottle of wine from the South Island's Marlborough region or grab a local craft beer brewed with Nelson Sauvin hops and prepare yourself for a trip to the North Island, where a different type of magic awaits: the "Hobbiton" movie set.

If You Go...

NEW ZEALAND GREAT WALKS: www.doc.govt.nz/greatwalks. Check DOC requirements for hiking the Great Walks and check on route conditions with local visitor centers. The routes are vulnerable to storm damage, weather and other factors.

THE DISNEY RACE:
IT'S ALL ABOUT THE COSTUME

By Anick Jesdanun

LAKE BUENA VISTA, Florida—Running at Walt Disney World isn't about your race time.

It's about your costume and your photo ops.

You might find Darth Vader, Tinker Bell or a classic Disney princess running alongside half-marathon participants.

But it's not the finish line they're most concerned with. It's getting to pose with costumed characters such as Donald Duck and Boba Fett before the lines get too long.

THEMES AND RUNCATIONS

Disney has races at Disney World in Florida throughout the year and one at Disneyland Paris in September. (Races at Disneyland in California are on hold pending construction on a new "Star Wars"-themed land and other expansion.)

In April, the Florida theme park hosts a Star Wars Half Marathon themed on the Dark Side. Along with 5- and 10-kilometer options, the races combine two of the world's biggest entertainment franchises—Star Wars and Disney—while capitalizing on Disney's $4 billion purchase of Lucasfilm in 2012.

Many runners come for the weekend or even the week, turning the trip into a "runcation" as they bring family to ride the rides and, for adults, drink the drinks at Epcot's World Showcase. It becomes less of a test of endurance than a challenge to get up early after full days at the parks. Races start before dawn to minimize disruptions.

COSTUMES

Costumes are a must for many participants.

"I have a thing about princesses," said Brooke Laing, who works at an investment bank in New York. "I wanted to dress up and have that all-girls weekend, getting to put on a tiara and have that childish experience."

You can even ride a roller coaster near the halfway point of a full marathon in January—though if you run too fast in an early-morning event, you may find the ride not yet open.

"Disney usually puts on a pretty good show for anything you go to," said Misty Hayes, a Fort Worth, Texas, police officer. "How many have the option of jumping on the roller coaster? It was pretty awesome."

The Disney races aren't free of gripe, though. Face masks are not allowed, while Princess Leia robes and Darth Vader capes can't be too long.

Darrell Saria, a federal government employee in Winnipeg, Canada, said he understands the need for safety and believes it pushes people to be more creative. He has run as a mashup of Goofy and Darth Vader, and another time combined the Muppets' Animal and Boba Fett.

He said the races turn into a social gathering. "I've met a lot of people," he said. "People who do make their own costumes give each other praises, and they intermingle. People will dress up just to have fun with it and make people smile."

WHY STOP AT ONE?

And hey, if you're going to Disney for a race, why not do two, three or even four on consecutive days? Finish multiple races for bonus medals featuring Dopey and Goofy (get it?). Wear them all as you visit the theme parks afterward and take pride as they clink and clank against each other.

Disney "figured out that if you're going to come down, especially if you're traveling from out of town, you might as well maximize your time out there and maximize your fun," said Mike Czernec, a software engineer who lives about an hour away in Melbourne, Florida, yet stays at a Disney World hotel for the weekend.

Mark Wietbrock, a security-technology salesman in Lake St. Louis, Missouri, does a Disney World race—or consecutive races—every other year. His wife and two children have done various races with him. He said the trips are also a chance for him and his wife to return to where they started dating in 2000.

"It's the best of both worlds to get to run and get to enjoy the parks," he said.

TIME AND MONEY

The races have gotten very popular, such that many have sold out within an hour of registration. Spouses and friends have been shut out for waiting too long.

The need to rush has eased more recently, though. For many, these races are "one and done"—especially as Disney races tend to be more expensive than hometown races. Multi-race challenges are even more so—pricier than signing up for the races individually. The four-race series in January costs more than $500.

Plus, there's airfare and hotels. Though there's no admission fee to run through the parks, the finish is in the parking lot, so you have to pay to re-enter.

Rob Biggar, a software programmer in Setauket, New York, said Disney's multi-race challenges become "much more a test of your wallet than your stamina."

If You Go . . .

DISNEY RACES: http://rundisney.com. Check time and date for race registrations well ahead. If a race has sold out, you may be able to register through tour groups and charities, with donations or fundraising required.

HO, HO, HO: YOSEMITE: A MAGICAL WINTER DESTINATION

By Don Babwin

YOSEMITE NATIONAL PARK, Calif.—Yosemite National Park might not seem like an ideal winter destination, particularly if you're from a part of the country where you'd like to trade in road salt for rim salt on your margarita and leave the words "wind chill" behind.

But Yosemite in winter is magical, as I discovered on a trip with my family just after Christmas. There's snowboarding and skiing, both downhill and cross-country, as well as sledding (pick up a plastic saucer at a sporting goods store on the way). You can also ice skate at a rink in the shadow of the famed granite formation known as Half Dome. Park rangers also lead snow-shoe walks.

Many of Yosemite Valley's shops and restaurants remain open. And at the Majestic Hotel, one of the country's most storied national park lodges, there are holiday decorations and a seven-course dinner with costumed performers called the Bracebridge Dinner. The wood-and-stone hotel, formerly known as the Ahwahnee, opened in 1927 and has hosted everyone from Presidents John F. Kennedy and Barack Obama to Queen Elizabeth and Walt Disney.

Winter can also be a time to enjoy the park's scenery without summer's crowds, though it can pose some challenges as well.

THE SCENERY

Naturalist John Muir once wrote that Yosemite was "full of God's thoughts."

Driving in, thick forests of snow-dusted pine and fir trees initially block your view of the park's famous granite monoliths towering over Yosemite Valley. But there's nothing like that first glimpse. El Capitan rises 3,600 feet (914 meters) from the valley floor, more than twice the height of the Empire State Building. On the other side of the valley is Half Dome, rising 4,700 feet (1,400 meters) off the valley floor.

In winter, options for seeing these landmarks from anywhere other than the valley are limited, as some roads in the park are closed until the snow thaws. The cables that climbers use to ascend Half Dome are also removed for the season.

But there are walking tours led by National Park Service rangers that explain how these huge chunks of granite came to be. They're not just the result of erosion, but were also formed by melting glaciers and forces under the ground that over the millions of years pushed them higher and higher. It's a way to understand the massive forces that formed the earth itself.

Visitors can also follow the footsteps of famed photographer Ansel Adams, who made his home here for a quarter century. You can even snap your own pictures from where Adams stood when he took some of his most iconic photographs. Classes cost about $100 but the Ansel Adams Gallery also offers free camera walks on certain days (tours fill up; reserve ahead).

GETTING THERE

Getting there can be a challenge on roads that are potentially snowy and icy. Car rental places may tell you—as they told me—that snow chains aren't necessary. They are, to be blunt, lying.

"California law says if you are entering a chain control area, you have to carry chains," said Scott Gediman, a park ranger and a public affairs officer in Yosemite. "Everybody needs to have chains, even if you have four-wheel drive."

Rangers don't enjoy checking car trunks for chains and cables but they do it and they will send you out of the park if you don't have them.

The good news is that chains are not that expensive, costing as little as about $40, and can be purchased at any auto supply store nearby. Snow chain technology has improved dramatically, making it far easier to put the chains on than it used to be. But if you still feel like you can't do it, there are services along the road that will put the chains on for you for $30 or so.

Yosemite Valley is about 210 miles (338 km) from San Francisco. But if the winter drive sounds intimidating, use the YARTS bus service which runs year-round between Yosemite and Merced, a city located about 130 miles (210 km) from San Francisco.

If You Go . . .

YOSEMITE NATIONAL PARK: https://www.nps.gov/yose/. Check for alerts, closures, schedules. Yosemite Valley is about 210 miles (338 km) from San Francisco. Things to do in winter: http://www.travelyosemite.com/winter/yosemite-winter-experience/

WEATHER, FEES AND SCHEDULES: Average temperatures range from the 20s to the 50s F (minus 6 to 10 above C). Conditions can change quickly and dramatically. Roads that are open one day may be closed the next. Tour schedules are also subject to change. Not everything is open on Christmas Day. For road conditions, call 209-372-0200 or visit http://www.nps.gov/yose.

MAJESTIC HOTEL: http://www.travelyosemite.com/lodging/the-majestic-yosemite-hotel/

YOSEMITE SKI AND SNOWBOARD: http://www.travelyosemite.com/winter/yosemite-ski-snowboard-area/

GRAND CANYON HIKING:
HOW TO PREP, PACK AND PAUSE

By Anna Johnson

GRAND CANYON NATIONAL PARK, Arizona—Nearly 5 million people visit Grand Canyon National Park each year, but many do not get far below its limestone rim. Even fewer head to the bottom.

Why? The simple answer is: It's hard.

The hike down to the banks of the chalky green Colorado River, and especially back up, is challenging, even grueling. Even if you've trained on stair climbers and hills with a 30-pound (13.6-kg) backpack, hiking the Grand Canyon will test your endurance and your ability to remain hydrated.

But the sweat and sore muscles are worth the experience as you gaze at the red-hued rock formations from the South Kaibab trail, cross the steel bridge over the fast-moving river and dip your hat in the cool waters of the Bright Angel Creek.

Here are some tips for making the most of your Grand Canyon hiking and camping experience.

PLAN AHEAD

Trying to hike from the rim to the river (or farther) in one day is possible, but extremely difficult. Even in spring and fall, the blazing Arizona sun can quickly turn dangerous, even deadly. Signs around the park and on corridor trails warn visitors not to hike too far down in a day for a reason.

Planning ahead will allow you to reserve a spot at the Bright Angel Campground or the rustic Phantom Ranch lodge at the bottom. For the campground, you should aim to get a backcountry camping permit several months in advance and plan to make reservations for Phantom Ranch even farther in advance.

TRAINING FOR LESS PAIN

Getting a permit and setting dates for the hike also will help with mapping out a training schedule so you can spend more time enjoying the hike instead of suffering through it.

If you have access to hiking trails, particularly in hilly locations, start walking there as soon as possible. On average, hiking down South Kaibab and up Bright Angel (the most common route) takes four to six hours down and five to eight hours back up. And if you're camping at the bottom, you will need to carry all of your equipment with you, so do some training while wearing a 20- to 30-pound (9- to 13.6-kg) backpack.

Other good options are stair-climbing machines.

TAKE YOUR TIME AND HYDRATE

Though your adrenaline will be pumping as you descend the switchbacks of the South Kaibab trail, stop every so often to soak it in and take some photos. The views on this trail are magnificent, but the excitement of getting to the bottom can propel you too quickly.

On the way back up, remember slow and steady is the way to go. Though you'll be tired, remember to pause not only to get your camera out but to eat and drink. And don't dismiss the first couple miles of the Bright Angel trail, which is fairly level along the Colorado River. This part has its own rugged beauty but can be overlooked in the eagerness to get to the top.

Both South Kaibab and Bright Angel have natural stopping points, including some where the parks service has installed bathrooms, and on Bright Angel, potable water (there is no water on South Kaibab). Take breaks about once an hour, eat salty foods like nuts and jerky and drink water and electrolyte drinks. Another rest tip: Elevate your feet each time you take a break to give them a rest and reduce inflammation.

PACK ONLY WHAT YOU NEED

You must pack essentials like enough food and water, along with a wide-brimmed hat, but don't overload your backpack.

You can weigh your pack at the national park's Backcountry Information Center on the South Rim before you head off. Aim for about 20 to 30 pounds (9 to 13.6 kg).

Water will likely be the heaviest thing you carry. Aim to bring all the water you need for the hike down. South Kaibab doesn't have any water and your next water stop will be at the Bright Angel Campground. On the way up, there is a shady resting area at Indian Gardens, which also has water year-round. If you do the hike in the warmer months, there's water every 1.5 miles (2.4 km) beginning at Indian Gardens on your way up. But, it also will be incredibly hot, around 90 plus degrees F (32 plus degrees C) in the late spring, summer and early fall, so consider doing this type of hike in the cooler months.

UNWIND AND HAVE FUN

Chat with fellow hikers at rest stops, soak your tired feet in the crisp Bright Angel Creek after setting up camp, and unwind at the canteen at Phantom Ranch after dark while writing postcards (the cards travel by mule to the top), playing cards and drinking a beer (the canteen sells beer, wine, other beverages and snacks). Though strenuous, the Grand Canyon experience has plenty of opportunities to relax and most importantly, have fun.

If You Go . . .

GRAND CANYON NATIONAL PARK: Permits are required for overnight camping trips but not for day hikes. Details: http://www.nps.gov/grca/planyourvisit/backcountry-permit.htm. Permits also are required for rim-to-rim or extended day hikes for organized, non-commercial groups (12-30 people). Details: https://www.nps.gov/grca/learn/management/sup.htm#CP_JUMP_2602654

GLAMPING IN YELLOWSTONE

By Traci Carl

WEST YELLOWSTONE, Montana—I planned our trip to Yellowstone National Park last-minute, and my family was divided over whether we should camp or stay in a hotel or cabin.

In the end, we couldn't find either. Everything was booked.

With visions of us trying to pitch a tent in the dark next to angry bison, I reluctantly coughed up $150 a night at the only place I could find that wasn't an overpriced motel: Under Canvas Yellowstone, a "glamping site" a few miles outside the park's west entrance.

WHAT IS GLAMPING?

I wasn't sure what to expect. Glamping—a blended word for glamorous camping—was something I knew existed but had never considered trying. Why pay for something you can basically do for free?

While the website showed canvas tents housing everything from cots to down comforter-covered beds, the woman who booked our reservation sounded more like a hotel concierge. She offered up a rundown of activities, with honest, helpful reviews, and ended up booking us a basic "tipi" with four cots and an afternoon on horseback at a nearby ranch.

I told my family I found a camping spot and left it at that.

The girls, ages 5 and 9, love roughing it. My husband loves not paying hotel prices. I loved the idea that I wouldn't have to pack, set up camp or even cook. (The tents don't allow food because it attracts wildlife, including bears. Campers dine at a great restaurant housed in a nearby lodge.)

PROBLEMS AND SOLUTIONS

The night before we arrived, my daughter got a stomach bug that had run its course with the rest of the family. The next morning, the prospect of camping seemed bleak.

I called Under Canvas Yellowstone and explained the situation. Despite the fact that it was high season and our reservations were nonrefundable, they promised to work with us and give us our money back, if needed. I came clean and told my family what we paid and what to expect: cots with sleeping bags, pillows and separate but heated bathrooms with warm water, towels and shampoo.

My daughter rallied so we went ahead with the trip. When we arrived, it was rainy and cold. Lightning flickered in nearby mountains. I expected whining, but the kids were excited and gladly got out of the car.

When we got to our tent, I discovered a small tear in the fabric. I asked the front desk, or the equivalent, located in another tent, for tape to repair it and they upgraded us to a tent with king-size bed, dresser and wood-burning stove. The kids and my husband were thrilled.

As night fell, my husband built a fire and we fell into a deep sleep under two layers of down. A steady rain pelted the canvas but never entered the tent. The front desk promised to wake us if lightning got too close.

The only glitch was when my husband got up to use the bathroom around 4 a.m., then returned and—because the tents all look the same—accidentally tried to unzip the tent of a family from China. After the initial shock, it gave us a funny story to tell around the campfire.

The rest of the trip ended up being one of the best we've ever taken, despite the fact that my daughter was still struggling with her stomach bug. The front desk helped us locate and make an appointment with an urgent care center nearby, gave us warm tea and helped reschedule our horseback trip to a day when she felt better.

We spent the days exploring Yellowstone and nights at the camp's roaring fire, meeting travelers from places like Sweden and South Korea.

When we left, the kids cried, and my husband and I decided we were glamping converts.

That's not to say we won't rough it with our own camping gear. But on trips where we want a unique adventure without doing all the work —where we'd like to fall asleep to the distant call of a coyote without packing gear and setting up tents—we'll definitely think about glamping.

TIPS

Some things to know if you're considering glamping:

Camping purists may scoff at amenities like cedar-sided, tiled bathrooms, or rules like the one at our site that banned food but allowed hot chocolate.

If you need privacy and comfort, consider how you'd feel about hearing other campers settling in for the night; sleeping in a tent that's open to the outdoors or has just one layer of canvas; or managing without running water or electricity if they're optional or unavailable. If bathroom setups and locations matter, research before you book.

Glamping is offered around the world, from South American rainforests to African safaris. Lodging ranges from yurts, treehouses and Airstreams to luxurious bedrooms set up in the wild with hot tubs, air-conditioning, white-linen dinners and minibars. Some affordable, bare-bones options exist but glamping is often expensive, running anywhere from a few hundred dollars a night to more than $1,000.

If You Go...

UNDER CANVAS YELLOWSTONE: https://www.undercanvas.com/camps/yellowstone/

GLAMPING: http://www.glamping.com

BASQUE CULTURE
ON A BLOCK IN IDAHO

By Kimberlee Kruesi

BOISE, Idaho—Idaho is home to one of the biggest concentrations of Basques in the United States, and the best way to learn more about that heritage is by visiting the Basque Block, tucked in the center of Boise, the state's capital city.

Basques began settling in southwestern Idaho as early as the late 1800s, with many coming from the Basque region on the border of Spain and France to work as sheepherders in Idaho. Nearly 8,000 residents of the Gem State identify as Basque today.

Boise preserved the Basque Block's rich history with a massive conservation effort during the early 2000s. Green, red and white Basque flags now adorn the streetlights, and the street, which lacks raised sidewalks and curbs, is frequently closed to cars thanks to festivals celebrating Basque culture.

The single block offers a crash course in all things Basque. A sprawling mural along a brick wall depicts seafaring Basques of the 1500s as well as traditional dancers in red and white attire. The Basque community is largely Catholic, and the mural also depicts Boise's St. John's Cathedral.

For more in-depth history, The Basque Museum and Cultural Center is packed with exhibits that explore the lives of the first Basque sheepherders, including a sheep wagon and full-size sheepherder's tent. Between April and September, the museum also offers guided tours of a restored Basque boardinghouse, which is also Boise's oldest surviving brick building.

Next door, The Basque Center has evolved into a local gathering place. The center is home to two traditional dancing groups and hosts tournaments for traditional Basque card games.

At The Basque Market, visitors can find one of the Northwest's largest selections of Spanish and Basque wines while shopping for specialty foods from the Iberian Peninsula, a rarity in land-locked Idaho. The market has become famous for preparing large portions of paella, served with homemade baked bread every Wednesday and Friday right on the patio for $8.99. The market also serves a revolving tapas menu every day from 11 a.m.

Other Basque eateries include Leku Ona, which in the Basque language means "good place," 117 S. Sixth St., offering casual and formal dining, or Bardenay, a restaurant and distillery, at 610 W. Grove St. Bar Gernika, 202 S. Capitol Blvd., is an old-fashioned pub in a landmark 1948 building where you can get traditional favorites like the lamb grinder and croquetas, along with a wide selection of beer.

The traditional Basque language is classified as a threatened tongue, with fewer than 1 million people able to speak it worldwide. But it's easy to learn one term while you're here: "ongi etorri" (pronounced ohn-gee eh-toh-ree). That's Basque for welcome.

If You Go . . .
BASQUE BLOCK: Located in downtown Boise, Idaho, between Sixth and Capitol Boulevard on Grove Street.

MOUNTAIN BIKING IN NORTH DAKOTA: LEGENDARY

By Carey J. Williams

MEDORA, N.D.—For mountain bikers, North Dakota's Maah Daah Hey Trail is such a treasure that people come from all over to experience it.

I drove with friends more than 1,000 miles (1,600 km) to ride 100-plus miles (160 km) of the single-track trail, which is no wider than a bike. And we weren't the only non-Dakotans traveling long distances to do it. We met folks from Philadelphia,

Minneapolis, Denver, Montana and Wyoming.

The MDH is located where the Great Plains meet the Badlands. To use North Dakota's state slogan, it's legendary. It connects the northern and southern units of Theodore Roosevelt National Park in the western part of the state.

With elevation changes of over 10,000 feet (3,000 meters), only the fiercest of athletes complete the trail in one day, usually for the MDH 100 race held each summer. We opted for a multi-day, self-supported trip. That's the essence of bikepacking—or backpacking by bike.

Within the first hour of leaving the northern trailhead, we knew we'd be tested by the rugged landscape. The unrelenting climbs, sheer cliffs along the exposed layers of the Badlands, switchback descents and grassy plateaus with panoramic views were going to be our repeating scenery for three days.

After a two-hour opening night ride due to a late start, it took us three full days of 10 to 12 hours on the bikes to complete the trail. A fourth day would have made it a more relaxing experience with various side trips to the China Wall, Ice Caves and Roosevelt's Elkhorn Ranch.

BIKEPACKING EQUIPMENT AND GEAR

Bikepackers carry the same gear as backpackers with the addition of tools and spare bicycle parts. Ideally, the gear (including a multi-tool, chain breaker, spare tubes, tire levers, patch kit, chain lube and pump) should be distributed equally around the bike because riding single-track trails demands your attention and balance.

When the narrow track zigzags, the bike needs to follow as riders become one with the trail. The ideal bike would be a hardtail (with or without suspension) mountain bike with 27.5 or 29-inch wheels and bags for the frame, fork, handlebar and seat post.

But we're proof you don't need top-of-the-line gear to complete the trail. Two of our three riders used panniers, meaning saddlebags on racks over rear tires, though they did face more mechanical issues on 15-year-old bikes than the gearhead of the group. Plus the width of the bikes with panniers tended to disrupt the tall western wheatgrass and dense brush along the trail, leading to stops for tick checks and broken bike parts.

THE PACE AND THE SCENERY

Resting points were key to a successful trip, especially between the hottest times of day, 2 p.m. to 4 p.m. The cooler, north-facing slopes and pockets of wooded ravines were natural pit stops—usually in a grove of leafy cottonwood trees.

The drier, south-facing buttes lent themselves to purple cone-flowers, prairie roses, bright yellow blooming prickly pear cactus and the easily-recognizable yucca plant with its tall stalks. The wildflowers provided a contrast to the browns and greens dominating the landscape.

WATER AND CAMPSITES

We each carried a total of 4 to 6 liters of water in daypacks, frame cages and luggage bags. Each campsite (CCC, Bennett, Magpie, Elkhorn, Wannagan, Buffalo Gap, Sully Creek), located at least 18 miles (29 km) apart, had hand-pumped drinking water.

There are also water-cache sites that can be stocked before the trip by driving on dirt roads. The campsites can be accessed on those roads, making it possible for exhausted riders to catch a ride back to town or for sag wagons—support vehicles—to greet pampered riders at the end of the day with a cold beverage.

Finding the campsites was a breeze with wooden fence posts placed on the trail within sight of each one.

Roosevelt first came to the area to hunt buffalo but later returned to work as a rancher while grieving for his mother and wife, who died the same day in 1884. "The farther one gets into the wilderness," he said, "the greater is the attraction of its lonely freedom."

If You Go . . .

MAAH DAAH HEY TRAIL: https://www.fs.fed.us/visit/destination/ maah-daah-hey-trail or http://mdhta.com/trail-guide or http:// mdhta.com/product/trail-maps/ .

GETTING THERE: The town of Medora is the jumping-off point for the Maah Daah Hey trail and Theodore Roosevelt National Park. The CCC campground, the northernmost part of the MDH, is located about 70 miles (113 km) north of town along Highway 85.

FIRE AND WATER: Check for drought, wildfires and other issues that can result in closures or compromised trail conditions

TIPS: Visitors with bikes—even walking or carrying them—are not permitted on Theodore Roosevelt Park's hiking trails. There are alternative routes around the park's north and south sections.

GLACIER NATIONAL PARK BY TRAIN

By Erin Gartner

EAST GLACIER, Montona—Chicago skyscrapers faded into green Wisconsin, and as the sun set over the Mississippi River, we made our first vacation decision. We weren't driving, so yes, we'd have some wine.

We then sat back and watched as 1,500 miles (2,400 km) went by aboard the Empire Builder train bound for Glacier National Park.

The historic train, which debuted with the Great Northern Railway in 1929, carries travelers between Chicago and the

Pacific Northwest, with stops along the edge of the national park in western Montana. The park is home to seemingly endless snow-capped mountain peaks, cascading waterfalls, wildflowers and valleys of turquoise lakes.

So between the train and shuttle buses around the park, we left the driving to someone else.

THE TRAIN TRIP

It was partly a sense of adventure and partly our budget that prompted the decision to take the train, which was about half the cost of flying when my hiking companion and I stumbled across the option for our 10-day trip last summer.

It did take some creative maneuvering, however, to fit our mammoth backpacks with protruding hiking poles into the train's overhead compartments.

We boarded the double-decker Amtrak train in Chicago's bustling Union Station. Our coach seats had larger-than-expected seats with ample legroom, leg rests and power outlets for our iPad during a movie or two on the nearly 30-hour trip. The seats reclined, but not fully, which made sleeping manageable but not especially comfortable overnight through Minnesota and North Dakota.

Sunrise over the plains was the cue to head to the viewing and dining cars, where floor-to-ceiling windows offered panoramic views of ranchland, towns and distant oil rigs. Locals advised where to sit for best views of the Rocky Mountains emerging from the prairie. A National Park Service ranger offered brief histories of early Montana settlers and the Blackfeet Nation as the train passed through the Native American tribe's reservation, which borders Glacier National Park.

At the East Glacier Park station, we stepped off into crisp air and quiet.

THE CHALLENGES

The park operates free, easy-to-use shuttle buses to explore the many trailheads, campsites and stunning views along Going-to-the-Sun Road, the only roadway bisecting the park. But getting to other areas of the park without a car was tricky.

Private, fee-based shuttles operated by Glacier Park Inc. and Xanterra Parks & Resorts access areas including Many Glacier, East Glacier and Two Medicine. Unfortunately, we'd tracked down incomplete information, including an inaccurate departure time that, had we waited for the next shuttle, would have cost us half a day.

We ended up hitchhiking with two friendly Malaysian visitors who crunched us into their small car in East Glacier after spotting our cardboard plea: "Many Glacier."

Campgrounds can quickly fill up. The one in Many Glacier was full before 7 a.m. the day we nabbed a site in mid-August.

Backcountry camping permits weren't easy to get either. Half the sites can be reserved in advance starting mid-March. The rest are distributed up to 24 hours in advance at ranger stations, first come, first served. We failed on two mornings, in line before sunrise, to reserve backcountry sites for popular multi-day routes.

We did however snag the last hiker-only site at a small campground along Lake McDonald, one of the park's postcard gems, especially from a kayak, and called that home base for the last three nights.

SCENERY, WILDLIFE AND THE VANISHING GLACIERS

The 11-mile (18-km), out-and-back trail to Grinnell Glacier pulls hikers above lakes surrounded by pink, yellow, purple and white wildflowers. A nearby trailhead accesses the roughly 11-mile (18-km) route to and from Ptarmigan Tunnel. Rocky switch-backs climb to the dark tunnel, cut through the peak, and open to maroon-tinted cliffs dropping into a deep valley.

Another highlight: the cliffside views across vast layers of peaks while hiking roughly 12 miles (19 km) along the Highline Trail to Granite Park Chalet and descending to a shuttle stop along Going-to-the-Sun Road.

Hiking down from Grinnell Glacier was delayed thanks to a bighorn sheep blocking the trail. We also saw cliff-perched moun-tain goats and through binoculars, bears. Several backpackers we met reported close bear sightings, including grizzlies.

Only 25 active glaciers remain in the park, out of an estimated 150 that existed in the area in 1850. The National Park Service says those could be gone by 2030. So whether you go by car, train or tour, don't wait too long to see them.

If You Go . . .

GLACIER NATIONAL PARK: Glacier National Park: https://www.nps.gov/glac. Only a handful of vehicle-accessible campgrounds take advance reservations. Backcountry campsites require permits, so plan multi-day hiking routes early after reviewing the reservation process at https://www.nps.gov/glac/planyourvisit/backcountry.htm#CP_JUMP_850358

TRAIN: Amtrak's Empire Builder, http://www.amtrak.com/empire-builder-train, travels from Chicago to Spokane, Washington, before continuing to Seattle or Portland, Oregon. Stops in between include Milwaukee and St. Paul, Minnesota.

SHUTTLES: The National Park Service's free shuttles along Going-to-the-Sun Road usually operate July 1-Labor Day, depending on weather. Private shuttles to other areas: http://www.glacier-parkinc.com/plan-your-trip/shuttle-information and http://www.glaciernationalparklodges.com/red-bus-tours/shuttles .

TIPS: Read up if you're new to camping in bear country and take wildlife warnings seriously. Plan for weather extremes; temperatures swung from sweltering heat to cold pelting rain in August. Late summer-early fall wildfires can impact the park as well. Don't rely on mobile devices in the park. Even at some lodges, Wi-Fi is spotty at best.

MINNEAPOLIS:
A PRINCE PILGRIMAGE

By Leanne Italie

MINNEAPOLIS—Prince's hometown of Minneapolis offers many places where fans can pay homage to the late singer, from his favorite record store to the humble house used in his Oscar-winning "Purple Rain" film.

PAISLEY PARK

Paisley Park, Prince's massive, gleaming white studio and performance complex, was turned into a museum soon after his death on April 21, 2016. Visiting is a must for fans, even if it's just a drive-by to see the sprawling place rise up from the flatlands in Chanhassen, an easy 20-mile (32-km) drive from downtown Minneapolis. The least expensive guided tours average 70 minutes and include rooms where Prince created some of his biggest hits.

Optional add-ons include a VIP tour of extra rooms, a photo opportunity, dance party and meals featuring some of his favorite foods.

Photos and video are strictly prohibited on all tours.

FIRST AVENUE & 7TH ST. ENTRY

This downtown club in a former Greyhound bus depot is a mecca for Prince fans and an indie rock hot spot. Guided group tours are available.

Otherwise, a ticket to hear one of the many bands that play there gets you inside the club where Prince played several times, including his first time in 1981 when it was called Sam's, and a 1983 appearance when he unveiled his ballad "Purple Rain." That gig was recorded, including the mega-hit that became his signature and other songs used on the album and in the film.

Brick walls outside are adorned with painted, white stars for other artists who played there. Prince's star stands out in gold.

ELECTRIC FETUS

Prince frequented the Electric Fetus record store, visiting just days before he died.

When the store opened in 1968, National Lampoon magazine singled it out for the worst name of a business. But it remains an indie mecca for audiophiles—including vinyl-lovers—and drew grieving fans when Prince died.

PRINCE MURALS

There are some beauties.

Downtown near 10th Street and Marquette Avenue, a five-story, white-painted wall of musical notes is where Prince shot some of his first publicity photos at age 18. At the time, it was home to Schmitt Music Company, which sold sheet music, pianos and organs. The musical notes are from a piece for piano by French composer Maurice Ravel.

Not far from Paisley Park, at Chanhassen Cinema, 570 Market St., is a huge purple portrait of Prince by muralist Graham Hoete.

Another purple portrait, complete with a white dove like the ones Prince kept at Paisley, was created by Bloomington, Minnesota, graffiti artist Rock "Cyfi" Martinez. It's in an alley on one wall of the Sencha Tea Bar, 2601 Hennepin Ave. S., in the funky Uptown district Prince shouted out in song.

PURPLE RAIN HOUSE

Prince's famous Purple House residence in the woods of Lake Riley in Chanhassen was bulldozed more than a decade ago, but the simple "Purple Rain" home used in the movie for exterior scenes stands, empty and a bit worse for wear. Head to 3420 Snelling Ave. in Minneapolis' Longfellow neighborhood for a look at the outside. Prince never lived here but his character "The Kid" came of age within its walls in the 1984 film. Some purple flowers were tucked into the mailbox on a recent visit.

GRAFFITI BRIDGE

The famous marked-up railroad crossing from "Graffiti Bridge," his 1990 sequel to "Purple Rain," was replaced in 1991 by a popular bicycle and running path in suburban Eden Prairie. The original bridge—covered with messages dating to the 1960s—had a heady, counterculture feel. The movie led Prince fans to add their own graffiti. But the replacement bike path is pristine. After Prince's death, devastated fans left farewell messages in black marker and purple spray paint on a highway underpass near Paisley Park, using the "love" symbol he created for himself. Getting there can be tricky. One way is to cross the busy highway leading to Paisley Park at the exit side of the parking lot, look for a West 78th Street sign and turn toward a walking path. The tunnel is marked Riley Creek.

MARK TWAIN'S RIVER TOWN:
A TRIP BACK IN TIME

By Beth J. Harpaz

HANNIBAL, Mo.—Mark Twain only lived in Hannibal, Missouri, for 13 years, but many of his most famous stories were inspired by this humble Midwestern city. A visit to Hannibal today, with its excellent museums, preserved historic sites and old-timey antiques shops, offers a way to appreciate the impact this place had on one of America's best-known writers.

And of course, Hannibal sits on the banks of the Mississippi River, which figured so large in Twain's life and writing.

MARK TWAIN BOYHOOD HOME & MUSEUM

A mere $11 gets you a look at nine historic sites and museums, all within a few blocks of one another. They include the actual houses where Twain and the real children who inspired his characters Huckleberry Finn and Becky Thatcher lived in the mid-1800s. You'll see the bedroom window the adventuresome Twain climbed out of as a boy. You'll see the fence that his character Tom Sawyer got other children to whitewash when he was supposed to paint it.

You'll also get a real sense of what Hannibal was like when Twain lived here in the 1840s and early 1850s, and how this place fed his imagination and sensibility. This was no lonely rural spot; it was a bustling river town, with three blacksmith shops, a distillery, tobacco factory and two slaughterhouses, with pigs herded through the streets.

Twain's real name was Samuel Clemens and he was not a privileged child. After his father died, his mother couldn't afford his 25-cent weekly school fee. He was apprenticed at age 11 to a printer, which led to work as a newspaperman. Later he was a steamboat pilot on the Mississippi. His pen name, Mark Twain, was a river call that described the water depth.

An interpretive center behind Twain's boyhood home offers photos, exhibits and wonderful quotes from Twain's writings that put his life and work in context. A museum gallery at 120 N. Main St. is filled with artifacts, from his top hat to 15 Norman Rockwell paintings created for special editions of "Tom Sawyer" and "Huckleberry Finn."

Twain's quips, prominently showcased, can seem as fresh and cynical as a 21st-century tweet, like this one: "Suppose you were an idiot. And suppose you were a member of Congress. But I repeat myself."

You can't miss the statue of Tom and Huck at the foot of Cardiff Hill on Main Street. Sculptures of Twain stand in Schwartz Gardens and Riverview Park.

CONTEXT AND CONTROVERSY

The museums also tackle the controversies over Twain's writings. In his own lifetime, "Adventures of Huckleberry Finn," about the wild, ragged son of the town drunk who runs away on a raft with an escaped slave, Jim, was banned because it was considered vulgar. In the late 20th century, the book was banned because Twain's language and depiction of Jim were considered racist.

One exhibit offers context for Twain's views: Slavery was legal in Missouri during his youth; his family rented or owned slaves when they could afford it, and he's quoted as recalling that nobody he knew ever questioned it. But one incident made him think twice about it, when he complained to his mother about a slave boy who sang and laughed incessantly. She responded tearfully that the slave child would never see his own mother again, and at least when the boy sang, "it shows he is not remembering."

THE TOWN AND THE RIVER

For a small city (population 18,000), Hannibal offers some good eating. LaBinnah Bistro, 207 N. Fifth St., has friendly service, charming Victorian-era decor and an inviting dinner menu that includes fish, steak and Mediterranean dishes. LaBinnah is Hannibal spelled backward, named for the town's LaBinnah

Club, where Twain spoke on his last visit to Hannibal in 1902. The Mark Twain Brewing Co., 422 N. Main St., offers burgers, a big selection of beers and other pub fare.

Hannibal has a wide variety of lodging.

Treasure-hunters should check out the half-dozen antiques and gift shops on and around Main Street.

If you're driving to Hannibal from St. Louis, about 120 miles (190 km) away, get off the interstate and take the Great River Road, Route 79, which winds through tiny towns, fields and farms, with scenic stretches along the Mississippi.

Between March 15 and Nov. 1, riverboat cruises are offered on the Mississippi from Hannibal.

If You Go . . .

MARK TWAIN BOYHOOD HOME & MUSEUM: 120 N. Main St., Hannibal, Missouri, http://www.marktwainmuseum.org

HANNIBAL, MISSOURI: http://www.visithannibal.com

MISSISSIPPI RIVER CRUISES: http://www.marktwainriverboat.com

MISSISSIPPI DELTA SINGS THE BLUES

By Beth J. Harpaz

CLARKSDALE, Miss.—The Mississippi Delta has no shortage of museums, historic attractions and clubs devoted to the blues. But visitors will find the region has many other stories to tell, from the cotton plantations where African-American families worked and lived in desperate poverty, to culinary traditions that reflect a surprising ethnic diversity.

THE BLUES TRAIL AND MUSEUMS

You can't miss the big blue guitars marking the famous crossroads of Highways 61 and 49 in Clarksdale. This is where, according to legend, Robert Johnson sold his soul to the devil to learn how to play the blues.

Roadside signs for the Mississippi Blues Trail make it easy to find other sites as well, from Clarksdale's Riverside Hotel, where Bessie Smith died, to the Dockery Farms cotton plantation in Cleveland, where many pioneering bluesmen lived, worked and made music, among them Charley Patton, Roebuck "Pops" Staples and Howlin' Wolf.

A sign in a field at Clarksdale's Stovall Plantation notes that Muddy Waters' songs were recorded here in 1941 by musicologist Alan Lomax as he collected folk music for the Library of Congress. The sharecropper's shack that Waters lived in has been restored and relocated to the nearby Delta Blues Museum.

In Indianola, the B.B. King Museum and Delta Interpretive Center pays tribute to King's life and legacy. He's buried there as well.

These museums and others use photos, artifacts, videos and other exhibits to explore the blues' roots, beginning with African musical traditions brought to the South by slaves. Because Delta cotton plantations were relatively isolated, musical styles developed here were uninfluenced by trends elsewhere. But eventually many African-Americans who barely eked out a living working for white landowners in the decades after the Civil War migrated away from the South, seeking economic opportunity elsewhere along with an escape from segregation and racial terror.

Muddy Waters left the Delta for Chicago in 1943. B.B. King left Mississippi for Memphis, where he got his big break at radio station WDIA. These and other bluesmen were worshipped by 1960s music giants like Bob Dylan and the Rolling Stones. "Muddy Waters' music changed my life," said Eric Clapton. As the title of one of Waters' songs puts it, "The Blues Had A Baby And They Named It Rock And Roll."

CAT HEAD, CLUBS AND FESTIVALS

Stop in Cat Head, a Mississippi blues music and gift store in Clarksdale, for a chat with owner Roger Stolle, a blues fan who moved there to "help pull the blues scene together in a way that would get people to come." Local clubs stagger their schedules so you can hear live music every night. Stolle keeps a list online of who's playing where .

Clarksdale's best-known club is Ground Zero, co-owned by actor Morgan Freeman and Clarksdale Mayor Bill Luckett, but blues fans may be disappointed by party-vibe bands playing songs here like "Sweet Home Alabama." A more interesting venue is Red's. Don't be fooled by its rundown appearance and tiny, informal living room-style interior. Red's showcases under-the-radar, brilliantly talented musicians like Lucious Spiller whose performances will make you realize why the blues still matter.

Delta festivals include the Sunflower River Blues & Gospel Festival in August, the Deep Blues Fest in October and the Juke Joint Festival in April.

FOOD, LODGING AND CURTAINED BOOTHS

Mississippi cuisine isn't just catfish and barbecue. Doe's, in Greenville, where a security guard watches over your car as you dine and walks you to the parking area when you leave, is known for steaks the size of your head and has been recognized by the James Beard Foundation.

Chamoun's Rest Haven in Clarksdale, founded by a Lebanese family in the 1940s, serves some of the best kibbe you'll find outside the Middle East. At Larry's Hot Tamales, ask owner Larry Lee to share stories of how Mexican tamales became a scrumptious Mississippi staple. For upscale bistro fare like ceviche and roasted vegetables, try Yazoo Pass in Clarksdale.

Delta accommodations range from motels to the Alluvian, a luxury boutique hotel in Greenwood. The city, once a major shipping point for Delta cotton, is also where the movie "The Help" was filmed. Today Greenwood is headquarters for Viking Range, the kitchen appliance manufacturer, and a Viking cooking school (classes fill up fast so book ahead).

Other Greenwood spots include the excellent Turnrow bookstore and the tasting room for the Winery at Williams Landing, which specializes in wines made from Mississippi-grown muscadine grapes. Pick up a bottle for dinner at Lusco's, a BYOB restaurant famous for whole grilled pompano fish and for curtained booths that offered cotton traders privacy for business deals, romantic liaisons and alcohol consumption.

A unique lodging option in the Delta is spending the night in a preserved sharecropper's shack at the Shack Up Inn in Clarksdale or at Tallahatchie Flats in Greenwood. Some travelers may find the concept offensive as a sugarcoating of the misery experienced by those who had no choice but to live this way. But for others, a night spent in a rustic cabin that rattles with the howling wind or shakes to its foundations in a thunderstorm may evoke the very vulnerability that makes the blues so haunting.

If You Go...
MISSISSIPPI BLUES TRAIL: http://msbluestrail.org/

CATHEAD DELTA MUSIC CALENDAR: https://www.cathead.biz/music-calendar

MEMPHIS, TENNESSEE:
MUSIC AND CIVIL RIGHTS

By Beth J. Harpaz

MEMPHIS, Tennessee—Seems like Nashville gets all the attention when it comes to music in the South. But make no mistake: From Elvis Presley to the sound of soul, Memphis is an essential stop for any music fan.

Memphis is also one of America's most important cities in the history of civil rights. It's the place where Martin Luther King

Jr. was assassinated. A museum built on the site where he was murdered tells that story and many others.

STAX MUSEUM OF AMERICAN SOUL MUSIC

One of the first things you see at the Stax Museum of American Soul Music is an exhibit portraying a Mississippi country church. That's because the DNA of soul, like so many genres of pop music, is in the Mississippi Delta, rooted in traditions brought here by enslaved Africans and in the blues played by African-American laborers eking out a living on cotton plantations.

The Stax recording studio was founded in Memphis in the 1950s by a white sister and brother, Estelle Axton and Jim Stewart. But in an unusual arrangement for the era, Stax was also a place where whites and blacks worked together. Stax's roster of black stars, including Otis Redding, Isaac Hayes and the Staple Singers, proved enormously popular with both black and white audiences, first in Europe and ultimately at home.

Stax eventually went bankrupt but the museum was built on the original site and does a terrific job showcasing everything from costumes to cars to walls of hit records. Videos of TV and concert performances will have you dancing your way through the exhibits.

SUN STUDIO

Sun Studio calls itself the "birthplace" of rock 'n' roll, and as every music fan knows, there's a straight line from the blues to rock. Among the Mississippi natives who recorded at Sun Records were B.B. King, Howlin' Wolf and Ike Turner.

But it was an 18-year-old who wandered into the studio in 1953 named Elvis Presley who took Sun's fortunes big-time. Presley recorded two dozen songs with Sun before switching to a national label to manage his rocketing career. An iconic photo displayed at the studio, dubbed the "Million Dollar Quartet," shows Presley back at Sun in 1956, sitting at a piano with Jerry Lee Lewis, Carl Perkins and Johnny Cash.

Lively guided tours of Sun Studio walk visitors through its hit parade with music clips and engaging anecdotes. You'll stand in the footsteps not only of the label's early stars but also more recent visitors like rock giants U2.

NATIONAL CIVIL RIGHTS MUSEUM

The story of music in Memphis can't be told without looking at black history.

One place to put that history in context is the National Civil Rights Museum, located in the former Lorraine Motel where the Rev. Martin Luther King Jr. was assassinated. The museum has extensive exhibits on slavery, segregation and the protests that powered the civil rights movement. Allow several hours to take in the engrossing displays, which include video footage of marches, riots and news reports from the era, along with engaging interactive exhibits that offer interviews with ordinary people reflecting on their personal experiences.

King was in Memphis to support striking garbage workers when he was shot while standing on a hotel balcony. On your way in, you see the balcony from outside, but at the tour's end, you'll see the spot where he was murdered from inside the hotel. It's a stunning, heart-stopping vantage point that brings you face to face with that watershed moment. April 4, 2018, marks 50 years since that day.

GRACELAND

No trip to Memphis is complete without visiting Graceland, the mansion Elvis Presley bought in 1957 and lived in until his death 20 years later. The house—which feels remarkably small by 21st century standards—is a time capsule, complete with green shag rugs and carved animals in the famous Jungle Room. Guests are shuttled through by the hundreds in a remarkably efficient fashion, with each visitor issued an iPad and headphones so you can get information about what you're seeing at your own pace. The King is buried in the onsite Meditation Garden, along with his parents and grandmother. There's also a memorial gravestone for his stillborn twin brother.

But the house is only part of what there is to see. Newer displays at Graceland look at Presley's career from his start at Sun Records, to his work in Hollywood, to his Vegas jumpsuit era. One area showcases his cars, another looks at his influence on other entertainers.

FOOD

You can try what was supposedly one of Elvis' favorite snacks, a peanut butter and banana sandwich, at Graceland's Gladys' Diner, named for Elvis' mom.

Gus's World Famous Fried Chicken is worthy of its boastful name.

For truly excellent Italian food with nouvelle flair and a Southern accent, visit Hog & Hominy.

BEALE STREET

Beale Street is packed with bars and clubs. So how do you find the right vibe for your taste in music? Just wander the street from one end to the other, stick your head in the door of any place that seems appealing, and if you like what you hear, go on in, grab a beer and a seat. If you enjoy the performance, don't forget to throw some money in the tip bucket.

OUTSIDE MYRTLE BEACH, TRANQUILITY IN A KAYAK

By Beth J. Harpaz

MYRTLE BEACH, SOUTH CAROLINA—Condo towers with ocean views. King Kong hanging off a mini-Empire State Building. A zipline, escape room and helicopter rides.

Myrtle Beach is all of this and more. But just a few miles from the city's busy boardwalk and roadside attractions, a different type of thrill awaits.

THE WACCAMAW RIVER

Here, the Waccamaw River meanders through a cypress swamp in a wildlife refuge. Spanish moss drapes the trees, turtles sun themselves on stones and spider lily plants bloom with bright white flowers.

Spend a few hours kayaking the calm waters and who knows what you might encounter. A dragonfly could land on your arm. A water snake could slither by. A bright yellow bird might pierce the quiet with a loud call as it flits from tree to tree, but good luck pronouncing its name: prothonotary warbler.

Duck your head if a low-hanging branch comes up too fast to paddle around, and move to the side if the modern world intrudes: Motorboats turn up on the waterway too.

KAYAK OUTING

I did a two-hour kayak trip here with a group of friends, booking through the Black River Outdoors Center. Our guide, Mandy Johnson, was brilliant at spotting wildlife and generous with her knowledge. And her love of the natural world was infectious: We smiled as she picked a flailing white moth out of the water and let it cling to her hat until its wings dried.

The kayak outing was one of many excursions I took on a five-day getaway to the Myrtle Beach area. But while I enjoyed the destination's other pleasures—including brunch at the Tupelo Honey restaurant and a visit to Fat Harold's, a North Myrtle Beach club famous for the swing dance known as the Carolina shag—the kayak trip stands apart.

Exciting activities are easy to come by in a place like Myrtle Beach—not to mention restaurants, bars, fireworks and shopping. What's harder to find is tranquility. But there it was, in a kayak.

If You Go . . .

BLACK RIVER OUTDOORS CENTER: Myrtle Beach, South Carolina; http://www.blackriveroutdoors.com/ or 843-546-4840.

WACCAMAW RIVER: https://www.americanrivers.org/river/ waccamaw-river/

THE ALABAMA TOWN BEHIND 'TO KILL A MOCKINGBIRD'

By Jay Reeves

MONROEVILLE, Alabama—Harper Lee's novel "To Kill a Mockingbird" is always nearby in Monroeville, Alabama.

This quiet town of 6,200 people was Lee's birthplace, where she lived most of her life and where she died at age 89 in 2016. And it inspired the fictional town of Maycomb in Lee's Pulitzer Prize-winning book about race and injustice in the Deep South of the 1930s.

Fans of "Mockingbird" have been visiting Monroeville for

decades, searching for remnants of that "tired old town" where the book's hero, attorney Atticus Finch, defended a falsely accused black man. Finch's daughter Scout—the character Lee based on herself—and her brother Jem watched the trial from the courtroom balcony.

The community puts on an annual stage adaptation of "Mockingbird" in April and May that includes a recreation of the fictional trial. The event draws visitors from around the world.

"Mockingbird" was published in 1960. A companion book to "Mockingbird" called "Go Set a Watchman" was published a year before Lee's death and brought a whole new wave of publicity and fans to Monroeville.

Most of what tourists see here are attractions inspired by the book. There's a Mockingbird Inn, a bronze statue on the courthouse square and a wall-size "Mockingbird" mural on the side of a building, all constant reminders of the town's claim to fame.

But other spots have a more authentic connection to Lee.

Start at Mel's Dairy Dream on South Alabama Avenue, a busy main road, and walk north toward the square.

The small restaurant, ringed by service windows and a counter where customers plop down money for ice cream cones, stands on the site of Lee's childhood home, which was torn down decades ago. Mel's is just a short walk from the school where Lee attended classes and where her alter-ego Scout and Jem began their "longest journey together" at the book's climax.

Lee shared the old house with siblings, her mother and father A.C. Lee, an attorney and Alabama legislator who was the basis for Atticus Finch. Finch returned in "Watchman" as his daughter went home to Maycomb as an adult. The Atticus Finch portrayed in "Watchman," however, was not the noble humanitarian depicted in "Mockingbird," and some fans found that disheartening.

Next door to Mel's and across a weathered stone fence is a grassy lot with the remains of a house foundation and a historic marker that recalls the site as the one-time home of author Truman Capote, Lee's childhood friend and the inspiration for the character "Dill" in Mockingbird. As adults, the two collaborated on Capote's classic crime story "In Cold Blood," published in 1966.

The homes of Lee's and Finch's neighbors are long gone, replaced by parking lots and stores, and the paved street is no longer shaded by big trees or transformed by rain into "red slop," as Lee described in the book.

But the courthouse and jail that recall pivotal moments in "Mockingbird" can still be seen on the courthouse square.

Now a museum, the old Monroe County Courthouse was completed in 1903 and is home to the balconied courtroom that served as the model for the crucial legal scene in the film version of "To Kill a Mockingbird." A tall white dome tops the building; magnolia trees shade the lawn outside.

Inside, visitors can walk across the shiny wooden floor and sit in the old witness chair where Robinson would have defended himself against false charges of raping a white woman before an all-white jury. A pot-bellied stove stands beside the jury box. The jail where Atticus would have protected Robinson from a lynch mob is now an office across the street.

In the atrium outside the courtroom, part of a gnarly old tree trunk taken from near the original Lee home site is encased in plastic. With a notch in the side, the log evokes the knotty hardwood in "Mockingbird" where Scout's strange neighbor Boo Radley hid gifts for her and her brother.

Radley was believed to be based on a seldom-seen neighbor of the Lees, Alfred Boulware, who died in 1952 and is buried in the same cemetery as Lee's father, who died in 1962. The graveyard is beside the town's United Methodist Church, just a few blocks from the courthouse. The author was buried here as well.

After Lee's death, plans were announced to create a museum in a 1909 bank building that once housed the office of Lee's father.

Lee lived out her final years in an assisted living facility. Mostly, though, like Boo, she was seldom seen around town.

If You Go . . .

MONROEVILLE, Alabama: Located halfway between Alabama's capital of Montgomery and its seaport city of Mobile, about 25 miles (40 km) west of Interstate 65, the nearest major highway.

MARDI GRAS IN NEW ORLEANS:
A GUIDE

By Kevin McGill

NEW ORLEANS—New Orleans is synonymous with Mardi Gras, and visitors who want to experience Carnival season face an abundance of choices on how, when and where to take it all in.

WATCH A PARADE

This isn't as simple as it sounds. Deciding where, when and how to catch any of the dozens of New Orleans area parades—and which ones to watch—involves planning.

The date of Mardi Gras changes from year to year, depending on when Easter falls, but it's always the day before Ash Wednesday. It can be as early as Feb. 3 and as late as March 9.

New Orleans' major parades, the ones with marching bands and masked riders who throw beads and other trinkets from elaborate floats, run for about two weeks before Mardi Gras. Most follow a route along historic St. Charles Avenue onto Canal Street, the broad downtown boulevard at the edge of the French Quarter, though the giant floats of Endymion lumber through the Mid-City neighborhood.

The throngs turning out to watch the parades come well supplied with lawn chairs, ice chests, trays of barbecue, buckets of fried chicken and step ladders with little seats bolted to the top to give the kids a better vantage point.

Alternatively, you can pay big bucks at one of the fine-dining restaurants that erect bleachers out front so you can catch the processions while sipping a Sazerac cocktail.

Often overlooked are smaller processions, like Krewe du Vieux's satirical and raunchy parade through the French Quarter with smaller, hand-drawn floats. Sci-fi, fantasy and horror fans don costumes evoking any of a variety of pop culture icons from Ewoks to zombies for the Intergalactic Krewe of Chewbacchus stroll through the Marigny neighborhood.

BE IN A PARADE

Getting a spot in a Carnival parade is the ultimate participatory Mardi Gras experience.

Some of the old-line parade "krewes" are famous for their exclusivity (some so exclusive that they stopped parading years ago rather than comply with a city non-discrimination ordinance). But others are open to anyone who can afford it, although spots are limited and sometimes have to be reserved well in advance.

Costs including membership fees, costumes and "throws" (beads, little stuffed toys, etc.) can add up. Some travel agency and hotel packages include parade spots for big bucks. On the other end of the cost scale are the walking clubs, like Chewbacchus, which has annual dues of less than $50.

SEE THE COSTUMES

Mardi Gras is a day-long costume party in the French Quarter and along the parade routes.

Sometimes the costumes are simple: multi-colored wigs, glittery masks, oversized hats.

Sometimes they are elaborate: shimmering bodysuits with huge feather headdresses fanning out from the wearers' heads and shoulders like peacock tails.

Some of the most intricate, elaborate and, sometimes, outrageous are on display at the annual Bourbon Street awards, usually at the intersection of Bourbon and St. Ann, where prize categories include best drag and best leather.

WEAR A COSTUME

Feathered masks, funny hats and boas are available at souvenir shops in the Quarter and from vendors who wheel their goods up and down the main parade route.

Many visitors fashion their own, sometimes topical get-ups. Coveralls splotched with black were among the 2011 costumes lampooning BP after the Gulf of Mexico oil spill. Some go for professionally made store-bought or rented regalia.

BEHAVE YOURSELF

Yes, it's often touted as the world's biggest free party and it takes place in a city famous for all-night bars and drinking in the streets. But there are limits, and hundreds of arrests in the police district around the French Quarter in the days leading up to Mardi Gras are not unusual.

FALL FOLIAGE:
6 SPOTS IN THE NORTHEAST U.S.

By The Associated Press

The Northeast's fall foliage dazzles locals and draws millions of tourists. Here are six spots for autumn vistas off the beaten path in New England and upstate New York.

CONNECTICUT

The Heublein Tower in Simsbury, Connecticut sits at the top of Talcott Mountain State Park.

The 165-foot (50-meter) tower was built in 1914 by liquor

magnate Gilbert Heublein as a summer home and offers spectacular views that on a clear day extend north to the Berkshires in Massachusetts and south to Long Island Sound.

Getting to the tower involves a relatively easy 1¼-mile (2-km) hike up a foliage-filled trail that winds up the mountain with plenty of overlooks of the Farmington River Valley. There's also a nearby pumpkin patch where visitors can enjoy hayrides and pumpkin picking. 　　　　　　　　　　　　　—*Pat Eaton-Robb*

MAINE

Nestled in tiny Turner in the foothills of Maine, Ricker Hill Orchards combines two of New England's most beloved autumn activities: picking your own apples and admiring the turning leaves. The orchard's hillside "u-pick" area offers a stunning view of Maine's western lakes and mountains region, with views of foliage stretching all the way to New Hampshire.

The ninth-generation orchard also offers fall staples such as cider and cider doughnuts along with its apples and views. It's about an hour's drive north of Portland—a ride with its own superb views of the fall spectacle. 　　　　　　—*Patrick Whittle*

MASSACHUSETTS

Most people associate Cape Cod with summer, sand and surf, but the peninsula offers some postcard-perfect backdrops for foliage.

Cross over the Sagamore Bridge and take the first exit onto rural Route 6A, which winds and twists through the scenic and historic town of Sandwich. The Old King's Highway, as it used to be known, hugs Cape Cod Bay and is lined with ancient stone walls, white picket fences, ponds and pastures.

Two worthwhile stops in Sandwich: Heritage Museums and

Gardens, where you can meander paths bordered by stunning flora; and the Green Briar Nature Center, next to the conservation area where Thornton Burgess dreamed up Peter Rabbit and other characters. —*William J. Kole*

NEW HAMPSHIRE

Why limit your leaf-peeping to a single state—or, for that matter—country? Head to Milan State Park, where a fire tower offers simultaneous views of the mountain ranges of New Hampshire, Maine, Vermont and Canada.

Brilliant leaves in the foreground contrast beautifully with fog that settles in the valleys and the mountains in the distance. The recently renovated park, about 125 miles (200 km) north of the state capital of Concord, includes a hilltop campground with a half-dozen campsites and four furnished yurts for rent.

Oh, and it's not pronounced like Milan, Italy. It's pronounced MY-linn. —*Holly Ramer*

NEW YORK

In the southern Adirondacks, the stony Sacandaga River and a series of forest-rimmed lakes reflect blazing orange and yellow leaves along a 50-mile (80 km) stretch of Route 30 from Northville to Indian Lake. There are long stretches of unbroken wilderness between the hamlets of Wells, Speculator and Indian Lake, with hiking trails leading to secluded ponds, waterfalls and small mountains with big views. —*Mary Esch*

RHODE ISLAND

For an urban leaf-peeping experience, there are few places more picturesque than historic Benefit Street in Providence, Rhode

Island. Hundred-year-old elms and other mature trees provide a canopy of spectacular color over brick sidewalks.

The street runs for a mile (1.6 km) past a collection of Colonial, Federal and Greek Revival-style homes, and several historic churches, including the First Baptist Church in America. Situated midway up the steep College Hill, it offers occasional glimpses of a more modern downtown, the Rhode Island Statehouse and rivers below. Above it is the main campus of Brown University, another lovely spot for fall color.   *—Michelle R. Smith*

VERMONT

The top of Owls Head Mountain, reached by a short hiking trail in the Groton State Forest off state Route 232, offers consistently world-class foliage displays.

With an elevation of 1,958 feet (600 meters), the view from the rock face near the peak includes spectacular views of Lake Groton, Kettle Pond, Peacham Bog and an unbroken expanse of forest that in late September and early October glows red, orange and yellow.

While the more adventurous can make a 1.5-mile (2.4 km) hike that's rated as easy to moderate, it's also possible to drive to a parking area near the top for a short walk that makes it an ideal outing with kids.   *—Wilson Ring*

HIDDEN HAMILTON HISTORY IN AND AROUND NEW YORK CITY

By Beth J. Harpaz

NEW YORK—Historic sites connected to Alexander Hamilton are getting a lot more attention than they used to, thanks to a little Broadway show you might have heard about.

Fans of the musical "Hamilton" have hunted down every Hamilton spot they can think of, from his home in Harlem, to his burial site in Lower Manhattan, to Hamilton Park in Weehawken,

New Jersey, near the dueling grounds where he was shot by Aaron Burr.

Tourists have always visited Hamilton's tomb in the graveyard at Trinity Church in Lower Manhattan. Now, not only are more people paying their respects, but they're also looking for the graves of Hamilton's wife, sister-in-law, son and his buddy Hercules Mulligan. "Visitors also now leave flowers, stones, coins, notes, even a potted plant, at Hamilton's monument and on Eliza's stone just in front of it," said Trinity spokeswoman Lynn Goswick.

The show's creator, Lin-Manuel Miranda, wrote part of "Hamilton" at the Morris-Jumel Mansion in Manhattan's Washington Heights. The mansion is known for a dinner party hosted there by President George Washington for his cabinet, attended by Hamilton, John Adams and Thomas Jefferson. (A different dinner party depicted in the show's song "The Room Where It Happens" took place at Jefferson's residence, now marked with a plaque at 57 Maiden Lane in Lower Manhattan.)

The Morris-Jumel Mansion has an odd Burr connection too: Burr married the rich widow who owned the house. She later divorced Burr, and her lawyer was Hamilton's son.

Also uptown, in Harlem, is Hamilton Grange, a National Park site that was Hamilton's home. It includes artifacts like a piano that Hamilton's daughter Angelica played. A replica of the instrument is featured in the show.

In addition to the dueling grounds in Weehawken, another significant Hamilton site is located across the Hudson River from New York: the Schuyler-Hamilton House in Morristown, New Jersey, where Hamilton courted his wife Eliza. A sculpture on the Morristown Green also depicts Hamilton with Washington and the Marquis de Lafayette. Hamilton was Washington's right-hand man in the Revolutionary War, and with his fluent French, he served as a translator between Washington and Lafayette.

Other pilgrimage sites include Hamilton statues in Central Park and at Columbia University. There's also an Alexander Hamilton Room at the Museum of American Finance on Wall Street, where Hamilton founded the Bank of New York.

One more spot in Manhattan is connected to Hamilton's tragic death. After the shooting, the dying man was rowed in a boat back to Manhattan. He died at the home of a friend in Greenwich Village, and a sign outside 82 Jane St. marks the site.

LAKE PLACID:
WINTER FUN AND THE OLYMPIC SPIRIT

By John Kekis

LAKE PLACID, NEW YORK—Lake Placid, New York, welcomes visitors year-round. But its most appealing season might well be winter. Part of that appeal is wrapped up in Lake Placid's famous connections to winter sports: This is a village that embraces the Olympic spirit like nowhere else.

Lake Placid is one of only three places to host two Winter

Olympics. (St. Moritz, Switzerland and Innsbruck, Austria, are the others.) The heroics of the U.S. hockey team and speed skater Eric Heiden helped make the 1980 Lake Placid games one for the ages, one with an enduring legacy. The town also hosted the 1932 Olympics.

Today, it's nearly impossible to go anywhere in the village without encountering somebody in training for something, whether it's skiing, bobsledding, mountain biking or the region's Ironman triathlon.

"It's a beautiful place, but the number of athletes going to the Olympics who live and train here speaks to the kind of lifestyle and activities people engage in every day," said Lisa Weibrecht, a former luge athlete for the United States whose son Andrew has won Olympic medals in downhill skiing.

Lake Placid's Olympic venues have been maintained and are open to the public—unless they're hosting the athletic competitions that are still periodically held here. And all are located within 8 miles (13 km) of Main Street.

Visitors can make the short drive down Route 73 to Mount Van Hoevenberg to ride in a bobsled or on a skeleton (sled), ski the cross-country network of groomed trails used during the 1980 Winter Games, or ski and shoot at the biathlon center. (Reservations are highly recommended for sliding sports, which are dependent on track and weather conditions.)

On the edge of town sits the Olympic Jumping Complex. Today, the complex comprises 120-meter and 90-meter ski jump towers. Visitors can zoom up the 26 stories in an elevator to get a bird's-eye view from the top. You can also ride a chairlift to the base of the jumps.

Seven miles down Route 86 sits Whiteface Mountain, which

hosted Olympic Alpine events in 1980 and boasts the greatest vertical drop (3,166 feet or 965 meters) in the East. Whiteface features 11 lifts and 87 trails with varying terrain for skiers and snowboarders.

In town next to Herb Brooks Arena, where the U.S. hockey team pulled off its "Miracle on Ice" upset of the powerful Soviet Union, sits the same outdoor speed skating oval where local hero Jack Shea won two gold medals in 1932 and Heiden accomplished his stunning achievement of five golds. Plunk down $8 to skate, or walk to the converted ski jump trestle that sends toboggans down two ice-covered chutes onto frozen Mirror Lake. The Olympic Museum next to the hockey rinks inside the Olympic Center has exhibits spanning the history of the 1932 and 1980 games.

For most of the last three decades, Ski Magazine has ranked Whiteface-Lake Placid No. 1 for off-hill activities. Its readers selected it the No. 2 resort overall in the eastern United States. That's partly because overnight options are more varied than ever, from bed-and-breakfasts like Cobble Mountain Lodge and the Interlaken Inn, to chain mainstays Marriott, Hampton Inn, and Crowne Plaza, to the stately Mirror Lake Inn Resort and Spa operated by Ed and Lisa Weibrecht since the late 1970s.

Food options are varied, too, from Caffe Rustica and its Mediterranean fare, to excellent barbecue at Smoke Signals, to Lisa G's and Lake Placid Pub and Brewery. The Cottage at the edge of Mirror Lake is one of the area's most popular apres ski sites.

For non-skiers and visitors who prefer their thrills to be just a bit tamer than zooming down a luge track, try snowshoeing or cross-country skiing on the area's beautiful wooded trails. Or plop yourself down on a sled, cover your lap with a blanket, and let a team of dogs pull you across Mirror Lake.

PART II

DESTINATIONS AND INSIDER GUIDES

ETHIOPIA:
ANCIENT CHURCHES,
MYSTERIOUS TOWERS AND LUCY

By Marcus Eliason

ADDIS ABABA, Ethiopia—Ethiopia has always held me in thrall. It is a cradle of prehistoric humankind. It embraced Christianity long before the missionaries arrived. Its people carved subterranean churches out of solid rock and built mysterious towers of stone.

The country's mythology included serving as keepers of the Ark of the Covenant (the legendary chest containing the Ten

Commandments) and the biblical story of King Solomon and the Queen of Sheba. And in the modern era it was the only African nation to repel a European colonial invasion (by Italy in 1896).

I visited not long ago wIth my wife Eva, taking a mere 4½-hour flight from Israel recently on Ethiopian Airlines. The airline also arranged all-inclusive tours, and for six days, by plane or car, we toured the north of the country from the source of the Blue Nile to the stone obelisks of the vanished empire of Axum.

LAKE TANA AND THE BLUE NILE

After our first night in Addis Ababa, the huge and crowded capital, we flew to Bahir Dar, a pleasant town on the shore of Lake Tana, and were driven south to see the Blue Nile, a tributary of the Nile River. It had rained overnight, and the trip was a slow and slithery affair on an unpaved road. Then we hiked for about a mile through bright green fields, across a wobbly wooden footbridge, and through patches of shoe-swallowing mud. We encountered women herding cattle and a man working his small plot with a plow harnessed to a bull.

Then the sun shone and we were looking at a wall of white water thundering over a cliff: the Blue Nile at its first great cataract on a journey to Khartoum in neighboring Sudan to merge into the White Nile and continue north to the Mediterranean.

Back in Bahir Dar, we traveled by boat across Lake Tana, one of the largest lakes in Africa. Its islands are dotted with monasteries and churches, one of them a circular chapel with a richly thatched roof. The ecclesiastical art on the inner walls was exuberantly colorful, but my own favorite touch was a boulder suspended from a tree branch which, when struck, sounded like a gong, summoning the faithful to prayer.

Next morning, after waking to a sunrise that streaked Lake Tana in gold, we set out on a three-hour drive north to Gondar, a past capital of Ethiopia whose highlight is a royal compound of 17th and 18th century palaces and castles.

Gondar was also once home to Ethiopia's Jewish minority until they emigrated en masse to Israel in the 1980s and 1990s. We did, however, bump into a high-spirited party of Ethiopian-Israeli teenagers on a visit to the place their families had come from.

MYSTERIOUS AXUM

Next stop, the mysterious kingdom of Axum (or Aksum) in northern Ethiopia. It's a junction of early Christian, Muslim and Jewish civilization in the Horn of Africa. Although the Axumite empire lasted hundreds of years, little is known about it. But it was clearly advanced for its time, judging by its most visible highlight, the obelisks.

These so-called stelae, some roughly 10 stories high with intricately carved stone, are thought to have demarcated royal burial places. The largest weighed 520 tons and still lies where it collapsed. Others survive upright.

MAGICAL LALIBELA

Another flight took us to Lalibela and its 12th-century churches—another reason for my wanting to visit Ethiopia. They are magical, baffling, awesome. Defying all conventional rules of architecture, they were carved out of soft volcanic rock, and are seen by looking down into the light-filled crevices that surround them.

The churches are decorated with religious art and other orna-mentation. Attesting to the religious mix that makes Ethiopia so interesting, we spotted a Christian cross inside a Jewish Star of David.

MOMENTS, MEMORIES AND LUCY

Ethiopia endeared itself to us in many ways: its impossibly complicated calendar; the complete absence of smokers (we were told the Church discourages the habit but Ethiopia has also begun banning smoking in public places); the Ethiopian currency, called birr (rhymes with grrr); our driver fighting through traffic not by leaning on his horn but by tapping it gently, almost apologetically; the exquisite little sauce dish we bought, only to see it melt back into mud under our all-vanquishing detergent.

We came across multitudes of people walking on roadsides in rural areas, often too poor to afford public transport. On the dusty unpaved road from Lalibela, at an elevation of 8,000 feet (2,440 meters), we saw crowds of children marching home from school. Our guide mentioned Haile Gebrselassie, the great Olympic long-distance runner, who walked and ran 12 miles (19 km) a day to and from school (not at all uncommon, so great is the hunger for education).

And traipsing uphill came a family in weathered robes and sashes, belongings lashed to a donkey, straight out of the Old Testament.

Finally, to get a sense of proportion after all the antiquity we had encountered, we stopped at the National Museum of Ethiopia in Addis Ababa to see Lucy, whose bones were discovered in northern Ethiopia in 1974. At 3.2 million years, she's the most famous human ancestor.

ROAD TRIPPING SENEGAL

By Nicole Evatt

DAKAR, Senegal—From dizzying Dakar to vibrant Saint-Louis, Senegal pulsates with rich culture, history and charm on Africa's colorful west coast.

All you need for a road trip to explore its bustling cities and sleepy seaside villages is a rental car, a navigation device or app and a little conversational French.

DAKAR FOR THE MUSIC, ART LOVER

Senegal's largest city perched on the tip of the Cap-Vert peninsula is an ideal starting place.

Spend the afternoons shopping for trinkets and T-shirts from the capital's many frenetic street markets. For a more serene shopping experience, head to La Galerie Antenna. This African art mecca boasts an impressive collection of sculptures, paintings, masks and jewelry from across the continent.

Rest up and head out after midnight to experience Dakar's thriving music scene at a local bar or club. After your late night, regroup by the beach at one of Dakar's luxury hotels: Terrou-Bi or Radisson Blu.

While most of Senegal is surprisingly drivable, Dakar traffic is not for the faint of heart. Be prepared for a general disregard of road signs and discombobulating roundabouts. Some rental car packages include drivers or one can be arranged through your hotel. Or hop in taxis for short trips. They're abundant and inexpensive. Be sure to check rates with a local before hailing a ride and negotiate the fare with your driver in advance.

GOREE ISLAND FOR THE HISTORY BUFF

An afternoon (at least) spent exploring the tragic history of Ile de Goree is a must when visiting Dakar. The UNESCO World Heritage site was a shipping point for African slaves during the 16th through 19th centuries. The island's most famous and sobering attraction, Maison des Esclaves (Slave House), has had many high-profile visitors, including President Obama in 2013. It is now a museum and memorial site serving as symbol for the larger slave trade throughout Africa.

You can easily book a tour guide when you arrive, but the small, tranquil island is quite walkable on your own. Take in the scenic ocean views, colorful, crumbling architecture, shops and street vendors before dining on fresh fish at the hilltop restaurant, Dolce Vita.

Ferries leave regularly from Dakar's main port.

SAINT-LOUIS FOR DAY TRIPPERS

Craving a quick trip outside the city? Head 200 miles (320 km) north to the French colonial settlement Saint-Louis.

This lively fishing community connects to the historic city center, a small island in the Senegal river brimming with colonial charm. Reminiscent of New Orleans, Saint-Louis boasts boutique hotels, trendy restaurants, galleries and an annual jazz festival.

Don't miss Senegalese designer Rama Diaw's boutique, which features colorful and wearable clothing and accessories for women, at Rue Blaise Diagne, Ile Nord.

If you have the time, head farther north to the lush wetlands of the Djoudj National Bird Sanctuary, another UNESCO World Heritage site.

On your way back to Dakar stop by Lake Retba, Senegal's "pink lake," about an hour outside of the capital. The water may appear more murky than rosy depending on the season and time of your visit.

GLAMPING AND WILDLIFE

Fathala Wildlife Reserve offers glamping, with three-course meals and luxury air-conditioned tents, near the Gambia border, about 160 miles (258 km) from Dakar, depending on your route. Excursions range from jeep safaris to mangrove boat tours. The attraction started as a conservation project for an antelope, the giant derby eland, but animals from other parts of Africa can be seen here too such as zebras and giraffes.

The lone rhinoceros is known for his nightly pilgrimage to the smartly-placed watering hole in front of the dining area. It's dinner with a show.

PETRA AND MEZZE IN JORDAN

By Amir Bibawy

AMMAN, Jordan—Looking for a Middle Eastern fix of ancient sites, sun, mint tea and falafel, but unsure about safety?

Consider Jordan. It's a world apart from the region's instability and conflicts and Jordanians warmly welcome tourists year-round.

Jordan's sites are spread out, but there's a good road and transportation system, and not an overwhelming number of things to see. It's easy to meet and talk with locals, many of whom speak English.

AMMAN

The serene capital, Amman, was originally built on seven hills on the ruins of ancient Philadelphia. The modern-day city has developed over 100 years into a hip town full of young people and a regional hub for tech start-ups.

The capital's most prominent sight is a Roman amphitheatre that's right in the middle of Amman. The amphitheatre grounds house the Folklore and Popular Traditions Museum where you can see displays of traditional dress from Jordan and Palestine and learn more about the cuisine and ways of life of the nomadic Bedouins.

The Citadel on Amman's highest hill is impressive, home to a Roman temple, Islamic palace, cistern and Byzantine church. From its vista you can get a full appreciation of the massive 2,000-year-old amphitheatre a stone's throw away.

FOOD

What the capital lacks in ancient sights, it makes up for in food. In a short span of several days, and accompanied by local friends, I was able to feast on the country's famed kebabs and mezze—small dishes—and even had pretty good sushi. Whatever you do, do not miss a late-night meat fix from Reem on the 2nd Circle (roundabouts in old Amman are numbered). Find the line of hungry Jordanians waiting outside this takeout shack for sandwiches ($1), and you're in good hands. The meat is marinated, grilled and topped with onions, tahini, tomatoes and salad for an unforgettable pita sandwich. The wait is long but worth it.

Jafra, also in the old city, combines a radical intellectual ambiance with a robust menu of traditional favourites. Photos of pro-Palestinian activist Edward Said, Palestinian poet Mahmoud Darwich and Western left-wing celebrities adorn the walls, but the crowd is split between decidedly hip young Ammanis and middle-class families. Sit on the terrace to soak up the street atmosphere below you.

PETRA

Outside Amman your travels could take you to ancient castles and Christian and Judaic sites or to wild natural reserves. But all paths will lead to Petra, an ancient city built in rose-red rock that remained largely undiscovered till the 19th century.

Petra was built by the Nabataeans, Arabs who controlled the region's trade routes over 2,000 years ago. The structures they left behind are so fascinating they were voted as one of the new Seven Wonders of the World in a global poll six years ago. This led to more visitors, so early morning is the best time to beat the crowds. To get to Petra, you can take a JATT bus from Amman (three hours) or hire a car and a driver.

Entering from the official gate, you pass through a tourist market in a street that descends into a wide valley where Petra's architectural gems begin. Walking through the winding Siq, a gorge formed when land movement split the massive rock mass, you come to appreciate the site's enormity. You may even gasp out loud when you first glimpse the majestic "Treasury" building through the narrow gorge. The Treasury is actually a burial building and not, as myth had it, a place where treasures were hidden. The intricate facade of the building is Petra's most famous image, made even more famous as a setting in "Indiana Jones and the Last Crusade."

Continue along a wide and sunny route past the Theatre, High

Place of Sacrifice, Royal Tombs and other structures. The site's undiscovered gem, at its highest point, is the Monastery, a first century B.C. building. There's good reason few people make it there: It's at the end of a 45-minute climb of 800 rocky steps. But it's worth it. Beyond the Monastery at that elevation is a spectacular view of the entire city of Petra and the colorful valley, Wadi Araba.

JUDEO-CHRISTIAN SITES

I ventured also to Jordan's well-preserved Judeo-Christian sites, including Mount Nebo, where Moses saw the promised land. A map there shows the distance to towns in Israel and the Palestinian Territories; Jerusalem is less than 30 miles (48 km) away.

Close to Mount Nebo is the historically Christian town of Madaba, whose St. George's Church houses an unusual floor map of the Middle East, done in colorful mosaics almost 1,500 years ago. Another unique mosaic is the large and almost-intact floor piece at the Church of Saint Lot and Saint Procopius in the nearby town of Khirbet al-Mukhayyat. These mosaics were discovered in a family's house when a cooking fire ruined the plaster hiding the original floor. The keeper of the church and son of that family holds the keys. He'll let you in and proudly explain that the house belonged to his Muslim family before they donated it to the government, which in turn made it into a church. He earns very little as the guardian of the site, according to my guide, and appreciates a tip of a dinar.

Beyond all this, there's the Dead Sea, along with more ancient Roman sites, Islamic castles and natural wonders—all beautiful and worth visiting. But if you are tempted to simply lounge about with a glass of Jordanian shiraz and a water pipe, staring at the stars in Amman's clear skies, go ahead. Enjoy it.

If You Go . . .

CURRENCY: You'll need local currency. Jordanian dinars. ATMs are common. At tourist sites, there are two prices: a high one for foreigners and a lower one for Jordanians and Arab nationals.

GETTING AROUND: It's too hilly to easily walk between neighborhoods in Amman, but cabs are cheap. Even a long taxi ride across town runs well under US $10. Just make sure the cabbie turns on the meter.

PETRA: Petra is a whole city, not a temple or two, and visitors are typically told that it's too big to see in one day. But it can be done. Arrive early in the morning for eight or nine hours of exploring, which allows you to see most everything. The terrain is not particularly difficult with good shoes and lots of water.

A SIGHTSEEING LAYOVER IN DUBAI

By Dean Fosdick

DUBAI—Dubai International Airport is one of the world's busiest international airports. Just as the Middle East bridged cultures in ancient times, long-haul flights from one continent to another often connect here.

And if you can arrange a layover that lasts a day or two, Dubai is a great place for a quick fix of sightseeing.

Dubai sits in desert country but that's part of its appeal. It makes a handy stopover point for lazing on a beach, doing wheelies in the sand with a dune buggy, bargaining with merchants at a traditional souk or taking high tea in the world's tallest building.

But beware: "Dubai has only two seasons—hot and hotter," my for-hire driver said with a shrug and a smile while taking me on a private tour of the city (about $125 U.S.).

Here are a few suggestions for things to see and places to go while pausing in Dubai.

BURJ KHALIFA

The Burj Khalifa, the world's tallest building, is the icon of Dubai's fast-growing vertical cityscape. It's the world's tallest structure at 2,717 feet (828 meters), making it nearly twice as tall as New York's Empire State Building. The building was completed in 2010 and houses a luxury hotel, residential apartments, corporate offices and suites. It takes a little over a minute by high-speed elevator to reach the observation decks (124th, 125th and 148th floors). Splurge by reserving a window table at the building's 122nd story At.Mosphere restaurant. Prices aren't cheap but then it's all about the views.

Fronting the building is the Dubai Fountain. It has quickly become popular for its choreographed, multi-colored displays, especially at night.

THE SOUKS

Getting to the most popular of the city's traditional souks is more than half the fun when you ride across Dubai Creek on a motorized abra. These small wooden water taxis can squeeze in 16 to 20 people seated shoulder to shoulder. Scores of the boats work the Creek daily, taking about five minutes to cross from Bur Dubai to the Deira district with its souks or small markets selling everything from gold and spices to perfumes and belly dancer outfits. Hone your haggling skills. Few things are sold at listed prices. Take a wharf walk to soak up the many fascinating street scenes. Buy a bottled beverage along the way to hydrate.

THE DESERT

Consider taking a trip into the surrounding desert if you have time. Tour options range from wildlife watching and sand-skiing to dune bashing—racing four-wheelers up and down the many steep sandy slopes. Another desert-trek alternative is sunset safaris. These are half-day, late evening outings to pseudo Bedouin encampments featuring buffets set around campfires. Entertainment varies from camel rides and belly dancing to falconry. One operator offers an exceptional after-dinner treat simply by turning out the lights. Stargazing in the unpolluted dark of a desert night is an unforgettable experience.

If You Go . . .

BURJ KHALIFA: Head for the lower level of The Dubai Mall near the food court and walk to the Burj Khalifa ticket counters. Book online in advance to avoid the long lines of daily visitors. That also may earn you a discount; http://www.burjkhalifa.ae/en/the-tower/ObservationDecks.aspx . Access the At.Mosphere Web site to make a dinner reservation, http://www.atmosphereburjkhalifa.com .

ABRA RIDES: Make your way to any of these departure points: Deira Old Souk Abra Station, Bur Dubai Abra Station, Sabkha Abra Station. Ticket prices are minimal: 1 dirham or about 27 U.S. cents per person per trip. No reservations are required. Simply pay the abra operator and board. The boats leave when both benches are full.

DESERT TOURS: Find a tour package in any of the local guidebooks at airport magazine stands or from sales reps stationed in nearby hotels. If you're flying Emirates airline, you can arrange a variety of stopover tours via its website: http://www.emirates.com/english/destinations_offers/dubai_stopovers/dubai-stopovers.aspx

GUANGZHOU:
A TASTE OF CANTONESE CULTURE

By Nicole Evatt

GUANGZHOU, China—The southern Chinese city of Guangzhou offers all the hustle, bustle, culture and commerce of other major Asian metropolises minus the massive tourist crowds.

And it's an easy stopover destination. There are affordable flights, it's a two-hour train ride from Hong Kong and visitors from many countries can visit for 72 hours without a visa.

COME HUNGRY

Often touted as the birthplace of dim sum, Guangzhou takes its Cantonese cuisine seriously. Head west to the historic Liwan district to stroll through the shop- and restaurant-lined Shangxiajiu Pedestrian Street. Pick up a traditional mooncake filled with lotus seed paste at Lianxiang Lou.

Just off the main strip are side streets brimming with tasty food stalls and bustling markets selling fresh produce and traditional remedies such as live scorpions and dried snakes.

If like me, you're overwhelmed by Guangzhou's copious culinary choices, book a local guide though Eating Adventures Food Tour and tackle this foodie's paradise like a pro.

A BIRD'S-EYE VIEW

Canton Tower is one of Guangzhou's top tourist attractions and for good reason. At 1,968 feet (600 meters), the modern monolith offers panoramic views of the cityscape and winding Pearl River. It also features rotating restaurants and, for thrill-seekers, a 100-foot (30-meter) free fall ride. I opted for the leisurely bubble tram and snapped the stunning sunset views while slowly rotating in a glass pod on a track atop the tower.

CULTURE VULTURE

Craving a creative boost? Head to the Tianhe District for the Redtory Art and Design Factory. This sprawling canning factory-turned-sleepy artists' village boasts a bevy of contemporary galleries, exhibits and restaurants. Pick up a milk tea from one of the trendy cafes and peruse the small shops of artsy handicrafts, clothing, books and accessories. Redtory is similar to Beijing's

798 Art Zone, but not yet quite as developed. Still, you can easily lose a few hours in this off-the-beaten path cultural compound.

SOUVENIR SHANGRI-LA

Cross off your entire shopping list with a visit to OneLink International Plaza. This massive wholesale mall off of Haizhu Square is a winding, multi-floor maze of toys, home goods, electronics, clothing and accessories. I spent three hours in this shopper's wonderland and barely scratched its surface.

GO UNDERGROUND

If you can overcome the language barrier, taxis are affordable and abundant in Guangzhou. But I'd recommend beating the traffic and hopping on the metro. The subway is clean, quiet, air-conditioned and cheap. It's also easy to navigate with most maps, and the announcements are in English. Keep in mind the Chinese government blocks thousands of websites. You'll need a virtual private network, or VPN, if Google Maps is your go-to navigation tool.

SHENZHEN:
SIGHTSEEING ON A BUSINESS TRIP

By Kelvin Chan

SHENZHEN, China—With its anonymous sprawl of skyscrapers and factories linked by busy highways, the southern Chinese manufacturing megacity of Shenzhen might not appear at first to be the best place to do some sightseeing during a business trip.

Yes, the city is a magnet for foreign business travelers, many of whom come expressly to visit factories and meet suppliers, but it's still far off the beaten tourist path. And that makes any effort to discover local attractions more rewarding than prowling the cliched and overpriced nightspots of neighboring Hong Kong or jostling with the crowds at the shopping malls and historical sites of Beijing and Shanghai.

OCT LOFT

On a recent trip to Shenzhen from my base in Hong Kong, I discovered the tranquil charm of OCT Loft, a cluster of old factory buildings that's been converted into an art and design zone.

A visit to OCT Loft, located in the Nanshan neighborhood, was a welcome antidote to Shenzhen's hyper-urban intensity. I took a cab from downtown and 20 minutes later, as we left the wide main road, high-rise tower blocks gave way to narrow streets lined with leafy trees and bicycle paths.

The district's low-rise buildings are filled with design studios, architects' offices, art galleries, bars and restaurants.

Finding your way around is easy thanks to metal maps set into the walkways. Buildings are helpfully denoted by simple combinations of letters and numbers: A4, B3.

INDUSTRIAL PAST

Disused pieces of factory equipment painted bright red were set up on the pathways as a reminder of the area's recent industrial past. An oversized machine press stood on a walkway paved with skinny red bricks. Nearby were two rustic cafes, their outdoor seats hidden by an array of potted plants and shaded by mature trees, and I stopped at one of them for a glass of iced lemon tea.

The district is also a great place to see contemporary art. Murals adorn walls and the sides of buildings; paintings and sculptures are on display at galleries; and big exhibitions are held at OCT Contemporary Art Terminal, or OCAT.

OCT Loft itself is part of a wider tourist district that includes theme parks and hotels known as Overseas Chinese Town. The state-owned company that runs it also operates an ecotourism resort called OCT East on the other side of the city. There's also a shopping district called OCT Bay.

If You Go . . .

OCT LOFT: By subway, the closest station is Qiaocheng East but you'll still have to walk about half a kilometer (a third of a mile). By cab, point your driver to the map at the Guide section at www. octloft.cn .

OCAT: ocat.org.cn/index.php/home?lang=en

A CITY GIRL IN THE WILDS OF MONGOLIA

By Nicole Evatt

ULAANBAATAR, Mongolia—I'm a city girl. I did not grow up camping, have never pitched a tent and know nothing of the Girl Scouts beyond Thin Mints or Samoa cookies. Certainly no one would use the words "rugged" or "outdoorsy" to describe me.

So I definitely had a few reservations when my husband suggested a vacation in the wilds of central Mongolia.

My trepidation only grew as I binged on travel reviews bemoaning makeshift bathrooms and swarming insects.

But I ended up loving every minute in Mongolia, a country

steeped in history, stunning scenery and welcoming locals. I stepped outside my comfort zone and into the trip of a lifetime. And here's why you should too.

GET OFF THE GRID

Mongolia, a country of 3 million people slightly smaller than Alaska, is one of the most sparsely populated places in the world.

You can go hours, even days, without seeing another human while traveling through Mongolia's countryside. Instead, you'll find a vibrant blue horizon and empty, rolling grasslands dotted with horses, cows, sheep, goats and yaks.

You'll be forced to unplug as cell service and Wi-Fi is mostly non-existent outside of the larger cities.

So say goodbye to Facebook rants and traffic jams and say hello to a seemingly endless untouched landscape. Your only roadblock is the occasional cow.

BOOK A GUIDE

As avid travelers accustomed to DIY adventures, we rarely book tours. But my top tip for this wonderland is to find yourself an expert.

There are few road signs and English is not widely used, so a local guide with knowledge of the routes and language is highly recommended.

You will also need a four-wheel drive vehicle to navigate the mostly unpaved terrain.

Our expert, good-humored guide, Munkh Bileg, whom we hired through Nomadic Discovery, tailored our private tour to our interests and time constraints to maximize our Mongolian experience.

We rode camels across sand dunes and horses at sunset. We met herder families and sampled local cuisine, including fermented mare's milk and dried curds. Most of our days were spent off-roading over mountains and across rivers, simply soaking in Mongolia's other-worldly landscape.

MUST-SEES

For the history buff: Erdene Zuu Monastery is located in Kharkhorin, on the northern border of the Ovorkhangai Province. Get your fill of ornate Buddha statues, elaborate wall paintings and artifacts dating back to the 18th century while exploring the three remaining Chinese-style temples at one of the oldest Buddhist monasteries in Mongolia.

For the nature lover: The Orkhon waterfall (also called the Ulaan Tsutgalan waterfall) is located in Ovorkhangai Province, around 75 miles (120 km) from the town of Kharkhorin. A hike to the edge of this massive, 65-foot (20-meter) waterfall offers stunning views of dark volcanic rock surrounded by a lush valley.

Also, be sure to stop by the pristine Lake Ogii in the southeastern corner of the Arkhangai Province. Like most of Mongolia, it felt like we had traveled back to a time before humans as the only other visitors were a group of horses splashing and lounging about in the calm waters.

For a glimpse of desert dunes: Elsen Tasarkhai is a sand strip located in Bulgan Province. While we didn't have time to explore Mongolia's famed Gobi Desert, we made a quick stop at this 50-mile (80-km) stretch of golden hills for a relaxing tour via camels.

GER LIFE

As the sun sets there is little else to do besides stargazing and cozying in your ger (pronounced "gare"), a traditional nomad home.

Apparently we were right on trend as an $8,000 version of the circular tent, or yurt, was featured in a holiday gift guide from Gwyneth Paltrow's lifestyle website, goop.

Our home base was the Tsagaan Sum hot springs and tourist camp in Khoton Soum, Arkhangai Province (approximately 280 miles or 460 km west of Ulaanbaatar).

The hustle and bustle of city life was but a distant memory as we fell asleep to the crackle of a wood-burning stove and woke to the sounds of horses neighing outside our ger.

GOOD TO KNOW

The flies will swarm as soon as you step outside, as will the mosquitoes. So pack bug spray and long-sleeved layers.

Western-style bathrooms are few and far between outside of Ulaanbaatar. Be prepared to cop a squat when nature calls.

Ulaanbaatar is Mongolia's bustling, traffic-jammed capital city, but tourist attractions are few. Stop by a grocery store to load up on water, snacks and essentials. Then head to the countryside.

Speaking of food, get ready for meat, mostly lamb and lots of it. Mongolian cuisine is about as "farm to fork" as it gets. Refrigeration in the countryside isn't common so your dinner was likely plucked from the pasture that very day.

If You Go...
NOMADIC DISCOVERY: https://www.nomadicdiscovery.com/

TSAGAAN SUM TOURIST CAMP: https://www.facebook.com/Tsagaan-sum-Hot-Springs-tourist-camp-1414194985537890/

THAILAND:
FROM ISLAND BEACHES TO MOUNTAIN TREKS

By Courtney Bonnell

BANGKOK—Trudging up a lush mountainside to a remote village, plunging through a swift-moving river in the footsteps of elephants and cruising Bangkok's gleaming luxury malls: With each step, I walked into different worlds, each one beautiful, all in Thailand.

Not to mention glittering temples, bustling night markets and world-famous Thai massages to soothe weary muscles.

BANGKOK

The capital's malls and markets are endless, from Siam Paragon, filled with designer brands and an upscale food court, to stands of cheap goods where souvenir-seekers haggle over the price of utensils, bracelets and trinkets. After dark, with the heat of the day subsiding, the night markets come alive, bustling with shoppers grabbing cheap sunglasses and shoes while families and friends enjoy soups and curries.

Bangkok is also famous for its opulent temples, including Wat Pho, or Temple of the Reclining Buddha, with its stair-step monuments to royalty called chedis, similar to stupas. The centerpiece is a massive horizontal Buddha, its gold girth touching the temple walls from end to end.

The white-walled Grand Palace complex houses Thailand's most sacred temple, Wat Phra Kaew, or Temple of the Emerald Buddha, with sparkling, gold-decked buildings. The surprise is the size of the famed Buddha figure, carved from jade and dressed in gold, but just 26 inches (66 cm) high.

CHIANG MAI

The walled old city houses more famous temples, including Wat Chedi Luang. Its towering red brick is worn to black, its steps have all but crumbled, but stone dragons still stand guard.

The moss-covered Wat Pha Lat temple is tucked in a forest just outside Chiang Mai. From the university, you can get there by hiking Monks Trail, which is marked by strips of orange fabric. Head farther up the mountain to popular Doi Suthep temple or hail a songthaew, a shared taxi.

Hungry after hiking? Hit the street vendors and restaurant

options that abound back in the tourist center: vegetarian-friendly green curried rice, fried mushrooms and pad thai, plus plenty of beef and pork speared on sticks for meat-eaters. To cool off from the heat or spice, try fresh-cranked pomegranate juice or coconut ice cream.

TREKKING

Chiang Mai is the jumping-off point for trekking, elephant tours and other outdoor adventures. A friend and I booked an ecotour trek and overnight home stay in a village some 4½ hours away in the Mae Hong Son region. The Karen ethnic group lives there, farming rice and cabbage on vibrant green hillsides. Our guides cut down wild passion fruit for us to sample, pointed out spiders as big as a hand and chopped bamboo to whittle into cups. After reaching the mountaintops near the Myanmar border and making it to the village, we used those cups to slug homemade rice liquor.

We set up a bed of blankets on the wooden floor and rested between bags of rice as our hosts cooked dinner in a hearth built into the floor. Sleeping in a home open to the elements was the only time I got cold on the trip, and the only place I skipped a shower, passing up a tub of chilly water in an outhouse with a squat toilet.

ELEPHANTS

I wanted to enjoy these majestic creatures, iconic in Thailand but often exploited, in an ethical way. The Elephant Nature Park allowed us to travel alongside them, not on their backs. We kept them moving through the jungle by thrusting bananas and melon into their eagerly outstretched trunks. It was surreal and a bit unnerving as we led four mostly blind and elderly female elephants on a muddy, uneven path, trying to keep our balance while avoiding their feet. In another part of the sanctuary, we got a peek at a baby elephant.

PHI PHI ISLANDS

Thai authorities have closed some of their most popular beaches at times because of overuse, so check before planning an itinerary.

We were able to visit the Phi Phi Islands, pronounced "pee pee," and had looked forward to decompressing on an otherworldly beach there. But rain was falling as we arrived and promised not to let up.

Instead of the party-hearty main town on Ko Phi Phi Don, the largest island, we opted for a secluded resort. A long-tail boat plowed through choppy waters to get us there, leaving us windblown and wet from ocean spray and rain as we tried to photograph the green-topped rock rising from the Andaman Sea.

The weather cooperated enough the next day for a group tour to the smaller island, Koh Phi Phi Leh, and its hotspot, Maya Bay, which is breathtaking but overrun after the movie "The Beach" made it famous. Even early in the day, it was tough to find a spot free of people posing with selfie sticks.

Nearby, we reveled in an empty swath of sand framed by cliffs before winding through rock formations to the Blue Lagoon, a green-walled swimming hole packed with tourist boats.

After the beaches and long days in the devout atmosphere of temples, our nights turned to buying knockoffs of favorite overpriced sandals, swigging 70 baht ($2) beer and watching men in elaborate makeup and sequined gowns dance in a packed outdoor market.

That's Thailand, country of contrasts.

A TOURIST IN TOKYO:
Q&A

By Linda Lombardi

TOKYO—Tourism to Japan is booming, with more than 1 million Americans among the country's more than 20 million annual visitors. But language barriers and cultural differences may seem intimidating to some travelers. Here are answers to questions you might have if you're contemplating a trip to the capital city, Tokyo.

Q. Is it true that addresses don't really exist? How will I find anything?

A. There are addresses, but the Japanese system is different. Most streets have no names and buildings are not numbered in order. Use a map or an app. That's what the natives do.

Bilingual neighborhood maps are usually posted outside train stations in tourist areas. Carry a bilingual map so you can point to where you're heading if you need to ask a local for directions. Two tricks will help you pronounce Japanese destination names: Put equal emphasis on every syllable, and always pronounce the E at the end of words as a separate syllable (so "Kobe" is "ko-bay").

Q. I can't read Japanese. How will I figure out the trains?

A. Trains and stations have signs in English. Most trains also have bilingual recordings and electronic signage announcing the stations. Stops are also numbered, which helps both with figuring out distance and with names that seem like a jumble of random syllables.

The bigger problem is that the system is so elaborate, a mere human can't always figure out the best route. No map can include all lines. Again, use an app. English options include the Tokyo Metro app and a version of the Japanese app Navitime.

Avoid trains at rush hour if possible.

Q. Bathrooms are really different, right? Spraying water, heated seats! What do I need to know?

A. Most high-tech Japanese toilets are easy to use. Flush is sometimes labeled in English. Just don't touch the other buttons. And don't be freaked out when a fancy one opens the lid automatically for you.

But be prepared for traditional squat toilets. Some public toilets have both squat and Western-style toilets, often with doors labeled for each type. If there's a line, it's fine to wait for the Western style to be available.

Another small wrinkle: Toilets nearly always give an option for a big or little flush. If you want to be environmentally correct, learn the characters for those terms because they're rarely labeled in English. Not a bad idea to learn the character for "flush" also, just in case.

Q. I'm scared of eating strange things. How will I order food?

A. Some restaurants have photo menus posted outside, and there may also be plastic food samples, so you can usually point to what you want. English menus are not unheard of, but don't expect them. And if a server doesn't come to take your order, you're not being ignored. It's typical to call one over (usually by saying "sumimasen"—basically "excuse me"). There's no tipping and usually you pay at the register on the way out.

Other options include convenience stores, where food is much better than in similar U.S. stores, from wrapped sandwiches and bento to snacks and dessert. Most Japanese department stores also have food on lower levels that you can point at and take away.

For unadventurous eaters, there's always tempura and ramen. But Tokyo is also a world-class food city. In some neighborhoods it's harder to find traditional Japanese food than Italian or French. There are exquisite Western baked goods in many neighborhoods along with a heavenly version of white bread. You'll also find Western fast food chains, although don't be surprised to find local specialties on the menu.

Q. Do I have to drink tea? I really need my coffee.

A. The Japanese are serious about coffee. You will find Starbucks, local chains and many independent shops.

Q. What do I need to know about money?

A. Japan is still very much a cash society, partly because it's so safe that no one worries about carrying a lot of cash. Department stores, large chains like Uniqlo and hotels take credit cards, but you'll pay cash at most other places.

Q. I'm intrigued by onsens. But do I have to be naked with strangers?

A. Yes, in both onsen (natural hot-spring baths, usually at resort hotels) and sento (public baths in cities). But bathing is gender-segregated. When everyone else is doing it, it quickly seems natural. To avoid calling attention to yourself, follow the customs. Most critically, wash yourself thoroughly BEFORE getting into the bath, which is only for soaking. Also know that baths traditionally prohibit people with tattoos, which are associated with organized crime, though this is starting to change.

Q. Will I have to sleep on the floor? Or in a drawer?

A. Not unless you want to. There are innumerable Western-style hotels in Japan. But there's nothing quite like waking up on a futon to the smell of tatami mats, so why not try it? As for the famous beds in drawers, capsule hotels are mostly for short-term business travelers, not vacationers.

Q. Do I have to take my shoes off?

A. Historic houses, fancy traditional restaurants, temples and traditional inns may require visitors to remove shoes. If you're wearing sandals, bare feet may not be allowed, so pack socks.

SINGAPORE:
LEAVE THE BUBBLEGUM HOME

By Amir Bibawy

SINGAPORE—Singapore celebrated 50 years of independence not long ago but the tiny city-state has shrugged off all symptoms of a midlife crisis.

The country has instead embraced travelers—including the many air passengers who stop here en route to Asia—with more and better things to see, taste and experience than ever before.

Singapore became independent in 1965 after being thrown out of the Malaysian federation. Back then there was no telling what the future held; the nation's founder Lee Kuan Yew reportedly cried as he announced the split. But Singapore has emerged as one of Asia's most prosperous, multicultural and stable countries, with a standard of living the envy of many nations. It's also famously clean, with strict laws against littering.

For travelers catching flights here to more exotic Asian destinations, there's enough in Singapore for a longer stay. Attractions can be split into neat categories: colonial heritage, contemporary attractions, ethnic neighborhoods, food and shopping. Coupled with stunningly efficient transportation, it's easy to plan an itinerary lasting several days.

ARCHITECTURE

I started my visit with a walk exploring Singapore's British colonial past along the city's quays. Historic buildings here include the Gothic St. Andrew's Cathedral, Victoria Theatre and the Empress Place Building, which houses the intriguing Asian Civilisations Museum.

The famous Raffles Hotel is a colonial gem that has hosted the likes of Rudyard Kipling and Michael Jackson, while the Fullerton Hotel was the main post office until 1996. Off the Fullerton, I took time to admire the intricate Cavenagh and Anderson bridges, landing conveniently on Boat Quay, a buzzy waterfront of bars and restaurants. As I walked, I snacked on a mango wafer-ice cream sandwich, topping it off with a kopi, a traditional coffee drink made from beans roasted with butter and sugar, sometimes served with rich condensed milk.

Finish off your heritage walk with some of Singapore's striking contemporary architecture: the Norman Foster-designed Supreme Court, the Esplanade Theatres or the flower-shaped

ArtScience Museum, reached via the quirky Helix Bridge, shaped like DNA's double-helix.

The backdrop for all this is the Marina Bay Sands Hotel, one of the world's most photographed hotels. Designed to resemble three decks of cards, it's joined together at the 57th floor by a stunning SkyPark with the world's highest infinity pool, a lounge and bar. Anyone can visit the SkyPark Observation Deck for stunning 360-degree views of the harbor and skyline, but the pool is open only to hotel guests. Rooms are pricey.

CHINATOWN

Singapore is extremely clean. You're not allowed to bring gum into the country, and the U.S. State Department's travel advisory warns about physical punishment for vandalism. (I unthinkingly popped a soda open on the subway, then quickly hid it in response to other passengers' disparaging stares.) But ethnic and traditional neighborhoods are a little less sterile and more colorful than downtown streets.

Chinatown is dotted with temples and buildings attesting to the rich heritage of Malay-born Chinese who immigrated here in the 19th century. You'll see fine art deco homes on streets like Ann Siang Road. At the Buddha Tooth Relic Temple, a tooth ostensibly belonging to the Buddha is encased in a 900-pound solid-gold stupa. Little India is a jolting feast for the senses: busy shops selling anything from cellphones to spices, hole-in-the-wall restaurants with flavorful cuisine, mosques and colorful Hindu temples.

HAWKER CENTRES

Singapore's "hawker centres" are something of a foodie legend. You could spend days shuttling between the biggest ones, sampling from stalls of Singaporean, Indian, Chinese, Malay and Indonesian cuisine. Seating is usually outdoors on shared benches under a canopy. Walk up to a stall and look at the pictures. Then order, pay the cashier and wait for your food (sometimes it will be brought to your table). You can buy different plates from different vendors. Don't forget fresh juices (sugar cane is a must) and desserts (mango, please!). I ate satay every day. Also great: the ubiquitous, succulent stir-fried squid with onions, scallions and shallots in a spicy tomato sauce. Most dishes cost around $5. Food courts in malls charge a bit more for similar fare, but with air conditioning.

GARDENS AND THE ZOO

Speaking of malls, Orchard Boulevard is lined with luxury shopping centers, worth a visit for people-watching if not for browsing. Istana, the presidential palace, is at Orchard Road's southern end, while the Botanical Garden is at its northern tip.

I skipped the Botanical Garden in favor of Singapore's hippest attraction, Gardens by the Bay. Adjacent to Marina Bay Sands, the park is dotted with "Supertrees," structures as tall as 15-story buildings that function as vertical gardens, loaded with exotic plants. A spectacular sound and light show plays here twice every evening, creating a sci-fi forest.

At the Singapore Zoo, most animals live outdoors, cage-free, from penguins and crocodiles to white tigers and polar bears. A combined ticket to the zoo and nearby night safari by tram will save you some cash. Safaris sell out, so book ahead.

All in all, the mix of cultures, food, colonial heritage and modern—even futuristic—infrastructure and amenities makes the country an ideal destination. Just be sure to leave your bubblegum home.

If You Go . . .

SINGAPORE: http://www.yoursingapore.com/en.html. Tropical climate, frequent rainfall (heaviest November-early January). EZ-Link transit cards cover public transportation and taxis, as well as many food and drink outlets.

BUCKET LIST BORA BORA:
NOT JUST FOR CELEBS

By Jennifer McDermott

BORA BORA, French Polynesia—Somehow I convinced my husband that the fifth wedding anniversary is the Tahitian anniversary. The traditional gift, actually, is wood.

For years, I had dreamed of going to Bora Bora in French Polynesia. The lagoon's glimmering turquoise, jade and cobalt blue waters, the overwater bungalows, the seclusion—for me, it was the ultimate bucket list destination.

Some of the world's most famous celebrities vacation in Bora

Bora. Jennifer Aniston honeymooned there. Pictures of Justin Bieber swimming naked in Bora Bora circulated far and wide online. Usain Bolt celebrated his Olympic victories there.

That doesn't mean normal couples can't go too — if they can afford it, of course. Our trip for a week, including flights and our hotel stay (with breakfast), cost just under $10,000.

My husband and I spent a week lounging on the deck of our bungalow at Le Meridien Bora Bora. We woke early to catch brilliant orange and pink sunrises. We got up close and personal with sea creatures, from moray eels and trumpetfish to sea turtles, sharks and stingrays. We discovered that the saying heard in pearl shops, "You don't choose the pearl, the pearl chooses you" is surprisingly true. Most of all, we tried to relax and take it all in.

THE BASICS

Bora Bora, located about 160 miles (260 km) northwest of Tahiti, was formed by volcanic eruptions millions of years ago. Mount Otemanu, a remnant of the volcano, rises nearly 2,400 feet (730 meters) on the island and serves as the backdrop of many photos.

About 9,000 people live in Bora Bora. The temperature is a relatively consistent 80 F (27 C). The island is set in a lagoon and surrounded by a string of motus, or small islets, where luxury resorts are located. The colors are stunning. A friend said my photo looked like a watercolor painting.

We flew there from Los Angeles, where many U.S. flights to Tahiti converge. From Los Angeles, it's about an eight-hour overnight flight to Papeete, Tahiti. It's less than an hour by plane from there to Bora Bora. Then it's a short boat ride to the main city, Vaitape, or to one of the luxury resorts. We didn't need vaccinations or a visa.

ACTIVITIES

Our overwater bungalow faced outward to the lagoon, which we requested when booking. Others are turned in, toward the resort. It featured a glass floor for fish watching and a spiral staircase for climbing into the lagoon.

We splurged on massages early in the week, before our pale skin turned a reddish hue, and we fed baby sea turtles at the Turtle Center established at Le Meridien. We took the hotel's boat to The St. Regis Bora Bora Resort to dine at the exclusive Lagoon restaurant by acclaimed French chef Jean-Georges Vongerichten and to check out the lavish bungalows with private swimming pools over the lagoon.

We tried paddle boarding. Then we tried snorkeling to find the sunglasses we lost while paddle boarding. Adventurous couples buzzed around the island on jet skis.

Feeling adventurous ourselves, we signed up for a snorkeling trip to swim with stingrays and sharks. There are so many stingrays there, you feel their slick, rubbery bodies hitting your legs. One is an older, docile stingray the guides call "grandma." Our guide from Teiva Tours lifted grandma and kissed it—on the mouth!

But when the guides started "chumming" the waters with fish parts to draw blacktip sharks, we climbed back into the boat. The sharks were much more interested in the fish than in us, but we weren't taking any chances of a misdirected chomp. In deeper waters, we snorkeled at the surface as 9-foot (3-meter) lemon sharks glided along the bottom.

VAITAPE AND PEARLS

We also spent a day in Vaitape. There's a center where locals sell their crafts, a small marketplace to stock up on sunscreen, juice and inexpensive French wine, and a cafe. The mountainside is home to cannons left behind by U.S. forces during World War II.

The main thing we did though, was shop for Tahitian pearls. We were leaving one of the stores when I caught a glimpse of a pair of green pearl earrings. I walked away but no other pearl could compare, so we returned at the end of the day to buy the pearl that chose me.

There's a must-visit spot along the coastline, about 3 miles (5 km) from the city center: Bloody Mary's, a funky restaurant known for its seafood and celebrity visits. I enjoyed the restaurant's signature plate of teriyaki wahoo and the house drink, of course, while my husband loved trying meka, a broadbill swordfish found in the South Pacific. By the entrance there's a long list of famous people who have dined there.

At the hotel, we ended the week as we began. We lounged on the deck, telling each other how unbelievable it was that we got to see such beauty in person and check Bora Bora off the bucket list.

MALAYSIA'S PENANG ISLAND: ARTS, EATS AND OLD STREETS

By Adam Schreck

GEORGE TOWN, Malaysia—Penang is the rare tropical island where hitting the town beats lazing on the beach.

Fortune-seekers from China, Europe and India have been drawn to this Malaysian island for more than two centuries, creating along with local Malays an eclectic mix that can feel both seductively familiar and exotic at the same time.

The colonial capital they've left behind oozes a hauntingly

rustic charm, with colorful street art as much a draw as the historical architecture and one of Southeast Asia's tastiest street food scenes.

WANDER THE OLD TOWN

There are plenty of tourist-friendly stretches of sand if that's what you're looking for. The most popular are along the resort strip of Batu Ferringhi on the island's northern coast.

Where Penang really shines, though, is in the scrappy but alluring lanes of the provincial capital George Town. Its historical center is listed along with Melaka, another enchanting Malaysian city further down the coast, on the UNESCO World Heritage list.

Although founded by the British as a trading hub, Penang has strong Chinese influences, the legacy of waves of migrants who settled here for work generations ago.

Craftsmen still tinker away in Chinese-signposted shophouses nestled up against busy dragon-topped temples swaddled in incense, and gather for rounds of mahjong as the sun sets.

"Penang people ... are very slow and very relaxed. We are living on a small island so we are happy with the situation," explains local artist Ch'ng Kiah Kiean, who grew up in the shadow of a traditional Chinese clan meeting hall known as a kongsi. "We still keep a simple lifestyle in George Town."

A handful of restored heritage buildings such as the Penang Peranakan Mansion and the grand Khoo Kongsi clan house offer glimpses into how Chinese immigrants both shaped and were influenced by their adopted home.

SOAK UP STREET ART

Less than a decade ago, it was George Town's tumbledown architecture and umbrella-topped cycle rickshaws that first caught visitors' eyes.

Turn a corner these days and you're more likely than not to be wowed by some selfie-inspiring street art slowly fading away in the tropical sun.

On this multiethnic island, it is perhaps no surprise that some of the most popular were produced by an outsider, Lithuanian Ernest Zacharevic, who was inspired enough by George Town to put down roots.

"It was very fresh for me—to see all these walls and textures and inspirations that I get there," he said. "There's just something charming about it. It's a place which is hard to forget."

Other pieces to look out for are the more than four dozen cartoonish steel-rod sculptures by Malaysian artists detailing local history, including one memorializing Penang-born shoemaker Jimmy Choo, and a mural of a larger-than-life Indian boatman by Russian artist Julia Volchkova.

Feeling inspired? Rozana Mohamed runs classes teaching the traditional art of batik painting from her studio on Lebuh Aceh. Sessions start from as little as 35 ringgit ($8.40) for one hour, materials included.

EAT ON THE STREET

Even by the standards of Southeast Asia—a region that spawned pad thai and Vietnamese banh mi sandwiches—the street food of Penang stands out. Part of what makes it so good is the mishmash of cultures that have left their mark on this island.

Start the day with Indian roti canai, a flaky flatbread served with curry. Or try a true Malaysian favorite: nasi lemak—a mound of coconut-infused rice plus peanuts, crispy anchovies, sweet chili sauce and a hard-boiled egg, served with or without meat. It's an odd combination—often wrapped in a grab-and-go banana leaf parcel—that works amazingly well.

Wash it down like the locals do with a strong iced coffee sweetened with condensed milk.

From there it's on to a parade of Chinese-inspired stir-fried noodle dishes. Char kway teow, made with flat rice noodles, sausage, shrimp, cockles and eggs, is a must-try staple that's easy to find.

Mee goreng, another fried noodle dish, is sweeter and can have a subtle Indian curry kick, while the famous laksa noodle soup is all about the sour and spice.

None of the dishes costs much more than 6 ringgit ($1.45). One you'll struggle to find? Panang curry, which is more associated with neighboring Thailand.

If You Go . . .

GETTING THERE: Bridges and ferries link Penang to the mainland. Or catch a short direct flight from the capital Kuala Lumpur or nearby hubs like Singapore or Bangkok.

ACCOMMODATIONS: Some of the best hotels and inns are housed in renovated old buildings, such as the Blue Mansion built by 19th century magnate Cheong Fatt Tze. Another one to check out is Ren i Tang , a converted Chinese medicine hall in Little India where an ingenious pulley spares guests from hoisting bags up the narrow stairs.

PENANG: Official tourism site, http://mypenang.gov.my

MAGICAL REALISM IN COLOMBIA

By Beth J. Harpaz

CARTAGENA, Colombia—Tell people you're vacationing in Colombia and some react like you're going to a war zone.

But don't be fooled by the show "Narcos." Pablo Escobar—the notorious drug kingpin who presided over a reign of violence in Colombia—has been dead for 25 years. And in 2016, Colombian President Juan Manuel Santos earned the Nobel Peace Prize for efforts to end decades of civil war with leftist rebels.

Meanwhile tourism is growing, and sightseeing options are many and varied. You can visit farms in the country's coffee region or follow the footsteps of famed writer Gabriel Garcia Marquez, whose childhood home in Aracataca is a museum. Garcia Marquez's fiction was known for its magical realism, and visitors may find the phrase an apt description of the culture, scenery and colorful history found in so many parts of Colombia.

MEDELLIN

At one time Medellín was practically synonymous with Escobar. His cartel was based there and you can find tours that will take you to the place where he died in a police ambush in 1993. But don't let that define this city. Head to Botero Plaza, named for Colombia's most famous artist Fernando Botero, to see the sculptures on display. And if at all possible, time your visit for December to catch the city's massive outdoor show of 30 million Christmas lights.

CARTAGENA

Cartagena is located on the Caribbean on the northwestern coast of South America. That location made Cartagena a key port in Spain's colonial empire. Attractions include 400-year-old stone walls along the coast and the spooky tunnels and cannons of the fortress San Felipe de Barajas. In the old city, you'll find a museum of instruments of torture in the Palace of the Inquisition and a church honoring San Pedro Claver, a priest who baptized thousands of African slaves brought here in the 1600s. Street vendors and tiny shops sell broad-brimmed hats and jewelry, all in distinctive local designs.

THE AMAZON

A visit to the sleepy Amazon town of Leticia is nothing short of surreal, from the view out the plane window of a dense green jungle as far as you can see, to a nighttime ride on the river in the pitch dark, listening to a symphony of buzzing, whistling insects and birds. Silverfish leap in your boat on the river at night, and tiny green frogs cover your clothes. Daytime boat tours will take you to meet indigenous people, see pink dolphins and visit Isla de los Micos, where capuchin monkeys will climb on your head. Colombia's section of the Amazon is bordered by Peru and Brazil, and you can cross those borders without a passport here. Boats from Leticia typically stop in Peruvian river towns, and the bustling Brazilian city of Tabatinga is a short taxi ride from Leticia.

A lodging option in Leticia is the Amazon Bed and Breakfast, where exotic breakfasts included bright purple and green juices made from fruits you've never heard of. The B&B has no air conditioning, but ceiling fans and cool showers keep guests comfortable. The staff can arrange all your excursions.

You may or may not be bothered by mosquitos. On a visit in December, there were virtually none. But those who care to be prepared should bring DEET repellent and hooded mesh jackets. Consult with a doctor about getting yellow fever shots and prophylactic malaria pills (beware the side effects—vivid dreams), along with antibiotics and anti-diarrheal medicine in case of intestinal troubles. Plastic rain ponchos come in handy in the periodic Amazon downpours.

BOGOTA

Colombia's capital city of Bogota is grittier than some other parts of Colombia but offers plenty to do. In addition to the well-known Gold Museum, two other museums are worth a visit, both free. Botero is known for his rotund figures, and the Botero Museum houses many of them, including a plump "Mona Lisa."

The museum also displays other artists' work donated by Botero, from Picasso to Francis Bacon. Look for street vendors selling beautiful mochilas—patterned shoulder bags.

At the National Police Museum, tours are available from English-speaking young Colombians doing their required national service stints. The tour includes an extensive exhibit on Escobar, from artifacts like his watch and motorcycle, to details of how police ambushed him by tracking his cellphone calls.

Escobar's demise—and the positive changes that have happened since—are a legitimate source of national pride.

BUENOS AIRES:
EVITA, TANGO AND THE POPE'S HOMETOWN

By Albert Stumm

BUENOS AIRES, Argentina—During Buenos Aires' heyday, fabulous wealth flowed into the city from Argentina's agricultural heartland, turning the country into one of the world's richest by the early 20th century. The evidence of that era is still apparent in the grand architectural showpieces scattered around this sprawling city of 3 million.

But since the late 1940s, Argentina has experienced dictatorship, military rule, corruption and a succession of crippling economic crises. Artless graffiti scars nearly every building and much of the transit system, though efficient, hasn't been updated since the 1960s.

Still, it remains a marvelous destination. Meet a few Portenos, as city residents are called, and take advantage of the legendary nightlife and restaurant scene, and you'll get a buzz from the culture that invented the tango.

CLASSIC ATTRACTIONS

No trip to Buenos Aires would be complete without a swing past the blushing balconies of La Casa Rosada, or Pink House, where Eva Peron and her president husband Juan once addressed adoring crowds. The building faces Plaza de Mayo, the heart of the city that provides a good jumping off point for exploring the downtown. An organization of mothers of the 30,000 Argentines who disappeared during the dictatorship in the 1970s and '80s still gathers there, as they have every Thursday afternoon for decades.

Continuing the requisite Evita pilgrimage, head up the hill to the posh Recoleta neighborhood and its namesake cemetery, where the city's elite have been laid to rest for generations. The necropolis resembles a city in miniature more than a burial ground, with intricate gothic temples to the dead lined up like row houses along a network of stone-paved alleys. Evita's black granite gravesite is rather dull by comparison, and generally crowded, but parts of the cemetery offer plenty of opportunities for reflective solitude.

Afterward, stroll around the surrounding area, where the wealthy built palatial homes as they fled a yellow fever epidemic in the low-lying San Telmo neighborhood near the Plata River.

WHAT'S NEW

It wasn't long ago that the dining scene mostly consisted of steak, empanadas, Italian and more steak. But a flurry of restaurant openings has transformed the city into a worldly food destination. The craft beer craze arrived along with a burger invasion a few years back, but chefs have begun to draw on other cultures to spice up the mix. The Korean-Argentinian restaurant Kyopo in Flores serves a sweet and spicy kimchi burger as well as savory rice bowls. In Villa Crespo, I Latina serves seafood-focused tasting menu of Colombian fare in a renovated townhouse.

The Pope Francis story has become big business in his native city. A number of tours have popped up to show off the sites he used to frequent when he was known as Jorge Mario Bergoglio. Stops include where he grew up in Flores, his former schools and the Metropolitan Cathedral where he presided.

HANGING OUT

San Telmo, one of the city's oldest neighborhoods, today is an artsy enclave known for a Sunday afternoon market at Plaza Dorrego with hundreds of stalls selling antiques, leather goods, vintage gear and handmade accessories. The rest of the week, sidewalk cafes fan out from the plaza during the day, and late at night (some bars don't even open until midnight) a bohemian crowd mingles with tourists. One called Doppelganger serves more than 100 cocktails at its dimly lit mahogany bar.

Besides late nights, Buenos Aires is also known for its beef. Don Julio and La Cabrera in the Palermo neighborhood represent fine options at the top end of the steak-joint spectrum, particularly if you pair the meal with a bold malbec wine. In the riverside Puerto Madera area, La Cabana sources its beef from its own ranch and offers views of the spire that angles up from a pedestrian bridge by architect Santiago Calatrava, who designed the Oculus transportation hub at One World Trade in New York.

TIPS

Find a way to experience one of Argentina's signature attractions: the tango. You're bound to stumble across dancers performing for tips on the streets, and there are numerous tango shows catering to tourists, including in Cafe Tortoni downtown and El Viejo Almacen in San Telmo. But it's best to hit up a milonga, which is essentially a tango gathering. Usually lessons are offered before a milonga begins. I found one in Villa Crespo at a downmarket sports club called Villa Malcolm. A two-hour group lesson in the pink and blue room on a Monday night cost less than $5 U.S.

The vast transit system can be baffling, but rides are cheap and its six lines mostly lead downtown. It's convenient for sightseeing but less so for hopping between the outer neighborhoods. Taxis fill the gap and are incredibly cheap by U.S. standards, but traffic can be stressful. Buses, called colectivos, are also inexpensive and a particularly good option if you're trying to get somewhere along one of the wide avenues that have dedicated bus lanes.

GUATEMALA:
MAYAN CULTURE IN LAKE ATITLAN

By Kristi Eaton

PANAJACHEL, Guatemala—The boat zips across the water starting early in the morning, picking up local villagers and dropping them off at various points around the lake. A few passengers wear traditional Mayan dress in a kaleidoscope of colors, heading to the town of Panajachel in hopes of selling their handmade crafts to tourists.

This is Lake Atitlan, a tourist-friendly area located in Guatemala's Western Highlands. There are more than 20

Mayan ethnic groups in Guatemala, and the Lake Atitlan area is home to a handful of them, most notably the Tz'utujil and Kaqchikel people.

Each of the towns and villages surrounding the lake is known for something different—for example, textiles, ceramics or holistic therapies. The area is also known for Spanish language schools, with options for students to live with local families.

PANAJACHEL

Panajachel is the main town and where many visitors start their trip. Several other towns and villages surround the lake and are accessible by foot, tuk-tuk or lanchas (public boats) across the lake.

Panajachel, known as Pana, is home to several restaurants featuring local and international cuisine, coffee shops, street food vendors and more. Along the town's main street, Calle Santander, visitors can shop for textiles and artisanal pieces handmade by indigenous people from around the lake. During the day, the street is lined with vendors who set up shop, selling bags, wallets, scarves, coffee, jewelry and other items.

SAN MARCOS LA LAGUNA

Across the lake, the town of San Marcos La Laguna is known for its laid-back vibe and attracts tourists interested in spiritual and holistic therapies, including massage, yoga and meditation. Visitors can sign up for classes of varying lengths at studios and retreats run by expats throughout the town. Vegetarian, vegan and locally produced dining options also abound in San Marcos.

The entire town is walkable, though there are tuk-tuk drivers offering services as well.

San Juan La Laguna, meanwhile, is an up-and-coming town known for women's cooperatives and textiles created using natural dyes. One of the best-known cooperatives is called Lema. Started by Rosalinda Tay, indigenous women in the cooperative use dying and weaving techniques handed down from past generations. The natural dyes are made from various plants grown in the area.

Visitors to the cooperative can learn firsthand how to weave and create the natural dyes during classes or purchase a scarf, bag or other handmade item created by the women.

Just down the road, a community project in San Juan, the Utz'iil Eco-Centro, is being developed as a cultural exchange hub for the community, featuring a hostel, tea room, gardens, music stage and area for artisans. The goal of the project is to share the Mayan traditions of locals who are Tz'utujil as well as to promote environmentally sustainable practices.

Another town along the lake, San Antonio Palopo, draws visitors because of its ceramics. Cooperatives create a variety of intricate pottery pieces in different designs.

HABLA ESPANOL?

Though Spanish is often the second language for many of the indigenous people in the area, visitors can study Spanish at one of the schools in the region that offer one-on-one sessions and the option of a homestay or on-site accommodation.

I spent my mornings taking two hours of Spanish classes each day at a local school in Panajachel for four weeks. My teacher was a young indigenous woman who lived with her family in the nearby village of Santa Catarina Palopo, so I was able to practice the language with her while also learning more about the Mayan culture and way of life.

The lake area offers accommodations for any budget—from the luxurious Casa Palopo in the village of Santa Catarina Palopo that features breathtaking views of the lake and volcanoes, to hostels and funky bed-and-breakfasts in San Marcos catering to yoga and massage enthusiasts.

If You Go . . .

LAKE ATITLAN, GUATEMALA: The Lake Atitlan region is located about 70 miles (110 km) from Guatemala City, home to the nearest major airport. Visitors can rent cars or take a bus from Guatemala City to Lake Atitlan. Small public boats known as lanchas transport people to the different villages around the lake for small sums.

BUCHAREST:
GHOSTS OF COMMUNISM IN A VIBRANT CITY

By Alison Mutler

BUCHAREST, Romania—Bucharest was once known as "Little Paris of the East." But English, not French, is the preferred foreign language in Romania's capital city, and 96 percent of its inhabitants are native Romanians.

Bucharest buzzes with an energetic, round-the-clock vibe. The city also features an eclectic mix of architecture—from Oriental Byzantine to French neoclassical to communist-era apartment buildings—reflecting cultural influences across decades and even centuries.

WINGS AND THE PALACE OF SPRING

The Palace of Spring was the family home to communist dictator Nicolae Ceausescu until 1989, when he was ousted from power and executed. Richard Nixon, the late U.S. president, once dined there. The glitzy decor includes a bathroom decked out in gold, mosaics in the swimming pool and a movie theater where the walls are upholstered with plump gold cushions.A pair of peacocks roams the garden. Ceausescu's pants, his wife Elena's shoes and an old black-and-white TV are all on display.

The "Wings" monument, dedicated to the hundreds of thousands of victims of communism, is located in front of Bucharest's House of the Free Press, a Soviet-inspired building where a statue of Lenin once stood. It is 30 meters (98 feet) high, an intricate web of concrete wings. Though it's clunky rather than graceful, it is a massive concrete reminder of the political detainees who were held in communist prisons or deported and persecuted.

MUST-SEES

Ceausescu's giant palace in the south of the capital, the world's second-largest administrative building after the Pentagon, is a must-see. It houses the Parliament and important conferences are held there. In December, shepherds angry with government policy almost managed to storm the building. It's a 3-kilometer (1.9 mile) walk around the building. A large Orthodox cathedral, the Salvation of the People, is being built on its grounds, a cause for some controversy.

Other essentials include Revolution Square, the National Art Museum (housed in an old royal palace), the 19th-century Athenaeum concert hall, and the old Communist Party headquarters. Ceausescu and his wife Elena fled from the roof of that building in a helicopter in December 1989 to get away from the booing crowd. It was their last public appearance.

THEATER, SHOPPING AND HANGING OUT

Romanians love the arts, particularly theater. The National Theater and National Opera buildings have been refurbished in recent years.

Shopping is a favorite pastime, and many shops are open until 10 p.m., with some 24/7 convenience stores too.

Centrul Vechi or Old City is very popular, a maze of bars, clubs, restaurants, shops and the 16th century Old Princely Court Church, clustered on a few streets close to the imposing National Bank of Romania.

For those in search of peace and quiet, Bucharest's fabled parks have a lot to offer. There is the elegant 19th century Cismigiu Gardens, where you can watch locals play chess and backgammon or take a stroll.

Farther north, there is the fashionable and sprawling Herestrau park next to the ethnographic Village Museum, featuring different styles of rural houses. You won't be able to visit the royal Elizabeth Palace next door, but the small Botanical Gardens in Cotroceni district are worth a visit, or if you want to get to know the "real" Bucharest, head south to the splendid IOR park, by getting off at Titan subway station or taking the 330 or 335 bus.

TIPS

Take a Bucharest City Tour Sightseeing bus. With 14 stops on the route, you can hop on and off as often as you want within 24 hours. For the more energetic, there are bicycle rentals and bike lanes on some boulevards. There are hardly any hills (Bucharest is a mere 70 meters or 230 feet above sea level) but drivers can be aggressive. Otherwise, ubiquitous yellow Dacia taxis are cheap and zippy. A subway ride is a surefire way to avoid heavy traffic.

Exchange bureaus are generally reliable and don't charge commission.

HAMBURG:
CHOCOLATE, COFFEE AND TRADE

By Frank Jordans

HAMBURG, Germany—For centuries, the port city of Hamburg was a powerhouse in maritime trade. These days, Germany's second-largest city is still the country's main entry point for exotic goods. But it's also a magnet for foodies, fans of the arts and folks who prefer to wander rather than powerwalk their way around a new destination.

Attractions include a chocolate museum, a historic warehouse district and river boat rides. Just remember in Hamburg you're never far from the water—including the kind that falls from the sky, so go with the flow and bring an umbrella.

FEAST YOUR EYES, TICKLE YOUR TASTEBUDS
Maybe you want to start small. Really small. In Hamburg's old warehouse district an indoor model railway called the Miniatur Wunderland stretches across two floors and takes visitors on a humorous journey around the world. Book tickets in advance.

The warehouse district, or Speicherstadt, was once a free port and its distinctive red brick buildings on timber foundations helped the area gain UNESCO World Heritage status in 2015. It's hardly a museum though. The warehouses are still used to store goods from around the globe and with a little patience visitors can watch Persian carpets and sacks of spices being loaded and unloaded using old-fashioned pulley hoist systems.

Hamburg has a long tradition of appreciating coffee. Enjoy a good brew at one of several coffee roasters around town, including Nord Coast Coffee Roastery. At Hamburg's chocolate museum, Chocoversum, learn about the origins of chocolate, what makes a good bean and even try your hand at creating a unique bar of your own.

A DAY ON THE WATER
Start exploring mankind's complicated relationship with the sea on dry land at the International Maritime Museum in the warehouse district. It features replicas of ancient ships, including a Phoenician galley and a Viking dragon boat, as well as equipment that helped sailors navigate the seas before GPS and satellite phones.

Then walk or take a subway to the Landungsbruecken. During the week these piers are used by commuters traveling into Hamburg on public boats. For a modest fare, hop on the No. 62 for a ride down the river Elbe, passing some of Hamburg's impressive maritime industry and not a few towering cargo ships along the way.

Step off at Neumuehlen and head downriver past the charming old sailboats to the Oevelgoenne beach for pizza and a hoppy beer, or coffee and cake, at a riverside cafe or bar.

A NIGHT ON THE TOWN

The Reeperbahn is Hamburg's notorious red light district. At night it transforms from a quiet street into a gaudy, neon-light affair filled with bars, live music venues and seedy entertainment. Near the Reeperbahn light rail stop is a square dedicated to the Beatles, who spent their journeyman years in Hamburg.

For a less touristy and more family friendly evening head to the Schanzenviertel, a former working-class district that's become hip. There's cheap food aplenty and a thriving bar culture. Sternschanze is the closest S-bahn stop.

From there, walk to one of Hamburg's best-known clubs at Feldstrasse 66. Don't worry, you can't miss it. Known to the Nazis as Flakturm IV, this massive over-ground bunker was too difficult to destroy after World War II and so it was left standing. Nowadays it's home to media companies and the club Uebel und Gefaehrlich —which roughly translates as Nasty and Dangerous.

If you're out all night, greet the day at Hamburg's legendary Altona fish market. Business starts at 5 a.m. April to October (7 a.m. in winter). Stalls shutter around 9:30 a.m.

GRAND BURGERS AND HIGH CULTURE

For centuries Hamburg was dominated by a tight-knit ruling class known as the First Families, whose members had acquired a superior form of citizenship that made them Grossbuerger (grand burgher). With the title came lucrative economic and political rights that they used to amass great fortunes and shape the city in ways that can still be seen in Hamburg's center with its Venice-like arcades and bridges, fancy shopping streets and lakeside promenade. From the underground stop Rathaus, take a stroll past the imposing town hall toward the Binnenalster, or Inner Alster, a reservoir inside the old city perimeters.

For a bit of high art, head to the underground stop Jungfernstieg and take the U1 two stops to Steinstrasse. From there it's a short walk to one of Europe's largest contemporary arts centers. The Deichtorhallen, situated in two former market halls built in late art nouveau style, hosts art and photography exhibitions.

For a grand finale, end your trip at the Elbphilharmonie concert hall. If you can't nab tickets it's worth visiting for the architecture, which features a wave-shaped roof, stunning glass facades and a panoramic view of the harbor.

PALERMO:
THE ITALY OF YOUR IMAGINATION

By Cain Burdeau

PALERMO, Sicily—For many travelers, Italy is seen as romantic, mysterious and a bit chaotic, with torpid heat, gorgeously rich colors and irresistible food.

In reality, of course, every region has a distinct culture and identity. But Palermo, the ancient capital of Sicily and jewel of the Mediterranean, lives up to the Italy of popular imagination. It's joyful and colorful, rich in art and cuisine, but also disorganized, unable even to reliably collect the garbage.

Life is busily lived on the streets here. Clothes hang haphazardly from balconies. Motor scooters zip down narrow alleyways (often driven by children going the wrong way). People shout in Sicilian—a dialect incomprehensible to many Italian speakers—back and forth across streets and from windows. They gesture, sing and openly observe others.

All this plays out in a city steeped in religious rituals, intricate history, stunning art and stunning decay. It's a place living amid the past—a past lost in so much of today's modernizing Italy.

It's also a culture that can seem oddly familiar to outsiders, likely due to the waves of Sicilians who emigrated to the U.S. and made their mark on everyday American life in everything from food to pop culture. Part of "The Godfather" was filmed here and the Mafia remains a force despite government crackdowns and the public's outrage and resistance in the wake of bombings that killed two anti-Mafia magistrates and others with them in 1992.

PALERMO'S MOSAIC

Before being bombed by Americans in World War II and ransacked by the Mafia after the war, Palermo was for centuries one of Europe's most splendid cities, rich with churches, palaces, theaters, villas. Much of that illustrious past remains, albeit faded, but so does deep poverty.

There are medieval Arab-Norman palaces (La Zisa, La Cuba, the Norman Palace), fantastic churches (the main cathedral with tombs of Norman royalty and the Cathedral of Monreale with extraordinary mosaics), art-filled Spanish palaces, the grand Teatro Massimo opera house, and much more.

What makes the city unique is the mixture of cultures across centuries: a tapestry of Phoenician, Greek, Roman, Arab, Norman,

Jewish, French, English, Spanish and Italian influences.

"You need an encyclopedia to describe the Palermitan," says Pietro Tramonte, a retired accountant who runs an eccentric outdoor bookstore. "Here you find a laboratory, just like when life began. It's an impossible mosaic. But we're forced to live together."

Just then, a man in a car hails Tramonte from the end of the alleyway. He's dropping off a strange donation: hardbound books about fascism by the Italian dictator Benito Mussolini.

"Palermo is the fountain of serendipity," Tramonte continues. "When a foreigner comes to Palermo, he should let himself go. Let yourself be a feather in the wind and you can find that that wind can take you to beautiful places."

THE MARKETS

Outdoor markets are some of the best places to revel in Palermo.

Vendors shout out prices. Butchers slice, pound, weigh meat. Fishmongers' stands display decapitated swordfish. Things sizzle in pots and pans of kiosks: chickpea fritters (panelle), potato and egg rolls (crocche), stuffed rice balls (arancine).

Your head spins at the movement, the flashes of life: A fellow brushes by with a pushcart full of sardines for sale; another tries to catch your attention to buy a bouquet of flowers. You admire displays of oranges, lemons, apples, strawberries, lettuce heads, broccoli and tomatoes as mouth-watering works of art.

You're in a stream of people, moving, buying, looking, talking, bumping into each other with bags full of food. A scooter blows its horn and plows through.

Your senses are assaulted by mounds of olives and dried tomatoes, bunches of rosemary and bay leaves, cheeses.

"We were born here and we will die here," says Francesco Andolina, a fruit and vegetable vendor whose family has been getting up before dawn and working until dusk in the Ballaro market for generations.

But Palermo's most famous market, the Vucciria, is a shadow of its former self. Merchants now offer antiques and souvenirs to tourists. The streets are no longer slick with vegetable and fruit remains. "All the people want to go to the supermarkets with their carts," Andolina says and mockingly pretends to push a cart.

CAPITAL OF CULTURE

Palermo recently restricted most cars from the city center. "Now you can hear your own footsteps, you can hear your voice. That was taken away when there were cars," says Sara Cappello, a folk singer and storyteller.

Palermo was designated Italy's Capital of Culture for 2018. "We deserve to be the cultural capital because we are a wonderful city," Cappello says.

She then thinks of the city's continuing problems: Trash piling up, corruption, unregulated development, poverty.

"We mistreated our city so badly," she says. "But maybe this too is the fascination of Palermo."

FLORENCE:
GALLERIES TO GELATO

By Michelle Locke

FLORENCE, Italy—The skies were clouding over as I strode briskly across that famous bridge, the Ponte Vecchio, ready for a productive day checking off Florentine must-sees.

Slight problem: The first museum on my list was open, but the ticket office was closed.

OK, then, on to the Uffizi Gallery. Except this time both ticket office and museum were closed; I had forgotten it was Monday.

A fine rain began to fall as I wandered listlessly past the open arches of the building next door, the statue-studded Loggia dei Lanzi. This wasn't going at all as planned.

And then it hit me. Wait. This was the Piazza della Signoria, where novelist E.M. Forster's adorable Lucy Honeychurch witnessed a stabbing moments after complaining about the dullness of life in "A Room With a View." And those had to be THE steps where the brooding George Emerson carried Lucy's fainting form.

Sunshine filtered through. I had found Florence. Or rather, it had found me.

If you're planning a trip here, you could do worse than wander until you find what you didn't know you were looking for. Here are a few starting points.

CLASSIC ATTRACTIONS AND MORE

If there is one must-see in Florence it's Michelangelo's David. Yes, there are lines, crowds and a forest of smartphones waving in front of you, but all that falls away as you round the corner to the long gallery and confront this masterpiece of cool, concentrated, confident youth.

The Uffizi Gallery, set in an imposing 16th-century building, is home to outstanding art, including Giotto's altarpiece, the Ognissanti Madonna, which revolutionized painting by portraying the human figure in perspective, not just two dimensions.

You can't miss the Duomo, the Gothic cathedral encrusted in pink, green and white marble that is a striking feature of the city.

The Ponte Vecchio isn't the most beautiful bridge in the world, but it is interesting, with its lineup of stores, mostly jewelers and souvenir sellers.

Around sunset, head to the Piazzale Michelangelo, on a hill on the south side of the Arno, for terrific views of the city. You can get here by taxi, the No. 12 bus or by walking about 20 minutes from the Uffizi Gallery.

The Opera Duomo Museum, devoted to art created for the famous Florence duomo (cathedral), has been given a major makeover and expansion. A highlight is the exhibition hall featuring a replica of the former facade of the cathedral.

The Central Market (Piazza del Mercato Centrale on Via dell'Ariento) has a bright and bustling remodeled second floor, home to food stands, a restaurant, pizzeria, wine academy, cooking school and more.

CHIANTI COUNTRY

If you have a car or can hire a driver, head for the hills. You're in the middle of Chianti wine country with several estates to visit, including Poggio Casciano, a 14th-century villa that is part of the Ruffino wine company and about a 30-minute drive from the city. The estate produces Modus, a "super Tuscan" red blend of sangiovese, merlot and cabernet sauvignon. By appointment only; reserve tastings and tours, http://www.ruffino.com.

TIPS

If you're planning on visiting museums, consider buying tickets online; book entrance times to skip long lines.

More into shopping than sculpture? Check out the Santa Maria Novella, an apothecary at Via della Scala 16 that traces its history back 600 years. Don't miss the displays of antique remedies such as anti-hysteria pills as well as the beautifully packaged perfumes and other products available for modern consumers.

For a touch of local night life, the Piazza Santo Spirito on the south side of the Arno is lined with cafes and bars.

A hot spot for gelato is La Carraia, Piazza Nazario Sauro 25R. Work up a literary appetite and order something in honor of Miss Honeychurch, who "loved iced coffee and meringues." Enjoy your treats on the nearby Ponte alla Carraia where you'll have more room, and, naturally, a view.

LISBON:
FADO, SARDINES AND THE
AGE OF EXPLORATION

By Beth J. Harpaz

LISBON, Portugal—Have you ever heard a song so tender and soulful it brought you to tears, even though you couldn't understand a word?

That's how I feel about fado, a Portuguese folk music tradition that blends the drama and rhythm of flamenco with the sentimentality of a torch song. You don't need to speak Portuguese to appreciate these melancholy ballads. They are songs of love, loss and longing, rooted in Portugal's seafaring culture, which for centuries has bid farewell to sailors, not knowing when or whether they'd return.

On a quick visit to Lisbon—with my return guaranteed, unlike those early explorers—I managed in four nights to visit four fado clubs. By day, I toured Lisbon's Museu do Fado (fado museum), as well as the home of the late, great fado singer Amalia Rodrigues. I also visited many sites honoring Portugal's great explorers, who beginning in the 15th century established a colonial empire that spanned the globe.

FADO

My first fado club was Sr. Vinho. I feasted on seafood and vinho verde, Portugal's delicious white wine, then sat spellbound as three women draped in shawls performed in the darkened room, one after another, accompanied by a 12-string guitar.

The next evening, at Clube de Fado, I knew something special was unfolding when a well-dressed entourage of 10 swept in, with much hand-kissing and photo-taking. All the Portuguese-speaking waiter could say by way of explanation was "Famoso!" Gradually I learned the entourage included a legendary Brazilian singer, Fafa de Belem, along with Cuca Roseta, a popular singer who's part of fado's new generation.

Three house singers had already performed, but Fafa and Cuca gave impromptu concerts. The crowd went wild. It was the Lisbon equivalent of Tina Turner and Alicia Keys appearing unannounced at a New York blues club.

A third club, Casa de Fados, offered outstanding food and service but the show was comparatively staid. Then at midnight

Saturday, I hit the jam-packed bar scene at Tasca do Chico in the lively Bairro Alto neighborhood. Anyone can get up and sing there, and it was fun to hear heartfelt amateurs.

LIVE LIKE A LOCAL

Breakfast was simple and delicious: coffee and custard tarts called pasteis de belem, served at tiny cafe counters. Many of those shops also sell shots of ginjinha, a potent cherry liqueur. (The airport duty-free store sells small ginjinha bottles, a perfect souvenir.)

Grilled sardines are a summertime specialty but sardine pate is often part of a meal's couvert, a small plate that might include olives, bread, cheese or sausage. You'll also see stores selling nothing but rows of colorfully wrapped canned sardines.

Another yummy local dish is grilled chicken. And make time for the TimeOut Market, a modern food court in a historic market where dozens of vendors serve thin-sliced cured ham, Asian food, gelato and more.

Hang with the hipsters at Lx Factory, an old industrial complex now filled with antiques shops, home design stores and boutiques like Rutz, where everything is made from cork, from sneakers to pocketbooks. The Lx Factory's Rio Maravilha has a rooftop bar with expansive views of the Tagus River, the 25th of April Bridge and the statue of Christ that overlooks the city.

LIVE LIKE A KING

Portugal is one of Europe's most affordable destinations. Luxury lodging is priced like three- and four-star hotels in other capital cities. Metered taxis were so cheap—a few euros per trip—that I never bothered with city buses or subways. Elaborate, multi-course fado club meals, with the show, averaged 50 to 60 euros ($55 to $65) a person, but ordinary restaurants were much cheaper. At these prices, a middle-class American can live like a Portuguese king.

You'll get a sense of how real kings lived at the magnificent Palace of Sintra, 16 miles (26 km) from Lisbon, one of several places I visited on a Gray Line tour. My favorite spot amid the palace's tiled rooms and treasures was a ceiling decorated with 136 magpies, symbolizing a king's flirtation with one of the queen's 136 ladies-in-waiting.

Another bus from Lisbon took me to Fatima, where three shepherd children saw miraculous visions of the Virgin Mary in 1916. Pilgrims approach the sanctuary in the town on their knees. Even the non-religious visitor will be awed by these displays of faith.

Back in Lisbon, the National Coach Museum displays gilded, velvet-lined coaches used by royalty, some dating to the 1600s.

I also wandered the narrow streets of the medieval Alfama District; marveled at tiles covering walls, buildings and even sidewalks, and took selfies at the Belem Tower, a stunning 16th-century fort on the banks of the Tagus River. Another landmark on the Tagus is the Monument to the Discoveries, a stone ship erected in the 20th century to memorialize the Age of Exploration.

At Jeronimos Monastery, amid the vaulted ceilings and intricate carvings, lies the tomb of explorer Vasco da Gama, whose revolutionary ocean expedition reached India in 1498. I'd traveled a long way from the U.S. for a mere five-day visit, but it was nothing compared to that.

PORT WINE AND SUNSETS
IN PORTO, PORTUGAL

By Albert Stumm

PORTO, Portugal—I was lost, looking for port wine caves dug into hills across the bridge from Porto. I trudged up a hill and rounded a blind corner, sidling against a stone wall to avoid tour buses flying toward me, when I stumbled on the highlight of my day: a nearly empty tasting room and private wine-cellar tour.

It was a reminder that in Portugal's second city, everything cool seems to be right around the corner, or more likely, just up a hill.

THE SUNSETS

Porto's historic core is set upon two hills, with the rejuvenated downtown between them spilling down to the Douro River. A pedestrian promenade lined with medieval merchant houses and cafe tables runs underneath the two-level Luis I Bridge, which joins the upper and lower sections of Porto and the city of Gaia. On one side is the twin-domed Porto Cathedral, on the other is the circular Monastery of Serra do Pilar. When the sun sets, the colors of the white monuments, stone towers and terra cotta roofs blend together, and the entire city glows orange. It's one of the world's most spectacular cityscapes.

Porto is small enough to walk past the highlights in half a day, but I spent nearly a week hoofing it around, taking in one stunning sunset after the next. Lookout points are labeled on tourist maps as miradouros. Each is unique, though none is a match for Praia da Luz, or beach of light. A historic trolley runs from the center to where the river flows into the ocean in the Foz do Douro neighborhood. A short walk north through a seaside park brings you to the rocky beach, where I nursed a glass of vinho verde, Portugal's light, dry white wine, on a plush lounge chair. The sun dipped into the Atlantic where medieval maps once depicted fire-breathing sea serpents.

CRAFTS AND BOOKS

Fortunately, there's more to Porto than postcard-worthy pictures, with more to come. The thwack of hammers echoing off the tiled facades on nearly every street heralds a tourist boom. Already, the downtown around Avenida dos Aliados, which was seedy as recently as a few years ago, has new life.

Concept stores run by collectives of crafters have opened

along Rua do Almada. Workshop Popup combines four stores into one for cork handbags, locally designed clothes and handmade souvenirs actually worth buying. It also offers private cooking lessons for a bargain at a show kitchen in the back. For night-life, the string of bars and restaurants around Rua da Galeria de Paris has a range of choices, from sophisticated to rowdy. The bars get busy almost every night of the week but often not until 11 p.m. or later.

One of Porto's best-known sites is Livraria Lello, a bookshop in a grand neo-Gothic 1906 building on Rua das Carmelitas that features a massive curved staircase, elaborate painted plaster ceiling and a stained-glass skylight bearing the Latin phrase "Decos in Labore" (dignity in work). There's a fee to enter, but the fee entitles you to a discount on purchases.

PORT WINE

I waited until the end of my trip to dive into port wines, those supple, fortified dessert wines the city is known for. After dinner at a friend's apartment, my hosts, an architect and an owner of a design studio, pulled out a white port made by Taylor that's typically served chilled as an aperitif. They recommended visit-ing Taylor's tasting room, one of the biggest, and Croft, the old-est. They also urged me to stay away from the expensive, flashy options along the riverfront.

It was while searching for Croft the next day that I stumbled on Churchill's, which isn't listed on most maps of the port cir-cuit. Their wine was rich and full, and slightly less sweet than others. A guide led me through the "cave," a warehouse dug into the granite hill with a steady temperature in the 60s F (15-21 C). Hundreds of oak barrels were stacked four high, aging port for up to 40 years. Turns out the British commercialized a product the Portuguese had been making for centuries, which explains the Anglophile names.

At Croft, founded in 1588, the charming tasting room with tables and stools made from wine barrels led into an impressive cellar with stone arches and casks the size of small houses. Taylor was the most commercial of the three, but the 10-euro entry fee includes a three-wine sample and self-guided audio tour, so it's a good choice for a novice with time for only one stop.

Sufficiently buzzed, I asked a clerk to recommend somewhere for a quick bite before rushing off to the airport. The five-star Yeatman Hotel hit the mark with a cheese plate, a glass of dry Douro Valley red and an expansive patio overlooking the city. It was just around the corner, and just in time for sunset.

If You Go . . .
PORTO, PORTUGAL: http://www.visitporto.travel . Located three hours by train from Lisbon. Stay near the Clerigos Tower in the Vitoria neighborhood, the center of nightlife and only a 15-minute walk from the higher-priced tourist spots near the river. Also, try francesinha, a Porto specialty that's like a meatier croque monsieur. Cafe Santiago near the Coliseu music venue serves up a gut-buster drenched in a tangy beer sauce, and locals like the francesinha at Cufra on Avenida da Boavista.

GIBRALTAR: MONKEYS, NEANDERTHALS AND THAT FAMOUS ROCK

By Brian Witte

GIBRALTAR—Barbary macaque monkeys are the star attractions in Gibraltar. Still, this historic port town is steeped in military history around the landmark Rock of Gibraltar. The town wears its scars well with plenty to offer visitors.

The British territory next to Spain has a striking and unique landscape with sweeping views of Europe and Africa. Its long military history stems from being a strategic point between the Atlantic and the Mediterranean. The ancient Greeks referred to the Rock as one of the two "Pillars of Hercules."

Britain acquired Gibraltar from Spain in 1704 during the War of Spanish Succession. Spain has persistently sought its return ever since.

BARBARY MACAQUES

Europe's only free-ranging monkeys are sure to enliven an afternoon enjoying the views from its famous Rock. While some monkeys regard tourists calmly, others can be astute opportunists, eager to pounce and snatch items out of hands and bags. They were known as Barbary apes, but they are actually tailless monkeys. They are now found on Gibraltar and in Morocco and parts of Algeria, a region once known as the Barbary Coast.

Visitors can find them by taking a cable car up to the Rock, which includes a stop at the Apes' Den. They have lived in Gibraltar since the British first captured the Rock in 1704 and have remained through many sieges. Folklore says the British will leave the Rock only when the monkeys do. During World War II, Winston Churchill ordered that their numbers not drop below 24. Warning: They have long canine teeth and can bite if disturbed.

James Bond fans may recall that "The Living Daylights" takes place in Gibraltar, and one of the monkeys startles Bond (Timothy Dalton) as he makes his way along the rock.

THE TUNNELS

Gibraltar features a labyrinth of tunnels more than 32 miles long (51 km) that were built for military purposes. Some were dug by hand and gunpowder blasts during The Great Siege between 1779 and 1783, when France and Spain tried to recapture the Rock from the British during the American Revolutionary War. They were built to get guns to cover a vulnerable spot off the northern face of the Rock of Gibraltar. Visitors can walk in the tunnels, which have cannons pointing out of openings in the rock. During World War II, the British added on to the Great Siege Tunnels out of concern Gibraltar would be attacked. These tunnels were built between 1939 and 1944 by the Royal Engineers. Tours are available.

THE MOORS

The Moors occupied Gibraltar between 711 and 1309 and between 1350 and 1462. The Tower of Homage remains from an original castle complex that once stretched to the sea. The structure's outside walls bear the scars of conflicts during the many sieges on the peninsula. The Gibraltar Museum, which provides a historical overview of the town, includes well-preserved Moorish baths in the museum basement. The baths were built in the 14th century.

NEANDERTHALS

Gibraltar is home to a unique UNESCO World Heritage site called the Gorhams' Cave Complex where humankind's prehistoric relatives, the Neanderthals, lived for 120,000 years. Access to the upper part of the site is open to walkers along the Mediterranean Steps path, though it is a challenging walk. There is also a viewing platform with information panels and guides. Limited guided tours to the sea caves are also offered July-October though they fill up fast; details at http://www.gibmuseum.gi/world-heritage/gorhams-cave-complex

ST. MICHAEL'S CAVE

Gibraltar is home to a network of limestone caves in the town's Upper Rock Nature Reserve. It's used for concerts and plays.

ROCK HISTORY

Beatle John Lennon married Yoko Ono at The Rock Hotel in Gibraltar in 1969. The line from "The Ballad of John and Yoko" goes, "You can get married in Gibraltar near Spain."

If You Go...

GETTING THERE AND GETTING AROUND: Cruise ships often make port calls in Gibraltar. You can also fly directly to Gibraltar from various British airports, or walk or drive across the border from Spain. Malaga, Spain, is about 85 miles (140 km) away. Most visitors get their sightseeing done on foot but there are taxis.

WATER, FIRE AND STONE:
MENORCA

By Albert Stumm

MENORCA, Spain—Locals say Menorca can be reduced to three words: water, fire and stone.

The Spanish island's three essential elements are embodied in Cova d'en Xoroi, a natural cave that houses a sophisticated lounge halfway down a cliff. As the sun dips into the Mediterranean, waves crash on the rocks below and selfie-snapping patrons burn the same roasted-orange color as the sun-bleached limestone. Then the staff lights torches under the craggy roof, and the stunning yet laid-back venue transitions into a lively night club.

Although the scene may sound as summery as a frozen mojito, it's repeated nightly well into autumn, when Menorca remains as beguiling as it is in peak season. Through much of October, it's still warm enough to enjoy the spectacular beaches, but visitors will find the island has plenty to offer besides sun and transparent blue waters.

Here's a quick look at Menorca and its vibrant cities, Mahon and Ciutadella.

NATURE VS. NURTURE

Menorca is the farthest east of the Balearics, an archipelago between Spain and Italy that includes the better-known islands of Mallorca and jet-set Ibiza. All three enjoy an enviably mild climate in a picture-postcard setting, but Menorca's comes without the crowds or the 50-euro club cover charges. It has managed to hold on to an understated, calmer style by restricting development to a few existing, mostly low-rise resorts.

The entire 270 square mile (700 square km) island was declared a UNESCO biosphere reserve in 1993, and as a result, most of the 125 beaches that encircle Menorca's jagged coastline have very little, if any, development.

Along the south coast, walking paths that start at inland parking lots wind through forested ravines to the beaches. Cala Mitjana's powdery white sand is surrounded by cliffs, and the calm, shallow water makes it easy to explore a cave and the rocky crags with snorkeling gear. In the north, Cala Cavalleria is a little easier to get to but no less unspoiled.

The water may feel warm into autumn, but visiting after the peak summer months also means paying half-price for activities like hiring a boat with a private captain. Just plan ahead and check the weather for wind as well as temperatures.

CULTURAL LEGACIES

The ancient Phoenicians called it "Nura," or the Island of Fire. Legend has it that passing sailors saw bonfires built along the southern cliffs, which the original inhabitants used to signal each other. Signs of those first settlers—Iberian tribes that came from the mainland in the Bronze Age—are still apparent in more than 2,000 stone monuments spread throughout the island.

The Talaiotic society left stone temples, burial chambers and monuments that resemble smaller versions of Stonehenge. Some of the larger clusters require tickets and have English guides in high season, but there are so many monuments that most aren't even marked. You might stumble upon them while hiking along a walking path, hidden in tall grass. Taken together, they comprise one of Europe's largest open-air museums.

The following millennia brought ever more visitors and invaders, including the Greeks, Moors, French and Catalans, but no outside culture has left a more lasting stamp than the British. They ruled the island intermittently during the 18th century and moved the capital to Mahon from Ciutadella, which had been founded before the Romans arrived but was destroyed in the 16th century by the Turks.

The English legacy shines through in the sash windows of Mahon's architecture and in the active gin trade. The Xoriguer gin distillery is a cool spot for a pre-dinner tasting in Mahon, and I saw beach-friendly bottles of frozen gin and homemade lemonade frequently for sale, including at an ice cream shop in Cituadella.

FARM TO TABLE

Though beaches get all the limelight, much of Menorca's economy is agricultural, evidenced by the fact that there are more cows than people. Small farms, separated into miniature parcels by dry stone walls, cover the rugged hills of the interior, producing a shocking variety of produce (40 types of apples, for instance), olive oil, wine and the delicious Mahon cheese.

The cheese even made it into my ice cream cone at Ambrosia in the capital—not cheesecake, but chunks of sharp, near-cheddar cheese mixed with vanilla ice cream. Somehow, it worked.

Menorca's ecological sensibility resonates at spectacular restaurants in the atmospheric cities, which overlook natural harbors surrounded by battle-ready fortifications. In Ciutadella, check out Es Tast de na Silvia, the only Slow Food-certified restaurant in the Balearics. They serve updated takes on local dishes like fideua, a sort of seafood paella with noodles. Over the dining room, an arched stone ceiling is stamped with the year 1704.

If You Go . . .
MENORCA: Through the winter, several airlines offer direct flights to Mahon from the Spanish mainland and several European capitals. In nice weather, overnight ferries from Barcelona are the insider's way to go. Spanish and a dialect of Catalan called Menorquin are the local languages, but many people, especially in the tourism industry, speak some English.

EDINBURGH: THE PALACE, THE CASTLE AND THE STATUE'S TOE

By Michelle Locke

EDINBURGH, Scotland—Rain is pelting the black bulk of Edinburgh Castle brooding over the city. But inside Fingers Piano Bar on Frederick Street, it's warm and dry as I dance with a throng of cheerful Scots waving their arms and casually slapping strangers on the back as the piano man valiantly covers "Sweet Caroline."

Which is when it occurs to me that this city's reputation

as a bastion of gentility might not be 100 percent on point—certainly not at Fingers, which is known for a boisterous vibe.

In truth, Edinburgh has many faces. You might start your day researching the city's (sometimes bloody) past, move on to a wind-swept hike of green hills and finish up with a plunge into the lively dining and bar-hopping scene.

THE PALACE AND THE CASTLE

The Palace of Holyroodhouse, aka Holyrood Palace, is worth a visit for its stylishly decorated rooms as well as the chambers of the doomed Mary Queen of Scots. This was the site of the brutal murder of the queen's Italian secretary David Rizzio on the orders of her second husband, Lord Darnley. (Note the chambers are reachable by spiral staircase only.) Check before you go to make sure the palace isn't closed due to royal visits.

Edinburgh Castle is a must-see, although it's up to you whether you spend hours poking into its nooks and crannies or just have a quick stroll and a nice cup of tea. This is actually a collection of buildings including former military prisons and tiny St. Margaret's Chapel, built in the 12th century and the oldest building on site. Don't miss the Stone of Destiny, displayed alongside the Crown Jewels in the Royal Palace, which has a long history in British coronations. Afternoon tea can be had at the Queen Anne Tearoom, a nice diversion, especially if it's pouring, which is always a possibility.

For a less aristocratic window on the past, visit The Real Mary King's Close, set on the Royal Mile that stretches between Edinburgh Castle and Holyrood Palace. This is a warren of steep alleys that once teemed with life but were abandoned when construction at the top of the hill sealed off the area, turning it into an underground relic. Costumed guides lead you through the partially furnished houses which include interactive portraits that help paint a picture of what life was like in these once-crowded streets. Bonus: You will come away with a new appreciation for modern plumbing.

HILL AND GARDEN

At the opposite end of the Royal Mile is Holyrood Park, home to Arthur's Seat, a hill popular with hikers. There are various paths to the top, most relatively easy although it's a bit of a scramble at the end.

The Royal Botanic Garden covers about 70 acres and is about one mile from the city center. Highlights include a memorial garden to the late Queen Mother.

If jetlag has you up at sunrise and you're somewhere near the Royal Mile, consider walking up Calton Hill. You'll get outstanding views of the city that are all the better when gilded by the rising sun. The hill is home to the National Monument, which looks like an unfinished Parthenon and, in fact, is. The plan was to construct a massively ambitious war memorial to Scottish soldiers and sailors killed in the Napoleonic wars, but money ran out and the project stalled at a base and 12 columns.

GETTING AROUND

Edinburgh is very walkable, but be prepared for lots of hills and steps and a changeable climate. A good place to catch your breath is Princes Street Gardens in front of the castle. Dining options range from standard pub grub - try the haggis, you know you want it—to innovative takes on Scottish classics. Recommended: The Bon Vivant, 55 Thistle St. The menu changes seasonally, but local oysters are worth a try if available. Also good for a drink and a bite is The Devil's Advocate, 9 Advocate's Close.

THE STATUE'S TOE

Part of the fun of Edinburgh is its many traditions. Note the shiny big toe of David Hume's statue on the Royal Mile in front of the High Court Building. Philosophy students used to rub the toe for good luck in exams; now everyone does it, which might not sit too well with Hume, who abhorred superstition.

Another, slightly less charming, good luck custom is to spit on the Heart of Midlothian, a heart-shaped mosaic in the sidewalk near St. Giles' Church on the Royal Mile. It marks the spot where executions were once conducted. Make of that what you will.

CANADIAN ROCKIES:
RUGGED HIKES TO UPSCALE RESORTS

By Adam Kealoha Causey

CANMORE, Alberta—Canada's stretch of the Rocky Mountains is an outdoor paradise with something for everyone: upscale resorts surrounded by jagged mountains, isolated hikes offering an escape from urban life and crystal-blue water that dares you to feel the chill.

The mountains straddle the border of British Columbia and

Alberta, with two of its best-known destinations, Banff National Park and Lake Louise, in Alberta.

My family and I flew into Calgary, rented cars and spent a week exploring the wonders around Banff, setting up base camp in Canmore, about 60 miles (97 km) west of Calgary. Our accommodations were at the midway point between luxury and roughing it. Cabins at Banff Gate Mountain Resort have a full kitchen and electricity, but no air conditioning. That worked fine on summer nights when temperatures dipped into the 50s F (10-15 C). Late afternoon sun beating in got the cabins toasty. That's not a problem, though, in a place where there's plenty to do besides sit indoors.

JOIN THE THRONGS AT LAKE LOUISE

Banff is the most popular of the area's cluster of national parks—which also includes Jasper, Yoho and Kootenay—and Banff's crown jewel is the glacial-fed Lake Louise. The lake is exquisite, as evidenced by selfies snapped along its shoreline walking paths, capturing smiling families with snow-covered mountains in the background. If being on the water is your preferred way to experience the lake, canoe rentals are available through Fairmont Chateau Lake Louise, a decidedly more chic hotel than where we stayed.

If crowds aren't your thing, plan to get to Lake Louise as early as possible. We didn't venture that way until noon, and parking lots were packed.

HEAR THE ROAR OF TAKAKKAW FALLS

For a more rugged experience, we left the masses of Banff behind, bound for Takakkaw Falls in Yoho. Heading west into British Columbia (and the Pacific time zone) you pick up an hour, so that may have helped us beat the crowd a bit, too.

Even before we got out of the parking lot, about a half-mile (0.8 km) from the falls, we could hear their mighty roar. Tumbling from 1,246 feet (380 meters),its mist gave the 60-degree F (15.5 C) air a chill.

A refreshing start to the day preceded what eventually became a 12-mile (19 km) round-trip hike. From Takakkaw we took the Iceline Trail, which included views of the Yoho and Little Yoho rivers and Laughing Falls.

TAKE IN THE SIGHTS FROM THE BOW RIVER

Not everyone in our crew enjoys a hike, but we do all like the water.

Sections of the Canadian Rockies include whitewater, but we decided to go for a smoother ride with Canmore River Adventures. The six of us joined another family of three on a wide raft paddled by a guide.

At one point we stopped and were told to touch a finger or toe to the water if we dared. I did, but I didn't keep my hand in for long. The guide said the river's temperature was about 40 degrees F (4.4 C) and wouldn't get any warmer.

Our one-hour float down the beautiful Bow River included sightings of an elk that had swum to an island to munch on grass and—just before we exited the boat—a bald eagle that dove into the water and came up clasping a fish. It was a fitting end to a spectacular trip.

SEASONS

The weather remains relatively mild into September, when larch and aspen trees turn gold as fall arrives. Wildfires and drought have been an issue in some areas in late summer, so check for warnings and conditions. For winter, ski slopes typically open in November.

If You Go . . .
CANADIAN ROCKIES: http://www.canadianrockies.net/

CANADA'S NATIONAL PARKS: https://www.pc.gc.ca/en/pn-np

HAWAII'S LAHAINA:
THE PLACE WHERE KINGS WERE BORN

By John Marshall

LAHAINA, Hawaii—The beach town of Lahaina in western Maui was once the capital of the Hawaiian Kingdom, a place where kings were born. It later became a key port at the height of the 19th century whaling boom.

Though it transformed into a mostly tourist area in the 1960s, much of Lahaina's history can still be found sprinkled around town—including in the roots of a giant banyan tree.

"There's just a ton of historical spots in town, really precious, sacred places," said Amy Fuqua, manager of the Lahaina Visitor's Center.

Located about 40 minutes from Kahului Airport, Lahaina was known in ancient Hawaiian times as Lele, meaning "cruel sun." It was conquered by Kamehameha the Great in 1795.

Front Street, which runs along the shoreline, was known as King's Road, where only kings and queens could walk. It's now the town's main thoroughfare, dotted with historical sites—62 in all around town—as well as shops and restaurants with spectacular views of the Pacific Ocean and neighboring islands.

Among the historical sites is the Hauola Stone, a chair-shaped stone used by Hawaiian royalty as a birthing site starting around the 14th century. The smoothed-out rock at the north end of the harbor also was considered to have healing powers.

At the town center is the Lahaina's famous banyan tree, a 60-foot (18-meter), multi-trunked tree that covers nearly an acre. Planted in 1873, it is one of the largest banyan trees in the United States and is still used for celebrations, including one for the tree's birthday every April. It grows new trunks via aerial roots that sink into the ground.

And make sure to visit the tree around sunset, when hundreds of mynah birds sing inside its canopy.

"It's kind of the center of town," Fuqua said. "Everyone knows where it's at. It has an important significance to the town and it feels good under there."

Not into history? Lahaina offers plenty of other touristy things to do.

Instead of whaling, the harbor has now become the launching

point for fishing, parasailing, ocean cruising or whale watching in the winter. The restaurants along Front Street are top-notch, offering straight-out-of-the-ocean fish daily.

The tiny Lahaina Civic Center transforms from a local events center into the center of the college basketball universe during the Maui Invitational in the days before Thanksgiving every year.

Lahaina also is the hub of western Maui, a gateway to golf courses in Kaanapali and Kapalua, sandy beaches and some of the best snorkeling found anywhere in the world.

"There's a lot to do here, even for a small town," Fuqua said. "It's just a cool town."

If You Go . . .

LAHAINA, MAUI: http://www.gohawaii.com/maui/regions-neighborhoods/west-maui/lahaina/. Located about 45 minutes from Kahului Airport, Maui.

SEATTLE:
PIKE PLACE TO POP CULTURE

By Donna Gordon Blankinship

SEATTLE—It doesn't always rain in Seattle, despite its reputation, so pack sunglasses for your visit, and be sure to catch some of the city's newer attractions along with classics like the chewing gum wall.

PIKE PLACE

Most visitors to Seattle stop by the Pike Place Market, a mishmosh of flower sellers, craft tables, restaurants, fish shops and crowds. Don't miss Rachel the pig, a life-size bronze pig that's actually a piggy bank, near the corner where fishmongers play catch with salmon. Around the corner is the must-see gum wall, covered with wads of chewed gum.

Ick factor aside, elsewhere there are some beautiful places in the market to relax with a glass of wine and enjoy the view, including The Pink Door and Cafe Campagne. The very first Starbucks is at Pike Place as well. It's a small spot, typically with a long line.

Near the market is one of Seattle's newest attractions, the Great Wheel on the waterfront, with 42 enclosed gondolas. It offers a nice view of the Puget Sound and the city.

SEATTLE CENTER

The Space Needle at Seattle Center is a symbol of the city. It was built for the 1962 World's Fair, but new for 2018, there will be a multi-level, floor-to-ceiling glass experience along with an open-air outdoor observation deck and glass benches designed to make visitors feel like they're floating on air.

Next door to the Space Needle is the Chihuly Garden and Glass exhibit, showcasing the work of Dale Chihuly, a native of the state of Washington known for his colorful, other-worldly glass creations. The attached Collections Cafe is fun, offering a look at the artist's personal collections of everything from ceramic dogs to bottle openers.

Seattle Center is also home to the Museum of Pop Culture, formerly the EMP (Experience Music Project). The museum's collection and artifacts span music history, science fiction and other aspects of pop culture, from "Star Trek" to the Muppets to superheroes.

A few steps away is the International Fountain, a must stop for kids on a warm day. The Pacific Science Center and the Seattle

Children's Museum are also on the Seattle Center campus and worth visiting. Another fun stop for families and history enthusiasts is Seattle's Underground Tour below the Pioneer Square neighborhood. Learn true and nearly true facts about Seattle history, and you might even see a ghost.

WEIRD AND WONDERFUL

Seattle is full of weird and wonderful museums that don't make most tourist lists: from the Living Computer Museum to the Seattle Pinball Museum, The Museum of History and Industry and the Dialysis Museum at the Northwest Kidney Center.

Some adult visitors will enjoy a stop at one of Seattle's new recreational marijuana shops, but be warned that public smoking is outlawed. Seattle police would love to give you a special souvenir of your visit if you light up in a city park.

For a free view and some exercise, walk up Queen Anne hill just north of downtown and visit Kerry Park. A series of hidden stairways will take you most of the way up.

HANGING OUT

The neighborhood of Ballard, which used to be its own city, is filled with some of Seattle's newest breweries, hip restaurants, little shops and rock music venues. Ballard has a nice Sunday market, but outdoor markets can be found all over town on the weekends.

You can rent a canoe or kayak at the University of Washington Waterfront Activities Center and paddle around Lake Washington and near the Washington Park Arboretum.

PHOENIX:
IT'S MORE THAN GOLF AND SUNSHINE

By Terry Tang

PHOENIX—With hundreds of golf courses and 300 days of sunshine a year, it's easy to cast metropolitan Phoenix as a retiree's paradise that leaves everyone else out in the cold. But within the desert beats the heart of an actual urban core that has come into its own. There's an emerging restaurant-and-retail scene along with classic attractions like the view from Camelback Mountain, plus newfound treasures like peeking inside a little-known house designed by Frank Lloyd Wright.

TAKE A HIKE

With all the sunshine, take a hike. Two popular summits are the 2,704-foot (852-meter) Camelback Mountain and 2,608-foot (795-meter) Piestewa Peak. Both are north of downtown and offer views of the entire metropolitan Phoenix valley.

A less crowded alternative is South Mountain Park 10 miles (17 km) south of downtown, where you'll find ancient petroglyphs.

DESERT GARDEN AND MUSEUMS

The 140-acre (57-hectare) Desert Botanical Garden boasts more than 50,000 plants and five trails that illustrate the role desert plants play in the environment.

The Heard Museum is known for art and artifacts showcasing Southwestern tribal culture, including Hopi katsina dolls, Navajo textiles and Zuni jewelry.

Galleries at the Musical Instrument Museum in north Phoenix are organized by world regions. Special headphones play music samples when you near the corresponding display. One gallery spotlights instruments and clothes belonging to icons from Elvis Presley to Taylor Swift.

HANGING OUT AND HAVING FUN

Stop by Changing Hands Bookstore, about 5 miles (8 kilometers) north of downtown near a light rail stop, and grab a book with some beer or wine at the store's First Draft Book Bar. Next door, the Southern Rail restaurant, named for its proximity to the light rail and its "low-country" cuisine, serves tasty Southern and Creole-influenced food like red beans and rice and fried chicken.

DeSoto Central Market in downtown, once a vacant brick building and former car dealership, is now a market with food stalls, bar and patio. It's known for happy hour, live music and swing dance nights. Drool-worthy delicacies include lobster rolls and oysters at raw seafood bar Walrus and the Pearl.

include fried chicken-skin po'boys at the larder + the delta.

Phoenix's artsy Roosevelt Row neighborhood is the best place for quirky people-watching along a seven-block stretch with restaurants, bars, galleries and street art. The first Friday of each month, the neighborhood hosts outdoor musicians, artists and vendors.

For a respite from the desert landscape, the 10-acre (4-hectare) Farm at South Mountain in south Phoenix feels like a country garden party. Onsite eateries include a breakfast-brunch cafe and fine-dining restaurant serving locally-grown produce. You can also grab lunch in a basket and use picnic tables in the farm's pecan tree grove.

Mexican restaurants in Phoenix are like Starbucks: There's practically one on every corner, from gourmet taco houses to casual mom-and-pop joints. Barrio Cafe is a local institution known for its collection of some 300 different tequilas and for dishes made from cochinita pibil (slow roasted pork) flavored with sour orange and a blend of spices.

TIPS

Phoenix's roughly 23-mile (37-kilometer) light rail system makes the ideal hop-on-hop-off tour bus with an inexpensive all-day pass. Several stops have free park-and-ride areas too. The tracks run through downtown, the college town of Tempe and the suburb of Mesa.

In Tempe, stroll around Tempe Town Lake, popular for jogging, fishing and even dragonboat racing. Mill Avenue is lined with shops, restaurants and bars. In Mesa, get off at the Main Street/Sycamore stop and walk five minutes to Mekong Plaza. The shopping center is a smorgasbord of authentic Asian cuisine—dim sum, pho or Taiwanese specialties like simmered pig ear.

Also available: green Grid Bike Share bicycles all around central Phoenix. Download the app to find and reserve a bike.

Every March, spring training brings 15 Major League Baseball teams to Phoenix suburbs as part of the Cactus League. Because the stadiums are relatively small, fans who arrive early have a good chance of interacting with favorite players.

Out-of-state visitors, take heed of the heat: If you're hiking, dress properly, go with a buddy, carry a fully charged cellphone and hydrate (pets too).

FRANK LLOYD WRIGHT

Phoenix is home to a Frank Lloyd Wright building, the David and Gladys Wright House, named for the architect's son and daughter-in-law, who once lived there. The house has gotten a lot of publicity in recent years after being saved from demolition and donated to the architecture school Wright founded for use as a living laboratory for students. Neighbors balked at the prospect of turning the site into a museum, and there are no regular public tours.

But Wright fans can tour the architect's winter home and studio, Taliesin West, in Scottsdale. It's a 30-minute drive from Phoenix.

BLUE SKIES IN BOULDER, COLORADO

By Beth J. Harpaz

BOULDER, Colorado—Not every destination lends itself to a whirlwind tour, but in the beautiful city of Boulder, Colorado, you can sample five fun and scenic spots in one afternoon.

Of course, if you've got more time, everything on this list is worth savoring. But if you're just passing through, this doable itinerary offers an easy way to experience the city's top sights in a few hours. Boulder is also an easy side trip if your primary destination is Denver, about 25 miles (40 km) away.

The city's typically sunny, blue-sky weather, gorgeous mountain scenery and easily traversed streets make it a pleasant destination no matter how much time you have.

CHAUTAUQUA
The Chautauqua movement started in the late 19th century as a summer school for teachers. It later developed into a cultural phenomenon, offering lectures, music, the arts and recreation in thousands of communities around America.

One of the last remaining Chautauquas is located in Boulder, now a National Historic Site with original buildings surrounded by parkland. Take a walk, lie on the grass, relax in a rocking chair, or if you have time, buy a ticket for one of its many events: concerts, films and other performances, including unique hikes that combine theater with the outdoors. There's onsite lodging if you care to stay overnight, but if you're cramming in a quick stop, one way to enjoy the place is to grab a bite at the Chautauqua Dining Hall. Get a table outside on the wraparound porch and enjoy the views and terrific menu, which ranges from bison to burrata cheese to Brussels sprouts. You can pick up a free map of Boulder inside the dining hall.

FLAGSTAFF MOUNTAIN
Boulder's 45,000 acres (18,000 hectares) of open space and parkland is supremely accessible. One minute, you're dining, shopping or walking on a city street; a few minutes later, you can be up in the mountains, surrounded by pine trees, looking down on the city below.

From Chautauqua, it's a quick drive west to Flagstaff Mountain, past the rock formations known as the Flatirons.

The winding drive up the mountain is beautiful with many spots to pull your car over and go for a short (or long) hike. Be sure to see the Sunrise Amphitheater on the summit. Built by the Civilian Conservation Corps in the 1930s, it has circular seating, a stage and incredible views. It's a popular site for weddings.

BOULDER CREEK PATH
Another encounter with the great outdoors can be had just blocks from downtown. On the scenic 8-mile (13-km) Boulder Creek Path, you can stroll, bike or just sit for a few peaceful moments by the water. Kayakers, fly fisherman and wading dogs are all part of the scene. Part of it is paved, part is dirt and gravel.

DUSHANBE TEAHOUSE
Boulder is home to dozens of options for food and drink but do not miss the one and only Dushanbe Teahouse. Dushanbe offers a formal afternoon tea with a three-tiered tower of pastries, cucumber sandwiches and more, but it's worth stopping in even if you don't have the time or appetite for a sit-down just to see the building.

The teahouse is named for Boulder's sister city, the capital of Tajikistan, and its elaborate carved columns, ceramic panels and hand-painted ceiling were mostly handcrafted there by artisans, with some elements made or assembled here by visiting craftsmen. The menu offers breakfast, lunch, dinner or a snack in addition to the afternoon tea, but if you've only got a few minutes, head to the takeout counter in back and get a chai tea or hibiscus cooler to go.

PEARL STREET MALL

Pearl Street has been Boulder's main shopping district since the late 19th century and a pedestrian mall since the late 1970s. Today its historic storefronts have been restored and it bustles with shoppers, street performers and children at play. You'll find eateries, bookstores, boutiques, antiques and toys, along with art galleries and shops selling everything from skateboards to cigars.

SPRAWLING DALLAS:
UPTOWN, DOWNTOWN AND MORE

By John Lumpkin

DALLAS—Dallas is known for its sprawl, and traversing the city by anything other than car—or as some locals prefer, truck—can be challenging and sometimes impractical.

But it is possible to enjoy the city, at least some parts of it, on foot, especially with the development of the Uptown neighborhood, abetted by the expansion of Dallas' cultural district and millennials moving into the area.

KLYDE WARREN PARK

Ground zero for walking is Klyde Warren Park. Philanthropists and city planners put a roof here over a freeway canyon that separated Dallas' downtown from Uptown, added lawns, flowers, trees, a sound stage and food trucks, and throngs of pedestrians took over.

Near Klyde Warren is a range of hotels, including the upscale boutique ZaZa. It's a short walk to the Perot Museum of Nature and Science, a 15-story cube with interactive attractions for kids.

BIKING, TROLLEYS AND THE BUSHES

Rent a bike and ride the Katy Trail, a 3.5-mile (5.6-km) linear park that starts near downtown. Or pedal to the Trinity Groves entertainment district to see the soaring Margaret Hill Hunt Bridge.

The old-fashioned McKinney Avenue Trolley follows a 4.5-mile (7.2-kilometer) elongated loop to the Nasher Sculpture Garden and the Dallas Museum of Art, both highlighted by a Michelin Green Guide that raved about the city. The trolley takes you to Uptown's brasseries as well.

The President George W. Bush Library is a short cab ride to the shady campus of Southern Methodist University, First Lady Laura Bush's alma mater. The museum has a replica of Bush's Oval Office and includes a 22-foot (6.7-meter) section from the fallen World Trade Center. While there, visit SMU's Meadows Museum, called "Prado on the Prairie."

CLASSIC ATTRACTIONS

Neiman-Marcus' flagship store is a must, even if you can't afford a $15,000 Carolina Herrera gown. Prices are more reasonable in the store's Zodiac Room eatery, where the mandarin orange souffle with chicken salad follow recipes of legendary Neiman's cookbook author Helen Corbitt.

The downtown Sixth Floor Museum, reverent and not ghoulish, is dedicated to the "life, death and legacy of President John F. Kennedy." It's located on the sixth floor of the building on Dealey Plaza from which shots were fired on Nov. 22, 1963, killing Kennedy as he passed by in a motorcade.

The State Fair of Texas hosts 3 million visitors for several weeks every autumn. The required snack is a Fletcher's Corny Dog, but vendors will fry almost anything, including Jell-O and Twinkies. The Texas Star Ferris Wheel, 20 stories high, only operates during the State Fair, but Fair Park's renowned art deco buildings can be viewed year-round.

DINING

Happy hour patrons are two-deep at the Ritz-Carlton Hotel's Rattlesnake Bar and celebrity chef Dean Fearing's namesake restaurant is on the same floor. Less expensive is Uptown's S&D Oyster Co., where the menu includes raw and fried oysters, gumbo and hush puppies.

Pecan Lodge is a Dallas barbecue mecca. Justin and Diane "Boss Lady" Fourton sold brisket sandwiches in a Jiffy Lube parking lot, then a stand in Dallas' Farmers Market before opening their expansive current location. Feed your delegation with "The Trough," stacks of beef and pork ribs, beef brisket, pulled pork and sausage links.

In Kyle Warren is Savor, with ceiling-to-floor glass on four sides, and across the street, Lark on the Park, both with al fresco seating and New American cuisine.

AUSTIN:
MUSIC, TECH AND HANGING OUT

By Glenn Adams

AUSTIN, Texas—Austin is the capital of Texas, but it brands itself as the "Live Music Capital of the World." And for good reason: On any given night, 200 venues across the city host live performances. The city is also known for South by Southwest, its annual festival of indie arts, media and tech culture.

MUSIC AND SXSW

Austin's ever-changing musical scene is a melting pot of global styles. Clubs and other venues host rock, jazz, blues, hip-hop, punk and Latino performances.

Bands even play outdoors to serenade runners in the city's February marathon and half-marathon.

Austin City Limits Music Festival is held over two weekends in the fall.

South by Southwest, or SXSW, a showcase for new talent that has almost become synonymous with Austin, features original music, independent films and technical innovation. It's held each March.

THE CAPITOL AND TEXAS HISTORY

Austin is the capital of Texas and the State Capitol building is worth a visit, with its mammoth dome, hundreds of rooms and windows, and many paintings and sculptures (including a portrait of Davy Crockett).

Wash the experience down at The Cloak Room, an unobtrusive, dimly lit bar near the Capitol where legislators mingle with lobbyists. The cooler should be well-stocked with Lone Star, which labels itself "the National Beer of Texas."

The Bullock Texas State History Museum tells the story of Texas since France and Spain claimed the region centuries ago. Artifacts include the 17th century French expedition ship, La Belle, which was recovered more than 300 years after it sank in a storm. You could easily spend the day at the Bullock, so consider dining in the museum's Story of Texas Cafe. But save some time for the Blanton Museum of Art, right across the street.

UT

You're at the edge of the University of Texas campus, which dominates a good chunk of downtown and brings zest to the city. Look up and you'll see the 30-floor administration building, also the former UT library. Tours of the school's clock tower offer a spectacular vista of the city and its hill country environs. (The tower is also where, in 1966, a gunman killed over a dozen people and wounded more than 30.)

New in 2018 at the university's Blanton Museum of Art: a stone building with colored glass windows designed by the late artist Ellsworth Kelly. The work is called "Austin."

Also on campus, the Lyndon B. Johnson Library walks visitors through the turbulent and historically significant years of LBJ's presidency.

The Lady Bird Johnson Wildflower Center, a unit of the University of Texas located on a satellite campus, offers trails, gardens, an arboretum and more.

HANGING OUT

A million bats can't be wrong. The largest urban colony of Mexican free-tailed bats in North America hangs out under the Ann Richards Bridge on Congress Avenue between April and October, and at dusk the bats billow out as they commence their nightly feeding. This spectacle can be viewed from the bridge itself, from a park below (both free), or from a riverboat on Lady Bird Lake below, which can also include a tour of some of the city's other highlights.

Bars with personality include the Mean-Eyed Cat, a former chain-saw repair shop that's now known for Johnny Cash memorabilia.

Like countless other Austin bars on West Fifth Street, it boasts a big selection of local and craft beers. Other places to eat and drink include the bar at the historic Driskell Hotel, Posse East (walking distance to the UT football stadium, good sandwiches), Hole in the Wall (hot music, draft beer, real Texas atmosphere) and Spider House (eclectic spot to watch grad students work and drink). Coffee bars are everywhere. If you're hankering to huff on a hookah, you're in the right town for that too.

Barbecue is a must. The trendy spot these days is Franklin's but just outside of Austin, The Salt Lick in Driftwood is famous for beef brisket, sausage and pork ribs. It's well worth the ride and potential wait time for a table.

Ready to cool off? Try Barton Springs Pool in Zilker Park. This three-acre gem (where Robert Redford learned to swim) is fed by underground springs and has an average temperature of 68-70 degrees.

TIPS

Austin is divided into six entertainment districts: Downtown, East, Rainey Street, Red River, Sixth Street and South Congress.

The city is bicycle-friendly, with bike lanes on many main routes. Drivers tend to be conscious of bikers, and riding opportunities extend to open-road course, parks with dedicated biking areas and city trails like the 7.8-mile (12.5-kilometer) Barton Creek Greenbelt.

CapMetro bus service serves many stops along the MetroRail rail passenger line. Downtown, Capitol Pedicab drivers work for tips.

The Austin-Bergstrom International Airport is convenient to downtown (20 minutes barring heavy traffic) and has nonstop flights to and from scores of destinations.

WISCONSIN:
CHEESE CURDS AND FRANK LLOYD WRIGHT

By Beth J. Harpaz

MADISON, Wisconsin—Walking around Madison, Wisconsin, I felt a sharp pain in my leg. What was poking me?

Turned out my pocket was full of toothpicks from all the cheese curds I'd sampled at the farmers market. It was one of several "Welcome to Wisconsin!" moments, starting with a display of orange "cheesehead" gear—worn by fans of Wisconsin's football team, the Green Bay Packers—that greeted me at Milwaukee's airport. Later in my trip, I got these directions to a cheese store: "Take a right and look for the cow."

MILWAUKEE MUSEUM

I spent as much time admiring the Milwaukee Art Museum outside as I did looking at the art inside. From one angle, the white, winged Santiago Calatrava-designed building on the Lake Michigan waterfront looks like a bird in flight. From another angle, it's a ship setting sail. Inside, white ribs form a futuristic tunnel with a lake view.

But don't forget the art, including the spooky hooded figure of "Saint Francis of Assisi in His Tomb" and an excellent Georgia O'Keeffe collection. O'Keeffe was born in Wisconsin.

I bookended my museum visit with two terrific meals: a hipster lunch at The National cafe and an outstanding dinner of farm-to-table small plates at Braise, owned by chef Dave Swanson, a James Beard Award nominee.

MADISON FARMERS MARKET

It's so crowded at the Dane County Farmers' Market that you can't choose which way to walk. You can only flow with the sea of humanity in one direction past tables overflowing with fruits, veggies, flowers, baked goods and of course, cheese curds, those squeaky bits of fresh cheese goodness, in flavors ranging from dill to Sriracha. The market runs Saturdays mid-April to early November until 1:45 p.m. around the state Capitol.

Take a peek inside the Capitol at its beautiful dome, then walk down State Street to the University of Wisconsin campus. Once you're on campus, stop at Babcock Hall for ice cream, climb Bascom Hill and hang out with the beer-and-bratwurst crowd at the lakeside Memorial Union Terrace.

At nearby Middleton, make a quick stop at the National Mustard Museum (free admission, goofy mustard-inspired art and every type of mustard imaginable). Rent a bike from a Madison BCycle kiosk and go for the 12-mile ride (19 km) around Lake Monona. The lake trail often detours from the waterfront and it's hilly (you thought the Midwest was flat?). But the exercise balances out eating all that cheese.

SPRING GREEN

America's most famous architect, Frank Lloyd Wright, spent his teenage summers working on his uncle's Wisconsin farm. You can see how that landscape of farms and rolling hills influenced Wright's style and aesthetics at Taliesin, his house and estate in Spring Green. Wright set out to replace the vertical boxy shape that dominated home design in the late 19th and early 20th centuries with modernist structures that flowed horizontally like the Midwestern prairie. Taliesin was a lab for his ideas: open floor plans rather than walled-off rooms, large windows with expansive views and a structure built to suit the terrain. House tours are offered daily May-October and weekends April and November. Tours sell out well in advance.

Taliesin was also the site of a shocking crime: A house employee murdered Wright's mistress and six others in 1914 and set fire to the house. But Wright rebuilt and kept going. New York's Guggenheim Museum, was being built when he died at age 89 in 1959.

Nearby Taliesin is the quirky attraction House on the Rock. Its creator, Alex Jordan Jr., amassed a collection of strange artifacts—weird carousel animals, machines that play creepy music—and they're displayed in a series of odd rooms and buildings, some ornate, some musty and dark. An hour here was enough for me, but if you go, don't miss the infinity room, a disorienting cantilevered structure lined with windows.

NEW GLARUS AND MONROE
I caught the tail end of Oktoberfest in New Glarus, a town so proud of its Swiss heritage that street signs are in German and storefronts are decorated with Swiss flags and cowbells. I downed

DETROIT:
DON'T FORGET THE MOTOR CITY

By Beth J. Harpaz and Jeff Karoub

DETROIT—Detroit has made a lot of headlines in recent years thanks to the city's struggles to emerge from bankruptcy and an epidemic of abandoned houses. Online photo galleries of those decrepit homes even gave rise to a new term: "ruin porn."

Let's hope that most visitors aren't just going to gawk at old troubles, especially with so much restoration and reinvention going on. Detroit has more than its share of authentic and interesting attractions, from Motown to coney dogs.

MOTOWN

The Motown Museum, also known as Hitsville USA, at 2648 W. Grand Blvd., is located in the house where record company founder Berry Gordy launched a cultural and commercial music empire. Artifacts include an old orange sofa where stars napped, the candy machine that Stevie Wonder got his snacks from, and lots of gold records. You'll stand in the studio where Diana Ross and the Supremes and others recorded hits that made them superstars, and you'll even get to sing "My Girl" while learning the rock-and-turn steps of the Temptations' classic move.

DOWNTOWN

Take a selfie fist-bumping the giant sculpted fist that is a monument to boxer Joe Louis. Then spend a few hours seeing other nearby attractions: the bronze monument called "Spirit of Detroit"; Campus Martius park (a skating rink in winter); the expanding Riverwalk along the Detroit River with attractions and views of Canada across the water (locals like to say it's a rare place where people can look south to Canada); the GM Renaissance Center (lots of shiny cars on display); the People Mover, an elevated light rail on a 5-km loop that costs 75 cents per ride; and the Guardian Building, a historic landmark and Art Deco masterpiece with a lobby that feels like a cathedral.

Streetcars also have returned to the Motor City in the form of the QLINE, a 6.6-mile (10.6-km) round-trip route connecting the downtown to the New Center Area. Cost is $1.50 for a single pass.

The Westin Book Cadillac was the tallest hotel in the world when it opened in the 1920s, and it hosted everyone from presidents to movie stars. It closed in the 1980s and was abandoned for 20 years before reopening in 2008 after a $200 million renovation.

On West Lafayette Boulevard, check out two side-by-side eateries with a legendary rivalry: American Coney Island and Lafayette Coney Island. Coneys are hot dogs with mustard, onions and chili. Wash it all down with Vernors ginger ale (the brand originated in Detroit).

For the first time in decades, all four of Detroit's professional sports teams are playing in the city, with the 2017 opening of Little Caesars Arena. The arena, home of the NHL's Red Wings (hockey) and NBA's Pistons (basketball), is just north of the Tigers' Comerica Park (baseball) and the Lions' Ford Field (football) and is to anchor a 50-block neighborhood of offices, apartments, restaurants and shops.

A short drive from downtown is Belle Isle, an island and state park in the Detroit River that houses a beautifully maintained greenhouse and botanical garden.

MUSEUMS

At one point in the nail-biting negotiations over the city's bankruptcy crisis, a proposal was floated to sell treasures from the Detroit Institute of Arts. Ultimately an alternate solution was found, but a visit to the museum will honor what the city nearly lost.

Museum highlights include Diego Rivera's Detroit Industry murals, a tribute to workers and manufacturing; the first van Gogh and Matisse to be acquired by any U.S. museum; and "The Wedding Dance" by Pieter Bruegel the Elder.

At the Charles H. Wright Museum of African-American History, a chillingly realistic exhibit depicts slave ships and other horrors of the slave trade. Stand in the lobby beneath the beautiful domed ceiling and whisper to hear the extraordinary acoustics, designed to recall the echoes of those who tried to flee.

The Henry Ford Museum in nearby Dearborn is devoted to the history of American innovation, from manufacturing to social change. The eclectic collection includes the bus that civil rights activist Rosa Parks rode in when she refused to give her seat up to a white rider; the limousine in which President John F. Kennedy was assassinated in 1963; George Washington's camping supplies; and a Model T that is taken apart and reassembled daily to demonstrate its simplicity.

MIDTOWN

Like them or not, hipsters are a presence in Detroit these days. One happening neighborhood is Midtown.

For Midtown food and drink, start with a beer at Honest John's, get a burger at The Bronx and end the evening around a bonfire in the backyard of Old Miami. Spend the night at The Inn on Ferry Street, a charming bed-and-breakfast located in several restored Victorian homes in a Midtown historic district.

Be sure to check out the Shinola store, 441 W. Canfield St., which sells luxury watches, bicycles and other high-end lifestyle products. The company based the brand in Detroit to identify with the city's manufacturing heritage. Next door is Third Man Records shop founded by Detroit-raised rocker Jack White, which boasts a vinyl record pressing plant in the back. Nearby is Source Booksellers, 4240 Cass Ave., an indie bookstore owned by longtime Detroiter Janet Jones.

INDIANAPOLIS:
CONTEMPORARY COOL IN A RUST BELT CITY

By Beth J. Harpaz

INDIANAPOLIS—Indianapolis is an old Rust Belt city on a speedway to the 21st century.

Sure, there's old-school Indianapolis: massive stone monuments that swallow blocks of downtown, divine corned beef sandwiches at Shapiro's and shrimp cocktail with the world's hottest horseradish at St. Elmo's. The Indy 500 car race has been running for more than 100 years, and the racetrack museum is loaded with vintage cars and photos.

But the city's best days are definitely not behind it. A defunct Coca-Cola bottling plant on Massachusetts Avenue is being turned into a groovy West Elm hotel and food hall. The Children's Museum of Indianapolis has a new Riley Children's Health Sports Legends Experience, with 12 outside sports experiences and three indoor exhibits devoted to physical fitness and sports history. Also new in 2018: shipping containers turned into boutique hotels. The overnight lodging, called "Tiny Urban Escapes," is located near Eagle Creek Park and Traders Point Creamery. It doesn't get hipper than that.

Many areas of the city are bubbling with creative energy, from small shops along Mass Ave, to Canal Walk, lined with artwork and popular with joggers. The city's dining scene offers terrific eateries like Milktooth and Tinker Street. And Indy's old nickname, Naptown, is now used ironically, with a hashtag, because this city has woken up.

ATTRACTIONS

Downtown attractions include White River State Park, the Eiteljorg Museum of American Indians and Western Art, the Soldiers' and Sailors' Monument and the Indianapolis War Memorial.

A memorial to the USS Indianapolis, a ship that was torpedoed in the Pacific during World War II, is at the north end of the Canal Walk.

Enjoy artwork inside the Indianapolis Museum of Art, then head outside to the 100-acre park on the museum grounds. Outdoor art there includes "Funky Bones," a giant skeleton made from benches that was featured in the book "The Fault in Our Stars," written by Indy-born John Green; and "Park of the Laments," a hauntingly serene spot with stone walls, a tunnel and grassy walled field.

Nearby Crown Hill Cemetery, one of the country's largest cemeteries, has acres of hills, trees and statuary. Notables buried here include Depression-era gangster John Dillinger.

VONNEGUT

Indianapolis is dotted with tributes to one of its most famous sons, the late counterculture writer Kurt Vonnegut. The Kurt Vonnegut Memorial Library at 340 N. Senate Ave., displays his typewriter, rejection letters and other intriguing mementos. There's also a restaurant named for his novel "Bluebeard" and a German beer garden, Rathskeller, in a building his grandpa designed.

A mural of Vonnegut towers four stories high over a parking lot on Massachusetts Avenue, but the street has many other attractions worth seeing, including Stout's Footwear (founded in 1886) and "Ann Dancing," a hypnotic animated neon sculpture. At the other end of Mass Ave, the hipster Black Market restaurant faces Indy Reads Books, an independent bookstore that sells mostly donated used books to support a literacy program. In between are groovy gift shops and boutiques.

In the Fountain Square-Fletcher Place area, look for the "YOU ARE BEAUTIFUL" sign along with funky restaurants and vintage stores.

PITTSBURGH:
WARHOL AND AMERICA'S BEST CAKE

By Beth J. Harpaz

PITTSBURGH—If you're planning a trip to Pittsburgh, you'll need to learn a few things. Yinz is local for y'all. Carnegie is pronounced Car-NAY-gie (as in Andrew Carnegie, who made a fortune in Pittsburgh's steel industry, and whose name adorns libraries, museums and more.)

And you don't get French fries WITH your sandwich at Primanti's. You get fries ON your sandwich.

The city offers plenty for sports fans: Pirates baseball, Steelers football, Penguins hockey. But you can also build an itinerary around food and the arts. After all, pop artist Andy Warhol and playwright August Wilson are native sons, and Prantl's bakery is said to sell the "best cake in America."

FOOD

Primanti's sandwiches and Prantl's famous cake—a burnt almond torte—are hardly Pittsburgh's only classic local eats. The best way to start your day here is with breakfast at Pamela's, preferably a crepe-like pancake stuffed with strawberries, brown sugar and sour cream.

Besides Primanti's, another old-school sandwich with a twist is found at Max's Allegheny Tavern, a German restaurant in Pittsburgh's Deutschtown neighborhood. Here you can get a sandwich served on potato pancakes instead of bread.

The Strip District is lined with ethnic food markets (Asian, Middle Eastern, Mexican) and specialty shops, from La Prima, which serves excellent Italian coffee and pastries, to Penn Mac for cheese. The neighborhood comes alive with shoppers and vendors on Saturday mornings.

In the Squirrel Hill neighborhood, the Dobra teahouse offers cozy seating and a vast tea menu that includes unique drinks like cold "beer tea."

THE ARTS

The seven-story Warhol Museum traces artist Andy Warhol's life from his childhood as the son of working-class immigrants to his advertising career in New York to his emergence as an influential figure in pop art and underground culture in the 1960s and

'70s. Gallery displays explain the impact and genius of his work, including his famous images of Marilyn Monroe and Campbell's soup cans.

But the museum's not just about appreciating Warhol's legacy. It's also just a heck of a lot of fun. You can bat enormous Mylar balloons around; lounge on sofas while gazing at Warhol's massive silkscreened celebrity portraits; or watch video interviews—some mesmerizing, some downright wacky—that Warhol produced for a TV project.

Another place that makes art fun is the Mattress Factory. Installations include polka-dot-and-mirrored rooms created by Yayoi Kusama and a slightly spooky rowhouse overflowing with toys and furniture.

Nearby is Randyland, 1501 Arch St., an outdoor park-like space crammed with art, signs and other colorful objects. "House Poem," a house at 408 Sampsonia Way decorated with Chinese calligraphy, is part of City of Asylum, which provides sanctuary and forums for exiled writers.

A gigantic model of a Diplodocus dinosaur known as "Dippy" sits outside the Carnegie museum and library complex. The Carnegie Museum of Art's treasures include Giacometti's "Walking Man" and Van Gogh's patterned pastel "Wheat Fields after the Rain." The Carnegie Museum of Natural History is known for its T. Rex.

The University of Pittsburgh's Cathedral of Learning Tower has 30 Nationality Rooms, each one decorated to represent a different country or ethnicity—Korean, Ukrainian, Welsh and more. Check the peephole in every door to see if there's a class in session, and if not, step inside for a look.

Downtown, stop by PPG Place, with its 231 castle-like glass spires, and the August Wilson Center, housed in a striking silvery building designed to evoke a slave ship. A film of Wilson's play "Fences" was shot in Pittsburgh, not far from Wilson's childhood home in the Hill District. The home, at 1727 Bedford Ave., is being renovated and will eventually open to the public. Meanwhile, fans can find other sites in the Hill District connected to Wilson, including a mural honoring his work at 2037 Centre Ave. Also in the Hill District is a historic mark for Josh Gibson, the power-hitting Negro Leagues baseball player whose story is mentioned in "Fences."

RIVERS, HILLS AND CITY LIGHTS

Pittsburgh is a city of hills, rivers and bridges (446 of them). At Point State Park downtown, you can see the confluence of the Monongahela and Allegheny rivers as they flow into the Ohio River.

For a fun ride and spectacular view, take a funicular up to Mount Washington aboard the Monongahela or Duquesne Inclines. At night, from the top, you'll see those rivers and bridges amid a sea of city lights twinkling like a million stars.

PHILADELPHIA:
FROM ROCKY TO THE REVOLUTION

By Kathy Matheson

PHILADELPHIA—Think of Philadelphia and three things come to mind: cheesesteaks, Rocky and the Declaration of Independence. (Hopefully not in that order.)

Of course there's a lot more here for visitors than Independence Hall and the museum steps that Sylvester Stallone made famous. But before we get to beer gardens and neighborhood gems, let's get the biggies out of the way.

HISTORIC PHILADELPHIA

Independence Hall, where the Declaration and Constitution were signed, is a must. It's free to visit but timed tickets are required March-December. Reserve ahead online for a small fee or get same-day tickets at the Independence Visitors Center.. No tickets are needed to glimpse the Liberty Bell and its famous crack.

The new Museum of the American Revolution offers a fuller story of the rebellion. And at the National Constitution Center, don't miss Signers' Hall, a recreation of the room where the Constitution was written. It's crowded with 42 life-size statues of the Founding Fathers. You can shake their hands, whisper in their ears or pose for selfies.

At Christ Church Burial Ground on Fifth Street, Ben Franklin's grave is strewn with pennies in homage to his famous saying, "A penny saved is a penny earned." Nearby, at the Betsy Ross House, 239 Arch St., a costumed re-enactor tells her story: Ross, an upholsterer by trade, was persuaded by Washington and others to sew an American flag. She worked in secret because British colonial officials would have considered that treason.

ROCKY, RIVER VIEWS AND CHEESESTEAK

The Liberty Bell isn't Philadelphia's only famous bronze. The Rocky statue was a prop from the movie "Rocky III." Fans usually have to wait in a quick-moving line at the foot of the Art Museum steps to take their picture with the fictional hometown fighter. Cynics, please note Philly's real heavyweight champ Joe Frazier has his own impressive statue at the city's sports complex.

Spruce Street Harbor Park has revived a faded area known as Penn's Landing. The now-vibrant promenade along the Delaware

River includes a skating rink and seaport museum complete with historic ships. The Schuylkill Banks Boardwalk on the city's other river offers postcard views of the skyline from its entrance on the South Street Bridge. Bikers, joggers and pedestrians can take the path up to the Art Museum and beyond.

For a bird's-eye view of both rivers, try the One Liberty Observation Deck, on the 57th floor of one of the city's tallest skyscrapers. The space offers 360-degree views, day and night.

Need a cheesesteak after all that sightseeing? Pat's and Geno's, those dueling South Philly landmarks, are open 24/7. You can also try Reading Terminal Market, Jim's on South Street and Tony Luke's, which is somewhat off the beaten path. Tip: Many locals prefer roast pork sandwiches with sharp provolone and broccoli raab.

HANGING OUT

While the Art Museum, Barnes Foundation and Rodin Museum showcase famous names, Philly's street art is second to none. Take a mural tour or visit Magic Gardens, a folk art and mosaic installation at 1020 South St.

Venture into the buzzing East Passyunk and Fishtown neighborhoods for lively bars, BYOBs, gastropubs and unpretentious but world-class dining. The coffeehouse culture is strong, too, with many indie storefronts.

The phenomenon of beer gardens, which began popping up a couple of years ago, continues unabated. The immensely popular open-air spaces range from rooftops and restaurant patios to office building breezeways and reclaimed vacant lots landscaped by the Pennsylvania Horticultural Society.

But for the simplest respite, try one of the city's original green spaces as laid out by founder William Penn. Logan Circle has the beautiful Swann fountain with a gorgeous view of City Hall; Rittenhouse and Washington squares offer green lawns and park benches; and Franklin Square offers family fun with a carousel and mini-golf.

WAIT, THERE'S TOURISM IN NEWARK?

By Beth J. Harpaz

NEWARK—Tourism in Newark, New Jersey? You might not think of it as a destination, but boosters say Newark is ready for visitors as part of a comeback.

A company called Have You Met Newark? has taken more than 2,000 visitors on walking tours and bar crawls. Tour company founder Emily Manz points out everything from Nasto's ice cream parlor , made famous in an episode of "The Sopranos," to a church, St. Stephan's, that appeared in the movie "War of the Worlds."

The Greater Newark Convention and Visitors Bureau has started taking travel writers to see attractions like the Newark Museum and the Ironbound, a neighborhood known for Portuguese and Spanish restaurants and shops.

And the "100 Things to Do Before You Die" series in 2017 published a Newark guidebook written by Lauren Craig, who fell in love with Newark while attending Rutgers Law School and calls herself the city's "glambassador."

The year 2017 also marked 50 years since riots scarred the city. "The perception of Newark being unfriendly, dangerous, dirty is something that has been ingrained in people for many, many years," Craig said. "I fight against that every day."

HAHNE & CO., A SYMBOL OF REBIRTH

Officials point to a massive brick building, vacant since the Hahne department store closed in 1987, as a symbol of Newark's rebirth. The Hahne building reopened this year with apartments (one-bedrooms rent for $2,000 monthly) and businesses, including a Whole Foods and a restaurant from celebrity chef Marcus Samuelsson called Marcus B&P. The informal eatery was an instant success with hard-to-get reservations. Its eclectic menu reflects African-American culture, Newark's immigrant heritage as well as Samuelsson's ethnic background—born in Ethiopia, raised in Sweden—with items like corn bread, fried chicken, pizza, charred octopus and dorowat rigatoni.

Also in the Hahne building is an arts incubator, Express Newark, with workshops and exhibits onsite.

Another downtown gem, Military Park, is pristinely

landscaped and attracts visitors with its carousel and trendy onsite eatery, BURG.

ATTRACTIONS AND HOTELS

Destination Newark has a lot to offer: New Jersey Devils hockey games and more at the Prudential Center , concerts and shows at the New Jersey Performing Arts Center and Newark International Airport, among America's 20 busiest airports.

Newark Penn Station is also just 20 minutes from Manhattan via PATH, NJ Transit or Amtrak trains. That makes Newark a viable lodging option for visitors to New York City at rates well under what you'd pay in Manhattan.

Downtown Newark hotels include the historic Robert Treat, which has hosted four U.S. presidents; the Hilton at Newark Penn Station, popular with airline crews; and the Indigo boutique hotel.

Treasures at the Newark Museum, a 10-minute walk from Newark Penn Station, include an 1885 mansion called the Ballantine House, a room of paintings by Joseph Stella, a Tibetan altar visited by the Dalai Lama and impressive collections of Native American and African-American art. "I go there as much as I can," said Hrag Vartanian of Brooklyn, New York, editor-in-chief of online arts publication Hyperallergic.com. "But it's amazing to me how many people have never heard of the Newark Museum."

Before hopping the train back to New York, Vartanian heads to the Ironbound, where dining options range from old-school bacalhau at Seabra's Marisqueira to tapas with a hipster vibe at Mompou .

The Ballantine House and the Ironbound are featured in Craig's "100 Things to Do in Newark Before You Die" book, too. On a recent day, she also took a visitor to the Off the Hanger boutique, where "Newark Vs Everybody" T-shirts are prominently displayed; the Jimenez Tobacco cigar lounge and bar; Casa D'Paco, an Ironbound restaurant; and Gateway Project Spaces, an art gallery adjacent to Newark Penn Station.

At one point on Craig's whirlwind tour, a taxi driver disputed the idea that Newark was ready for tourists.

"I beg to differ," Craig said politely, then said to a guest, "You see what I'm fighting against?"

THE CITY PAST AND PRESENT

Of course, problems persist. Newark's population declined from 400,000 in the 1960s to 280,000 today. Thirty percent of residents live in poverty. Crime remains a top concern, though it's decreasing: Newark is statistically safer than Washington, D.C., Atlanta and Memphis, Tennessee.

But Newark's decline in the last half of the 20th century wasn't isolated. Many urban areas lost population as factories closed and white middle-class Americans fled to the suburbs. Even Newark's riots were part of a larger pattern: Riots rocked more than 100 cities in 1967, and many—including Newark's, which erupted after the arrest of a black cabdriver—were sparked by allegations of police brutality amid racial inequality and lack of opportunity in African-American communities. More than 20 people died in Newark's riots; millions of dollars in property damage was sustained.

Karin Aaron, CEO of the Greater Newark Convention and Visitors Bureau, left the city in the early '90s because she "didn't see any progress," even though her mother often spoke about "how great Newark used to be." Aaron moved back in 2016 and believes a renaissance is underway, saying: "Everybody loves a comeback story."

NYC:
SECRETS OF A BIG APPLE GREETER

By Beth J. Harpaz

NEW YORK—As a native New Yorker, a licensed city tour guide and a volunteer Big Apple Greeter, I've answered lots of questions from tourists over the years.

Among them: "Is it safe to drink the water?" (Yes.)

"What does 'curb your dog' mean?" (Dogs should not use sidewalks as a bathroom.)

And my favorite: "Where are all the supermodels?" (I don't know.)

The Big Apple Greeter organization matches out-of-towners with locals for free neighborhood visits and other outings. As a greeter, I've also shepherded tourists from around the world on their first subway rides, visits to Harlem and Brooklyn, and tastes of local delicacies (like bagels). Along the way I've given lots of advice on enjoying the city while staying safe, having fun and sticking to a budget. Here are some tips.

SAFETY

Crime is very low but safeguard your wallet from pickpockets and don't drape your purse over your chair.

Street food is safe to eat.

Many people will accost you, trying to sell you things. Keep walking.

It's not uncommon to hear of pedestrians hit by bikes or even cars. Look both ways when crossing the street. Use seat-belts in cabs.

THE BEST THINGS IN NEW YORK ARE FREE

Take the Staten Island Ferry: Great views of the Statue of Liberty, Lower Manhattan and New York Harbor, it runs 24 hours a day and it's beautiful at night with the city lit up. Reachable via the No. 1 subway to South Ferry or 4 or 5 trains to Bowling Green.

The 9/11 memorial park is powerful symbol of the city's resilience, with One World Trade rising above. Reflecting pools built in the footprints of the twin towers are a moving tribute to those who perished. Be sure to stop at the Survivor Tree. Check out the Oculus nearby, a cool and curious white-winged structure with shops and eateries inside.

Walk across the Brooklyn Bridge. Take the C or A train to

the High Street stop on the Brooklyn side and walk back to Manhattan.

Visit Central Park. New Yorkers live in tiny apartments. City parks are our collective backyards. Enter at 59th Street and Fifth Avenue.

Brave the crowds on the High Line. This vertical park built on an old rail line 30 feet (9 meters) above the street runs for about a mile (1.6 km) from 34th Street west of 10th Avenue to just below 14th Street.

Stop by Grand Central, 42nd Street and Lexington Avenue. Notice the famous four-faced clock, cathedral windows, grand staircases and zodiac signs in the ceiling. A small black rectangle in the northwest corner of the ceiling is a reminder of the days prior to a 1990s renovation when the entire ceiling was black from decades of tobacco smoke.

About Times Square: New Yorkers hate this place. But visitors can't seem to stay away.

THE SUBWAY

It's noisy, dirty and confusing, and those of us who live here believe that the service is getting worse. But it is generally safe, mostly efficient and definitely cheaper than taking taxis all over town. Chances are you will encounter homeless people, panhandlers, musicians and trains so crowded you can't get on. It runs 24 hours a day, though trains and riders thin out overnight. Trust your gut: If someone is acting strangely or aggressively, make like a New Yorker and walk away. If you bump someone accidentally, a sincere apology is expected.

Get a free map from a manned booth. There's also a map in every car of every train. Most New Yorkers can provide basic directions to neighborhoods and major attractions. This site can provide detailed routes: http://tripplanner.mta.info/MyTrip/ui_web/customplanner/TripPlanner.aspx. Trains are often rerouted on weekends for track repair work; see http://web.mta.info/weekender.html for advice or just head into a station and ask for help.

Each one-way ride costs $2.75. Best deal is an unlimited seven-day pass for $32. There's a $1 fee for the card, but you can refill it.

ATTRACTIONS

Buy online timed tickets for attractions when available. Otherwise arrive a half-hour before opening time to reduce your wait.

Empire State Building, Top of the Rock or One World Trade observatories? Each one is a bit different. The elevators are slow to the top of the Empire State Building, but the view is outdoors and the wind makes it thrilling. Top of the Rock's view includes both the Empire State Building and the One World, plus Central Park. Much of the view from One World is of the harbor and New Jersey.

Many museums schedule a few free hours each week. Expect lines.

The Metropolitan Museum of Art has a massive collection spanning the history of human civilization; the Egyptian wing is a highlight. Kids will enjoy the American Museum of Natural History's dinosaurs. At the Museum of Modern Art, do not miss the permanent collection and its star painting, Van Gogh's "Starry Night."

NEIGHBORHOODS

In Harlem, have a bite at Marcus Samuelsson's Streetbird on

116th Street and walk across the neighborhood's main street, 125th Street. Joe Shanghai on Pell Street in Chinatown is cheap, crazy, fun and good; be prepared to wait for a table and beware the hot broth inside the pork dumplings. From Chinatown, walk to Little Italy for dessert at Ferrara's, 195 Grand St. Among many options for great pizza, Lombardi's won't disappoint; take the C train to Spring Street. Ground zero for hipsters is Brooklyn: Try Bedford Street in Williamsburg, or Bushwick in the area around Troutman, Starr and Wyckoff.

In summer, ride the subway to the end of the line in Coney Island, Brooklyn, to New York's favorite gritty beach and amusement park, or check out the surfers' beach in the Rockaways in Queens.

BOSTON:
A WICKED GOOD PLACE TO VISIT

By William J. Kole

BOSTON—Call it Boston, Beantown or the Cradle of Liberty. Whatever you call it, it's a wicked good place to sightsee, from Fenway Park to the Freedom Trail.

CLASSIC ATTRACTIONS
Non-negotiables: lunch and shopping at Faneuil Hall Marketplace in the heart of downtown, where Samuel Adams and other

patriots agitated for rebellion against the British. Ditto a leisurely walk through Boston Common and the adjacent Boston Public Garden, the heart and lungs of the city.

You can't truthfully say you've done Boston without following the Freedom Trail, a 2.5-mile (4-km) route that takes in Old North Church, Paul Revere House, Bunker Hill Monument and a dozen other colonial sites.

A raucous alternative is a splashy ride on a duck boat: a World War II-style amphibious vehicle that rumbles past most of those landmarks.

Other must-sees: the interactive John F. Kennedy Presidential Library & Museum, devoted to the 35th president and Massachusetts' favorite son. Or, if high-end retail therapy is your thing, the fashionable salons and boutiques of Newbury Street.

For heaven's sake, don't go home without genuflecting before Fenway Park, a baseball shrine which deserves a visit even if the Red Sox inside aren't always worthy. Catch a game in season and consider an hour-long walking tour and a selfie atop the ballpark's signature Big Green Monster wall.

By now, you'll be ravenous. Head to the North End, a warren of narrow streets lined with Italian restaurants. Slake your thirst with a tour of the Samuel Adams Brewery.

THE MARATHON

If you're a runner or a history buff, or both, you'll be hot to trot for RunBase. Part interactive museum, clubhouse and retail outlet, RunBase is located near the finish line of the iconic Boston Marathon. It's a great place to find someone to share a run along the nearby Charles River, or simply to learn more about the rich lore of the marathon, which is held each April and began back in 1897.

A memorial to victims of the 2013 marathon bombing opens spring 2018.

CAMBRIDGE AND CONCORD

Make like a local and get out of town. No, really. Just across the Charles River is Cambridge, home to a certain Ivy League college and its eponymous Harvard Square. Fine, technically it's not Boston, but who'd quibble when it's replete with so many fabulous watering holes and seriously interesting indie bookstores? Pro tip: Don't even try to pahk the cah in Hahvahd Yahd; just take the T, which is what locals call the MBTA public transit system. You can buy reloadable CharlieTicket and CharlieCard passes for the trains and save a bundle.

A bit farther afield—20 miles (32 km) from Boston—is Concord, where you'll find Walden Pond. The bucolic site was made famous by Henry David Thoreau, who went there to live in the woods because, as he famously put it, "I wished to live deliberately." His 1854 book, "Walden," describes living simply in coexistence with nature. There's a trail around the pond, a reconstruction of Thoreau's tiny wooden cabin and a visitor center. It's most easily reached via car, but you can take the MBTA commuter rail (Fitchburg line) to the Concord stop, then get a taxi or Uber to the pond.

THE POPS AND THE TOP

Visiting in summer? Grab a blanket and some munchies and catch a free open-air concert on Boston's riverside Esplanade park. The city's beloved Boston Pops orchestra has been performing in the outdoor Hatch Shell for decades.

End your trip by getting high: Have a drink at Top of the Hub, a bar and restaurant 52 floors above the Back Bay. It offers stunning 360-degree panoramic views of the city that boasts it's the "Hub of the Universe."

MAINE:
SOMETHING FOR EVERYONE

By Beth J. Harpaz

HARTLAND, Maine—For me, summer vacation means spending time on a Maine pond where the sound of loons calling is about the most exciting thing that happens all day.

But I do venture occasionally from my little paradise to experience other things the state has to offer, whether it's the coast, a mountain hike, a whitewater adventure or the arts. Here are a few options.

THE SHORE
Maine's scenic coast has so many wonderful towns that you almost can't go wrong, but every spot has its own personality.

Old Orchard Beach just outside Portland has a sandy beach, busy pier with food, drink and souvenirs, and an old-fashioned amusement park. You could also make a day of visiting Popham Beach State Park in Phippsburg in the morning (the wide sandy beach is great for kite-flying) and nearby Reid State Park in Georgetown in the afternoon (rocky outcroppings, tidal pools and a lagoon). In Rockland, the man-made Breakwater jetty lets you walk nearly a mile from the shore into Penobscot Bay, and a ferry runs across to Vinalhaven island, where it's worth spending the night. Pemaquid Point Lighthouse Park is another popular spot.

HIKING

Acadia National Park and the gateway town of Bar Harbor are beautiful but busy in summer, so be prepared for traffic and crowded trails.

For a lovely, doable alternative, consider a day in Camden, with a hike up Mount Battie. A poem by Edna St. Vincent Millay, "Renascence," engraved on a plaque at the top, describes the stunning view, with references to "three long mountains and a wood" and "three islands in a bay."

For serious hikers, the Appalachian Trail runs through Maine, terminating atop Mount Katahdin in Baxter State Park. Depending on your route and fitness level, a hike up and down Katahdin's steep, rocky trails could take 10 to 12 hours, which means you'll run out of daylight if you don't start early. Parking for Katahdin hikes is also limited and often gone by 8 a.m., so consider driving up the night before.

The new (and controversial) Katahdin Woods and Waters National Monument doesn't offer many visitor services yet. Your car will need to be able to handle miles of uneven dirt roads to access hiking trails. For hikers, the Barnard Mountain Trail isn't particularly challenging (4½ miles or 7 km round trip), but the payoff is the view from the top, straight across, of Mount Katahdin. (The mountain is not in Katahdin Woods and Waters, but the unimpeded view is spectacular.)

WHITEWATER

Whitewater trips are available on several Maine rivers. My favorite outfitter is Moxie Outdoor Adventures, based in West Forks, which offers an all-day Kennebec River trip that's part paddling like crazy through Class IV rapids and part scenic wilderness float trip. Midday, boats are beached on an island where guides cook steak and chicken over a fire. On one trip, we even saw a moose en route to our launch spot. Warning: You will get soaked. Bring a quick-drying fleece to wear over a swimsuit and shoes (not flip-flops) to wear in the water.

MOOSE

You can find moose-watching tours on land and water. I've enjoyed sunset boat trips to see moose on Moosehead Lake, but as with any such excursion, there are no guarantees that you'll see the wildlife you came for. In rural and northern areas, moose present serious driving hazards, especially at dawn, dusk and after dark, so watch out (and be careful what you wish for).

FOR KIDS

Portland Children's Museum is fun for a rainy day. Aquaboggan Water Park in Saco offers slides, wave pools and mini-golf. Old-fashioned fairs take place around the state all summer, featuring rides, games, farm animal displays and more. One friend told me his little girl's favorite Maine outing was chasing butterflies at the Coastal Maine Botanical Gardens .

SHOPPING

Freeport is home to dozens of outlet stores along with the flagship for L.L. Bean. Take your picture in front of the massive boot by the Bean entrance. Note for insomniacs: Bean's flagship is open 24/7.

THE ARTS

In Portland, visit Henry Wadsworth Longfellow's house (he wrote the poem "Paul Revere's Ride") or take a Stephen King tour of Bangor to see places that inspired his spooky tales. In Cushing, tour the Olson House where Andrew Wyeth painted "Christina's World" and see Wyeth paintings at Rockland's Farnsworth Museum . The Portland Museum of Art offers tours of painter Winslow Homer's waterfront studio and house on Prouts Neck. Music festivals abound as well, from classical to folk.

BOAT RIDES

Rent a kayak or canoe, or take a ferry, like the ones to Monhegan Island or from Portland to the islands of Casco Bay . There are fancy yachts, schooner rides and dinner cruises, along with lobster boats where you can watch a lobster trap being pulled in. Many port towns also offer nature boat rides. Just know that you could pay a lot of money to spend a few hours on the ocean and not see the whales, seals, eagles or puffins pictured in the brochure.

SEAFOOD

Everybody has a favorite place for lobster rolls and chowder. Look for simple "lobster shacks" on the water where you order at a counter and wait for your number to be called. I like Harraseeket Lunch and Lobster Company in South Freeport.

LODGING

Take your pick: campsites, B&Bs, motels, hotels, even upscale resorts. Or rent a rustic cottage, what Mainers refer to as a "camp." If you're lucky enough to be on the water, sit back and listen for those loons.

APPENDIX

AP

TRAVEL TIPS

SAVING TIME AND MONEY

HOW TO MAKE AIRLINE SCHEDULE CHANGES WORK FOR YOU

By Scott Mayerowitz

NEW YORK—Airline schedule changes are often frustrating. Suddenly a mid-morning flight shifts to one leaving before sunrise or a leisurely layover turns into a mad dash to the next gate.

Savvy travelers, however, realize that sometimes schedule changes—usually an hour or more—allow the freedom to make itinerary adjustments without paying hundreds of dollars in fees.

Airlines typically publish schedules 11 months in advance. Southwest Airlines generally keeps to its schedule but American

Airlines, Delta Air Lines and United Airlines make many changes during that time. Some shift flights by a minute or two. But others dramatically alter itineraries, and that's where fliers can benefit.

Let's say a family is flying from Orlando home to Boston. They really want the 4:30 p.m. flight to get a few extra hours at the pool. But that flight is $60 more per person than the 9 a.m. flight. So they book the earlier, cheaper flight.

A few months pass and the schedule changes. That 9 a.m. flight now leaves at 7:15 a.m. Most passengers might grumble and accept the very earlier wakeup. But they shouldn't.

That big of a schedule change provides fliers the ability to change—for free—to almost any other flight the airline offers, including the costlier 4:30 p.m. flight originally desired. Sometimes passengers can even shift their flight a day earlier or later, as long as they depart within 24 hours of their original time. Normally, such changes would cost $200 per passenger plus any difference of fare.

"The fact that you can change is generally made clear. They don't make it clear what you can change to," says Brett Snyder, who runs an air travel assistance company called Cranky Concierge. "The rules are crazy and complex."

A good rule of thumb is to call the airline if your flight shifts an hour or more. Travelers should also be aware of smaller changes that might turn a tight connection into one that breaks the airline's minimum amount of time allowed for a layover.

Minimum connection times vary by airline and airport and even by terminal. For instance, on domestic itineraries Delta allows as little as 35 minutes to connect in Atlanta, United 30 minutes in San Francisco and American 25 minutes in Phoenix.

The general rule: if your connection has shrunk to under 45 minutes, call the airline.

"They tend to be pretty flexible as long as it is a legitimate change," Snyder says.

Fliers should be aware of alternatives. Go to the airline's website and search flights by schedule. When calling to for a change, ask for specific flights. Also, check other airlines. You might be able to get a refund and buy a new ticket on another carrier. However, airfare typically increases closer to the date of travel.

TSA PRECHECK:
HOW IT WORKS

By Scott Mayerowitz

NEW YORK—Flyers facing extremely long airport security lines might want to consider becoming members of the Transportation Security Administration's PreCheck, an expedited screening program that can speed travelers through the checkpoint.

Q. What is PreCheck?

A. The program allows previously vetted fliers to use special lanes at the checkpoint. Shoes, belts and light jackets stay on. Laptops and liquids stay in bags. And these fliers go through standard metal detectors rather than the explosive-detecting full-body scanners most pass through.

Q. How do fliers join?

A. Travelers get PreCheck if they are a member of one of the Customs and Border Protection's expedited entry programs—Global Entry, Nexus and Sentri—or by joining directly with the TSA. Membership in these programs ranges from $50 to $100 for five years. Travelers can fill out an application online and it then takes some time for the government to approve the application and schedule an in-person interview, typically at an airport. Those without a passport can just get PreCheck for $85.

Q. How do the airlines know who is a member?

A. Once approved, travelers get a "known traveler number." If they enter that in frequent flier programs or while making a reservation online, the airline knows of their PreCheck qualification. Then, when a boarding pass is generated a check is made with the TSA and usually PreCheck is granted and added to the document.

Q. Is it good on all airlines?

A. Most major U.S. carriers participate and many international airlines are signing on. The following airlines were members as early 2018: Aeromexico, Air Canada, Air France, Alaska Airlines, All Nippon Airways, Allegiant Air, American Airlines, Aruba Airlines, Avianca, Boutique Airlines, Brussels Airlines, Cape Air, Cathay Pacific Airways, Contour Aviation, Copa Airlines, Delta Air Lines, Dominican Wings, Emirates, Etihad Airways, Finnair,

Frontier Airlines, Hawaiian Airlines, InterCaribbean Airways, JetBlue Airways, Key Lime Air, KLM Royal Dutch Airlines, Korean Air, Lufthansa, Miami Air International, OneJet, Philippine Airlines, Seaborne Airlines, Silver Airways, Singapore Airlines, Southern Airways Express, Southwest Airlines, Spirit Airlines, Sun Country Airlines, Sunwing Airlines, Swift Air, Turkish Airlines, United Airlines, Virgin Atlantic, WestJet, World Atlantic and Xtra Airways.

CREDIT CARDS:
TRAVEL REWARDS VS CASH BACK

By Scott Mayerowitz

NEW YORK—Many frequent flyers love charging their way to a free vacation.

Rewards credit cards lure us in with dreams of a free trip to some warm tropical beach.

You're going to spend money. Why not get a vacation out of it?

The truth is, these cards make sense only for those who spend lots of money, and quickly.

The better value for most travelers, especially those flying domestic coach, is a cash back credit card.

There are a number of factors to consider when choosing a credit card. First, a major caveat: None of these cards—rewards or cash back—make sense unless you pay your bill in full each month. If you don't, any rewards earned will be washed away by interest payments.

CASH VS POINTS

The beauty of cash is that there are no restrictions. Forget desperately hoping that the airline opens up enough mileage seats on the flight you want. Or worse, locking yourself into one airline—just because you have miles—that requires a connection when there is a cheap, nonstop flight on another carrier.

The Citi Double Cash card and the Fidelity Rewards Visa Signature Card both offer 2 percent cash back on all spending. No special quarterly rewards bonuses to track. Just 2 percent back on everything.

Why is this better than frequent flier miles?

A typical domestic roundtrip ticket costs 25,000 miles on American Airlines, Delta Air Lines and United Airlines.

Having a credit card with one of those airlines earns you one mile for every dollar spent—more for purchases with the airline. That means you would have to spend about $25,000 on a credit card to get a free ticket.

That same $25,000 spent on a cash-back card would earn you $500. The average domestic roundtrip ticket is less than $400.

If you charge less than $25,000 a year, cash back makes even more sense. You might only earn $150 or $200 in rewards a year. But you can stash that money away to pay for part of your next flight instead of hoping to eventually have enough miles for that trip.

ANNUAL FEES

There are cards with higher cash back rates in certain categories as well as many travel cards but they come with sometimes steep annual fees. For many families, that fee can wipe away any savings.

Let's compare a no-fee, 2-percent cash-back card with a card that has a $95 annual fee. It takes $4,750 in charges on that 2-percent cash-back credit card just to earn $95 in rebates. If you are earning miles or some other currency with that annual fee card, your first $5,000 in charges basically cover the fee. For somebody who charges $80,000 a year, that might not be an issue. But for somebody charging $10,000, they are paying a fee and won't even get enough miles for a free trip.

But don't necessarily dismiss a card just because it carries an annual fee.

Most of the major airline credit cards offer free checked bags for the primary cardholder and—with some airlines—some of the people traveling with them; as long as everybody is on the same reservation. Since checking a bag typically costs $25 each way, that $95 annual fee could pay for itself if three bags are checked roundtrip a year. You don't even have to make other charges on the card, sticking to your cash-back card for everyday spending.

Amtrak's credit card, with a $79 fee, comes with a free companion ticket, potentially making it worthwhile for frequent train riders. A roundtrip ticket from Boston to New York could easily top $200.

SIGNUP BONUSES

Finally, there are those eye-popping signup bonuses.

The Chase Sapphire Reserve Card made headlines when it launched with a 100,000-point signup bonus after spending $4,000. Those points can be worth up to $1,500 in travel rewards. It carries a $450 annual fee but $300 of that is refunded for spending on travel. While that deal is long gone, many cards routinely offer anywhere between 30,000 to 50,000 miles in signup bonuses.

So, if you have good credit and can meet the minimum spend within the short time period, you can quickly pad your frequent flier balances.

In other words: Get the card for the signup bonus and then cancel it before the next annual fee hits.

Just be warned, credit card companies are starting to cap the number of cards you can have and are putting lifetime limits on signup bonuses.

AIRLINE MILES:
WHAT YOU NEED TO KNOW

By David Koenig

DALLAS—Airline loyalty programs are losing much of their allure even for frequent flyers, and the rules for navigating the system have changed.

Flying is no longer the best way to earn miles or points. The biggest bang for your buck comes from signing up for the right credit card.

And those come-ons from the airline to sell you miles? Ignore them unless you are very close to a qualifying for a big trip.

Frequent-flyer programs get relatively little attention from Wall Street, and their financial importance to the airlines is not widely understood by travelers, who just hope to earn a free flight now and then.

Airline profits are subject to vagaries like the price of fuel, the actions of competitors on key routes, even the weather. Amid all that uncertainty, the airlines have found a reliable source of revenue in selling miles to banks, which then use the miles to persuade consumers to sign up for the cards and use them as much as possible.

"The bottom line is that the business of selling miles is a very profitable one and has proven historically to be far less cyclical than the core airline," Joseph DeNardi, a Stifel analyst who tracks airlines, said this month in a note to clients.

The downside for airline customers is that the world is awash in frequent-flier miles, and the airlines are constantly making each mile, or point, less valuable. Many trips don't earn as many miles or points as they once did, and the price for claiming a reward flight keeps going up. In many cases, availability of reward seats on flights has gotten worse.

"It is harder to use miles at the price that people are expecting to pay," says Gary Leff, who writes the View from the Wing travel blog.

Even for frequent flyers like Leff, a once-cherished benefit of the miles—using them to upgrade to first class—has been diminished because airlines sell more of those upgrades for cash.

That doesn't mean travelers shouldn't sign up for the airline programs. After all, there is no charge for joining.

It does require rethinking how to earn, keep and redeem miles. Many of the strategies revolve around credit cards:

— Watch credit card offers for bonuses. Banks often offer the biggest bang. JPMorgan Chase shook up the sector in 2016 with a 100,000-mile bonus for signing up for the Sapphire Reserve card, which came with a hefty annual fee.

— Even if you make purchases with another card, consider getting the card of the airline you usually fly to enjoy benefits such as priority boarding and free bag-checking, even on so-called basic economy tickets. If you check a bag a few times a year, you will more than offset the annual fee.

— To stretch your miles, redeem them to fly midweek. Brian Karimzad of MileCards.com says it takes an average 30,574 miles for a Tuesday flight but 41,332 for a Sunday trip.

— Don't let miles expire. On American Airlines, which runs the biggest frequent-flyer program, you don't have to fly, you just have to make a purchase within 18 months on partners that range from other airlines to restaurants and flower shops. Miles on Delta Air Lines and JetBlue Airways don't expire.

— Ignore your airline when it sends yet another email asking if you'd like to buy miles. The exception is when you are just a few miles short of earning a big trip, says John DiScala, who runs the JohnnyJet.com travel website.

— Use 'em while you've got 'em. The value of your miles won't go up.

— Airlines often raise the number of miles needed for certain flights, with United Airlines being the most recent example. Airlines used to announce big mile-price increases once every several years but now make smaller hikes more frequently. "Either way you're going to pay more three years from now," says Karimzad.

— Over the past several years, American, Delta, United and Southwest have all linked rewards to how much customers spend, not how many miles or flights they take. That means frequent-flyer programs are a better deal now for people who buy expensive tickets, such as business class.

— The change has discouraged "mileage runs," the cheap but long flights that die-hards would take just to puff up their frequent-flyer accounts.

— "It has weeded out a lot of people who were gaming it —you can't blame the airlines for wanting to do that," DiScala says, "but it stings as a consumer."

TRAVEL SPOTLIGHT

CRUISING

CRUISING:
A CONVERSATION WITH EXPERTS

By The Associated Press

PORT MIAMI, Florida—What's new in cruising? What are the trends? What challenges does the industry face?

The Associated Press hosted a unique forum on cruising on Jan. 4, 2018, aboard the Seabourn Sojourn ship in Port Miami, Florida, where three experts talked about these and other issues. The panelists also offered advice and insider tips on cruising.

The event took place with a live audience of Seabourn passengers who asked questions. The forum was taped and aired as two episodes of AP Travel's weekly podcast "Get Outta Here!" (available on iTunes).

Here are excerpts from the conversation moderated by former AP Travel Editor Beth Harpaz with panelists Carnival Corp. CEO Arnold Donald, speaking in his capacity as chairman of CLIA, the Cruise Lines International Association (identified in the transcript as AD); Carolyn Spencer Brown, editor at large, CruiseCritic.com (CSB), and Jane Wooldridge, Miami Herald business editor (JW). The text has been edited for length and clarity.

WHAT'S NEW IN CRUISING?

CSB: People love the razzle-dazzle, the slides, the zip lines, the bowling alleys. But what we're seeing at CruiseCritic is a huge shift to people who are interested in small ship cruising whether it's luxury, river, expedition. People are looking at cruising as a way to be a traveler rather than be tourists. What that means for a lot of folks is picking itineraries, spending a lot of time in ports of call, overnight in ports of call, that give you shore excursion options that really help you meet local families or learn local culture or experience the regions and the destinations in a personal way.

The second trend is a really positive trend for cruise in general. We are seeing lines of every ilk in size embrace healthy eating, fitness, all sorts of positive, new kinds of approaches to yoga and all that kind of thing, so that you can go on a cruise and you can be healthy and you can continue your regimen from home or start a new one.

JW: The thing I'm most excited about that we're going to see this year and next year is a growth in the number of expedition ships and the good news is that they're going great places. There are more and more of them. I think the bad news is that the very nature of being able to go to a lot of these places and the necessity for a low-impact small ship means that the prices on those experiences are significant.

The other thing, there are a ton of new ships coming on. . . . And when you bring on ships, when any cruise line brings on new ships, and they've got the latest razzle-dazzle on it, then they go back and refit their older ships because you don't want to have one kind of experience on one of their ships and a really different experience on another ship the same brand. So I think that all bodes very well for consumers because there's going to be a lot of fresh product.

AD: Cruise has been growing quite a bit has grown since 2008. If you project into 2018, it's gone from a little over 16 million individual guests a year to 27.2 million, projected 2018. Overall an average of a million plus people a year additionally cruising each and every year. So with that many more people cruising, everything they said is true. There is an appetite for small ships, there's an appetite for expedition but there's also a huge appetite for the large ships.

There is absolutely a trend in general in society, more about experiences than about things. People often ascribe that to millennials. But as you know for every generation it's true, but at the same time it's all about fun.

There's actually 27 new ships coming in 2018 including river. . . . A third of all the people who cruise have average household incomes of less than $80,000. So it's accessible to everyone. And it's just such a tremendous vacation experience and still a tremendous vacation value because the equivalent land-based vacation costs considerably more than what you will cost you on a cruise.

IS THE OLD CRUISING STEREOTYPE STILL TRUE: CRUISES ARE FOR NEWLYWEDS, THE OVERFED AND THE NEARLY DEAD?

JW: Well when I first started covering cruising, that was true. The industry was saying, 'There's a cruise for everyone,' and I kept looking at them thinking, 'mmm, no, there really isn't.' Well today there really is. There is some sort of opportunity whatever your travel style is, with the exception of budget backpackers ... There are cruises for adventurous people, there cruises for people with mobility issues. . . . And there are cruises for really literally every sort of orientation, whether it's a cultural orientation or whatever it is, there is really a product that will suit almost everybody at some point in their life. . . . particularly with multiple generations. It is really hard to deal with a baby, an adult child or a grandparent all in one setting and very many kinds of arrangements. You can do it if you rent a house for a week but then you're a little too much on top of each other and you're always arguing about who's turn it is to do the dishes. I don't do dishes on cruises. Nobody does dishes on cruises except people who are paid to do that.

It is easy to be overfed on a cruise, but it is not as difficult to be judicious as it once might have been because there's been much more emphasis on healthy food, healthy eating.

AD: Certainly there are a lot of myths about cruising . . . There are so many different brands. Each one caters to a different psychographic segment. And all of us are in different psychographics segments at a given point in time. If you're traveling with a romantic interest, that's one experience. If you're traveling with your grandparents and your parents and your kids, that's a different experience. And so those experiences all are different but the trick for us in the industry is to make certain that the brands are consistent. . . . For us word of mouth is still the most powerful marketing tool. The brands sale full, ours and the rest of the industry. The ships are full. So people obviously love the experience. But once someone goes on a cruise and they've chosen the right one for them, they become a lifelong advocate.

I would tell anyone out there that are still questioning a cruise experience, just talk to someone they know that that has gone on one. And hopefully that person went on the right one for them and someone they trust and know it and they'll realize that it's probably very different than what they think.

CSB: What's really changed in 20 years is not only that the industry has grown so much but that it's grown in a way that every brand, every cruise line out there is really marketing a particular lifestyle. It's telling a story about who should be on that ship and if you and I go back to the whole multigenerational thing, you know you want to make sure you pick a cruise that has a spa for mom and tea and bridge for the grandparents and the kids club for the kids.

Also listen to travel agents. Travel agents are very well schooled in cruise and listen to them. . . . The worst thing you can do is pick a cruise based on price alone. Pick a cruise based on the story the line is telling about what it represents.

WHAT'S IN A CRUISE FOR MILLENNIALS?

AD: CLIA . . .reported from a study that was done that showed that millennials overindex on cruising. ...They have more of a preference for cruising than any other generation. The reason is simple: . . . A cruise is an experience. It's a community, it's an experience, you're not buying a thing. It's not a product, not a pair of pants or a phone. It's a real experience. And so millennials tend to overindex seeking out experiences and cruise is an affordable experience. And so it's a great value relative to land-based vacations.

A lot of these young people have been on cruises when they were younger. There are still a lot of newlyweds on cruises. Well guess who the newlyweds are these days. Primarily millennials. So the cruise industry is carrying lots of millennials.

JW: I live in Miami. People here do grow up with cruising. Every kid has been on a cruise with their parents. And so now that they are in their 20s and 30s, they've already had that experience. Two other things: It really is much less expensive to go on a cruise than it is to even spend a long weekend in some places.

The other thing is that cruise lines have become better, though I don't think they're there all the way there, but they've become better about excursions that do provide really authentic experiences, beyond walking around the town and looking at another jewelry store. There are really very good and more diversified excursions now than there were for a long time. I don't think you bridged the far end of that limit yet in the industry but you see things like overnight excursions to go trek with the gorillas in Africa. You see excursions where you can sail a tall sailing ship. There are a lot of different things that make it a real authentic experience than there were 20 years ago for sure.

CSB: Millennials . . . do not have a lock on wanting experiences over things. In fact I think the baby boomers are much further along in terms of wanting experiences over things. They've got all the things. They're trying to give them away and nobody wants them. They want cultural experiences. They want itineraries that are more immersive. They want more time in port. The things the millennials want actually have been developing for years and are already out there.

And millennials I know who I work with, who travel, say, 'We resent being marketed to as a generation that has a lock on these qualities of the cruise experience.' These are qualities of the cruise experience—being a traveler rather than a tourist, being active and recreational and healthy—that I think will serve the industry for the next 30 years. . . . All this focus on those millennials is obscuring the fact that everybody wants more immersive, more connections, more personal experiences when they travel. And that goes with being on board as well as onshore in terms of the community that Arnold referenced earlier. That's the thing I think that keeps people coming back that they don't expect is what it's like to build community onboard as well as how the experience is.

JW: It's a psychographic not a demographic. . . .It's a mindset. My husband who is not so young, he loves all the same things that his sons half his age love. And I think one of the quintessential aspects of baby boomers is that we are essentially the Peter Pan generation. We're never going to age, we're never going to grow up and we're never going to quit wanting to do all the stuff that we have been able to do. And so I really think it's a mindset. If you want to get out there, boy, you know it doesn't matter what age you are, you just want that experience. And for boomers it's maybe even more important because as you said you've had all this stuff. So that doesn't have as much meaning for you. And then you begin to see on the horizon some day when perhaps not all will be possible for you. And so then you start going, you know, I really need to get moving on this bucket list thing. And I think that that becomes a real motivator.

CSB: And I do want to add one thing that the most vibrant group we see coming into cruise who's never cruised before isn't necessarily millennials. It's the 60-plus who swore up down and sideways they would never try cruise. But now they still want to go to Tibet. They still want to go to Africa. They still want to do these things. But they want to be a little bit more comfortable than they were in the past. They don't want to give up being independent and finding their own way if they want to but they want to be more comfortable and they're really flocking to cruise in a big way.

AD: You know the demographic thing comes out of the old marketing where you marketed by age, income, geography, location, zip code, whatever. Those are demographics and the psychographic is attitude. It's your preferences. So we have a couple of brands and if you look at a distribution curve of the guests, they look identical, demographics, in terms of age and income distribution, you would say, well, it's the same people. But if you stood in Ketchikan, Alaska, any one of you can stand there and you will go, Holland America, Princess. You can tell who's on which ship just by looking at them and the differences, the orientation of the people. You know Princess is more Hong Kong luxury kind of hotel, it's Southern California-ish. They want to kayak to the adventure, to the museum or whatever. And then Holland America's kind of Midwest classic, you know Warren Buffett, plaid shirt orientation. They want a really nice bus to go to whatever museum they want to go to and it's just preferences. Neither one is right or wrong. They have as much money as each other, they're the same age. They just like different things.

DO WE NEED TRAVEL AGENTS FOR CRUISES?

CSB: I'm organizing a family reunion kind of cruise in June to Bermuda. I have very little to do with it. I've handed the whole thing over a travel agent. I must be prehistoric. But to me the question is, why wouldn't you use a travel agent. It's no charge to me. There are so many moving parts on a cruise that you really, why not take the help when you can get it. I probably know more than my travel agent about cruise, but she knows more about the ins and outs of what you need to book when and she gives us that information. ... I'm a big advocate of do your homework before you go to a travel agent. Go online. It's the best homework you'll ever have. You figure out which lines you like and then you and where you want to go and then you hand it to a travel agent and let them sort it out and figure it out and hand over your credit card. I can't imagine why you wouldn't use a good qualified travel agent.

JW: I have also done this family reunion thing. And we also handed it over to a cruise agent because I cannot possibly deal with everybody's air arrangements in this, that and the other. What's really important is having a good travel agent who is really knowledgeable about the brand that you want to sail and is smart enough to ask you a lot of questions about your preferences. . . . I would also say that while cruising as an experience is one of the most easiest things once you get on board, it is a very complex-decision making process. Where do I want the cabin to be. Do I want the package around the drinks, do I not want the package around the drinks. What exactly do I want and need. Is the itinerary going to be exactly what I want. And so I think that the complexity of that decision making upfront really benefits from somebody who can say, no, this is a little bit better cabin for you because of this and it's closer to the elevator and there are X number of elevator banks and this one's really good for you. Or you know, gee, if you're really particular about a certain food allergy, this line is very good at working with that. I think that kind of in-depth knowledge is not something that you can find easily on your own on the internet.

AD: Travel agents and travel professionals still book the vast majority of cruises. And that will continue for quite a while because all the things they just said. Our job is to exceed our guests' expectations and that's what we want to do every time. The best thing to get a good start on that is have the guests on the right ship. The right brand. And the best way for us to do that is to find a travel professional, a good one. And there are lots of good ones that really understand and they'll ask the right questions and they'll ascertain what's going to be best for this group, this family, this individual and if they get on the right ship then as an industry we have them for life. If they get on the wrong ship, they may have an OK time, but when they go back and tell their friends who have all these myths about cruising, 'How was your cruise?' 'It was OK.' That's not going to motivate those people to want to cruise. And so we need to exceed their expectations. The first step for us is the travel professionals.

CSB: One of the things the travel agency community is going through is a huge transition from being bookers to trip planners. While cruise ships and cruise lines have their own shore excursion programs, your travel agent may also have some really great access to unique bespoke experiences they can create for you in port. And one example I got from one passenger was he went to Prague for the first time and he was a pianist and he wanted to sit where Liszt played in his own house and so they arranged for him to go to Liszt's house, the composer, and actually play on his piano. The travel agent said bring your favorite piece of music. Who would ever forget something like that. So there are other uses for travel agents, plus the pre and the post, if you're going into town for a longer stay, they can really help you with that. They can make it seamless and you have someone to go to something does go wrong.

OVERTOURISM, WHEN TOO MANY TOURISTS HARM THE LOCAL QUALITY OF LIFE, IS AN ISSUE IN MANY PLACES. WHERE DO CRUISES FIT IN AND WHAT IS THE SOLUTION?

JW: Cruise lines could be more proactive about working as an industry together to see that there are not too many ships in port. One of the places that really works well is Antarctica. Only vessels with 200 passengers or fewer are allowed into Antarctic waters are allowed to make landings and the ships all talk to each other in the morning and at night to make sure that they're not going to be in the same place as another ship at that time because the ecology there cannot take it.

CSB: I used to live on St. Thomas for a year back in 2000. Let me just tell you on Tuesday and Wednesday when there's seven or eight ships in, you didn't go to town. You stayed away. Although I think the industry actually is doing quite a good job these days or better job of being more sensitive to the fact that some ports are not going to be great for their own passengers' experiences and by that I mean, they're creating itineraries, they're trying to take them out of the big cities and into the smaller ones. For example the country-specific itineraries is a big trend that CruiseCritic highlighted this year. So you can go around Japan, you can go around Iceland, around Croatia or through Croatia. . . .They're creating new itineraries. They're juggling itineraries so they're not in town on the same day that seven other ships are in town. So the experience is more pleasant and I think those kinds of activity, actions by the cruise industry are very, very critical.

The ports themselves have every right to just say no. You know, they're not saying no. And that's what's happening now is we're seeing locals rise up in Barcelona in particular. Locals have said we've had it but you know the port has to say no, no more ships or we need to balance them better and we're not really seeing that sort of approach that at this point.

AD: If the locals are not happy, the guests will not have a good time period. We're all about exceeding expectations and not about taking people to places that aren't going to have a good time. That's number one. The second thing is that I talked about all the cabins in the world don't add up to 2 percent of hotel rooms. ... Overtourism is a legitimate issue. And as part of tourism, we have to be part of the solution. We can't just say, 'look, those aren't our guests and we're only a small part.' . . . In the end even if it's one ship, our guests won't want to go to Old Town if it's overcrowded and they can't see the things they want to see. So in the end it's all in our self-interests to make sure Venice is Venice and Old Town Dubrovnik is Old Town and Barcelona is Barcelona. If it changes and becomes just a sea of tourists hanging out on the cathedral steps, buying one dollar items, smoking, then nobody wants to go. The locals hate it. And our guests hate it. . . .

We have to be very sensitive and we have to stagger, we have to communicate. We have to lead by example and I'm proud to say and often in all these places Dubrovnik, the mayor talked to us and these places, they actually want more cruise guests because they feel the cruise guests are real guests. They don't spend money? You know that's not true. The cruise guests do. They go into town. They dine and go into coffee shops, they don't buy a one dollar little thing. They actually get something made or they buy a piece of local art, they immerse in the culture and they're very respectful because they're there for that reason. And so again if we lead by example, publicize the kind of correct behaviors, encourage that, show people that, work with the locals to stagger times and flow the people into different locations instead of everybody coming at the same time to Old Town.

The reality is overtourism is a much bigger issue. Cruise gets blamed like in Venice. Often the locals see the big ship from Market Square. So it is visible. So it becomes a symbol but it's actually not where most of the people (are coming from).

AUDIENCE QUESTIONS

FORMAL WEAR

STEPHEN FELD: My question is about the trend I see—I've been cruising for a number of years—toward informality. I know that every cruise ship's dress code seems to be dumbing down a bit except Cunard. I mean you're still dressed up at night. Most people are in black tie. You need a jacket every night. I notice even on Seabourn when we used to have to wear a jacket and tie and black tie, now it's just a jacket. And I'm wondering is this a this is a trend, is this is this to attract a certain demographic, psychographic. I don't know. . . . Was it a conscious trend in order to attract people or was it just a reflection of where the world is going.

AD: It is conscious but it comes from our guests. So what we do in our case is we always ask our guests. So we're constantly asking the guests what they want. The brands are engineered for the guests that frequent those brands a lot. As the guest preferences shift then we will shift without changing the brand. We'll shift to the preference of the guests. Cunard is going to stay formal. I mean it is the classic cruise as you know: Queen Mary 2, high tea at 3. That's what it is.

CSB: I'm going to be a contrarian on this. ... We were on Regal Princess Princess Cruises a couple of months ago and they didn't have formal night every night. But they had a couple of formal nights and you could see these were not black tie folks. And you could see how excited they were about getting dressed up, getting their pictures taken, having a very special moment. Even more so with the kids who came with these fabulous outfits.

It was like Prom Night. People didn't want to do it every night.

But they when they did it, they did it with gusto. I did a prediction and I was being a little contrarian. But I did a prediction that where we've gone so far over here with casual wear that we're going to have to come back into the middle. Maybe we won't go back to where we were, where it's three nights of this cruise at this time in nice restaurant that's too complicated. But having an option on the cruise that fits the right psychographic is absolutely, makes for a magical evening.

SINGLE SUPPLEMENTS

JERRY AMOS: My question is somewhat personal since I'm traveling as a single now. And I'm going to put it to you because I'm looking now for to go to Antarctica next in February of 2019. Now I'm looking at two lines, looking at the Quest and I'm also looking at National Geographic. . . . When you first look at it, it looks like National Geographic is more expensive. It is in fact, if you're traveling with someone else. If you're traveling as a single, it's cheaper because they have eight single rooms. I just wonder if the industry is looking at that issue because there a lot of people who would like to travel are single but the cost could get pretty ridiculous actually.

AD: It depends on every brand and every brand is different and there are brands that have single rooms that are built in and there are those that have double rooms that they'll offer at single room kind of plus price as opposed to having to pay for the entire cabin. But every brand is different. And what happens in the industry, to be candid, is that when you're building a ship you think about this square footage and you know the revenue the recover the investment on the ship and so on and so single rooms often become a tough economic factor to make work. So usually end up with those when you have public spaces and you can't quite get you know the full cabins in and then later in terms of pricing them because the ships tend to be sold out, you know, it's tougher to get you breaks and stuff. But every brand is different. . . . The practical reality is that you know the ships are so full that it's hard to give up a cabin and give up the revenue from a real business practical standpoint.

JW: One thing I often see is in the early fall often there are a number of lines will come out waving the single supplements for the next few months because it's a slower season for them.

CSB: The solo issue, it's a really huge issue for our readers. Huge. And I think it's up to you guys in a big way. Make a lot of noise if you're unhappy with it, make noise, make a fuss because if you book Lindblad, let Seabourn know why you booked away because I think that if you're paying 200 percent for your cabin, you're paying the price of someone else. . . . I think single travel is a huge growing thing. But consumers have to make a fuss, make noise and get that rule kind of mixed up a little bit.

HOW TO FIND A TRAVEL AGENT

MELVIN: As a layman, who rarely goes on trips, I want to know is there any chance that you could guide me as to that professional travel agent that has your knowledge and has the moxie to give us the directions.

CSB: The best way to find a qualified good cruise travel agent is to go to professional organizations that train and really register them . . . certify them. So there's CLIA, which Arnold is serving as the head of. Cruise Lines International Association, Cruising. org, and there's ASTA, the American Society of Travel Agents, and they all put their travel agents through their paces.

You have to work hard to stay on those levels and you can go to those websites and find travel agents either in your area or in your specialty. You can search and dice and slice and then reach out. It's no longer necessary to go down to Main Street and walk in and meet somebody but you still can. So use those two organizations to get started and talk to friends who've worked with good travel agents as well. But those two organizations are bonafide.

SMALL SHIP CRUISING

By Beth J. Harpaz

Cruise ships carrying thousands of people have gotten all the headlines in cruising in recent years. But there's also been a boom in small ships, river cruises and what's known as expedition cruising on ships designed to sail in places like the polar regions.

But the experience of sailing on a ship that carries a few hundred or even 1,000 people is very different from the experience of cruising on a ship so big that it's practically a floating city with dozens of eateries and water parks with massive slides.

"It's not about the slides," said Eva Santiago, assistant cruise director aboard the Seabourn Sojourn. Santiago was one of 360 crew members on a recent sailing with 450 guests. That ratio of nearly 1:1 staff to passengers offers more personalized service than is possible on a ship four or five times bigger. Smaller ships won't have a full production of a Broadway show, like "Hairspray" on a Royal Caribbean ship this year, but you might find Santiago singing opera on the deck of the Sojourn under the stars.

Small ship cruises are usually more expensive than big ships but they're also usually all-inclusive. That means alcohol, shore excursions and other items that you'd pay extra for on a big cruise ship are covered in the fare for a small ship.

Smaller ships may also be more understated in style, with a casual elegance that's a stark contrast to the glitzy Vegas-style decor that's often a hallmark of massive spaces on bigger ships.

Or if they're expedition ships with a focus on rugged adventures to see wildlife and scenery in the Galapagos or Greenland, the ships may have fewer creature comforts onboard but a more compelling experience on land than you'd get in a typical port of call in a beach town.

But smaller scale doesn't preclude smaller ships, especially the newer ones, from offering special features.

Two new ships from Ponant in 2018, Le Laperouse and Le Champlain, have a lounge called the Blue Eye. Located beneath the water line of the ship, the Blue Eye has two windows and digital screens showing images from underwater cameras, and it also transmits underwater sounds and vibrations.

New in 2019 from AmaWaterways, the AmaMagna has a built-in expedition platform for watersports, making it easy for guests to use paddleboards, Zodiacs or kayaks.

New in 2018 from Scenic Luxury Tours & Cruises is a luxury yacht called the Scenic Eclipse, with a 228-guest capacity (200 for Antarctica, where passenger numbers are regulated). The Eclipse will serve both polar regions and everything in between in the Atlantic. Its amenities include helicopters and a submarine for guest use.

Many smaller ships also specialize in far-flung itineraries that may be unfamiliar to Americans more accustomed to Caribbean cruising. Paul Gauguin Cruises, named for the French painter who visited Tahiti in the 1890s, offers trips to French Polynesia. Celestyal Cruises homeports in Greece and specializes in the region, but also has seven-day trips to Cuba that offer more time on the island than big cruise ships with one or two nights in Cuba as part of a longer Caribbean sailing.

Even European river cruising has more options than many people may realize. "In Europe, you can cruise from Belgium and Holland all the way to the Black Sea," said AmaWaterways founder Rudi Schreiner. "That's 3,000 miles of uninterrupted waterways in Europe."

TIPS FOR FIRST-TIME CRUISERS

By Joe Kafka

What's not to like about cruising? Ocean views, exotic ports and beautiful ships with fine food, abundant activities and great entertainment.

Today's ships are like floating cities, carrying thousands of passengers, and each year, new and bigger vessels are launched with ever more unique features. New ships offer everything from menus designed by celebrity chefs to sophisticated fitness centers and spas, kids' clubs and recreation ranging from basketball to water slides to laser tag. Entertainment includes cabaret, dance clubs, blues clubs, Broadway shows, comedy and circus acts.

But if you've never done it, the idea of a cruise might be daunting. Here are some tips for first-timers.

BOOKING

Choose cabins according to your finances. Inside cabins are cheapest, ocean view is next, then rooms with a balcony, and most expensive, suites. If prone to motion sickness, lower decks and cabins closest to ship's center are the most stable. Peruse layouts online before picking a cabin and to familiarize yourself with the ship's features.

Every cruise line has a different style. To book the right ship for you, experts recommend using a travel agent. It doesn't cost extra and might save money, because agents often have access to deals.

PACKING, DEPARTURE AND BOARDING

Plan your wardrobe carefully, depending on itinerary and expected weather. Laundry and dry cleaning onboard are expensive.

The days of required formal wear—jackets, ties, evening gowns—at dinner are long gone, though some passengers will dress up.

Pack a power strip. Most cabins have only one or two outlets. Shampoo and soap are provided but you may bring your own—and there's no size limit like there is for flying.

If you're flying to your departure port, arrive a day ahead. If your flight is cancelled or delayed, you might miss the sailing.

Have reservation documents in hand when checking in at the terminal, along with required identification such as driver's license or passport. Lines can be long as departure time nears.

A mandatory muster drill—where everyone reports to a deck for safety and evacuation information—is held shortly after departure.

It takes a few hours for luggage to be delivered to cabins.

Smoking on ships is restricted to certain areas and not allowed in cabins.

WHAT'S FREE, WHAT'S NOT

No need for cash onboard. Cruises provide plastic cards (like credit cards) to charge purchases to your account and also as ID for exiting and reboarding the ship at ports.

Meals in dining rooms, buffets and poolside are included with cruise fare, and you may order more than one main course or dessert. Specialty restaurants charge extra and often get booked up, so make reservations ahead.

Water, coffee, tea, juice and milk are free. Alcohol and soda are not, except for the most upscale cruise lines. Cruises sell daily or weeklong alcohol and soft drink packages that may save you money, depending on your drinking habits.

Shows, gyms, water parks and many other facilities and activities are free. Some fitness classes are free, some are not. Spa services are extra. On a budget? Avoid the casino and gift shop.

Using cellphones at sea, if service is available, is costly. Consider putting phones in airplane mode. Most ships offer Wi-Fi packages but they're pricey, so you might wait to go online until you're at a hotspot in port.

On top of your cruise fare, cruise lines usually suggest an

amount to tip the staff, or automatically add daily tips to your bill for distribution among room stewards, wait staff and others. Tips are automatically added to alcohol.

EXCURSIONS

Shore excursions may be booked through the cruise line, or you can go off on your own in port or hire independent tour guides. Booking through the ship guarantees you will not be left behind if your tour is delayed for some reason. If you go off on your own and return late, the ship will leave without you.

ABOUT CARNIVAL CORPORATION

Carnival Corporation & plc, the world's largest leisure travel company, provides travelers around the globe with extraordinary vacations at an exceptional value. The company's portfolio of global cruise line brands includes Carnival Cruise Line, Fathom, Holland America Line, Princess Cruises and Seabourn in North America; P&O Cruises (UK) and Cunard in Southampton, England; AIDA Cruises in Rostock, Germany; Costa Cruises in Genoa, Italy; and P&O Cruises (Australia) in Sydney. Additionally, Carnival Corporation owns a tour company that complements its cruise operations: Holland America Princess Alaska Tours which operates in Alaska and the Yukon. Together, these brands comprise the world's largest cruise company with a fleet of 102 ships visiting more than 700 ports around the world. Learn more at http://www.carnivalcorp.com.

ACKNOWLEDGMENTS

The Associated Press would like to thank Beth Harpaz, Peter Costanzo, Scott Mayerowitz, Warren Levinson, Benjamin Snyder, Carolyn Lessard, Mike Bowser, Kevin Callahan and "Cruising Conversation" panelists: Arnold Donald, Carolyn Spencer Brown and Jane Wooldridge.

Additional thanks to Mike Flanagan and Ellie Beuerman of LDWW Group.

Special thanks to Roger Frizzell and the entire team at Carnival Corporation for making this project possible.

ABOUT THE PHOTOS

(In order or appearance)

1. A view from the deck of the Seabourn Sojourn cruise ship in the port of Miami, January 4, 2018. (AP Photo/Beth J. Harpaz)
2. A group of women wearing colorful woven clothes in Patacancha, Peru, October 3, 2015. (AP Photo/Fritz Faerber)
3. Shown is Edzna, a gem of a Mayan site an hour away from Campeche, December 19, 2016. (AP Photo/Amir Bibawy)
4. A member of the Dessena tribe poses for a picture in her village outside of Manaus, Brazil, October 11, 2017. (AP Photo/Peter Prengaman)
5. Bosnian Arian Kurbasic, the owner of the War Hostel in Sarajevo, stands with a lit candle in his hand next to a wall of one of the hostel rooms, November 12, 2016. (AP Photo/Amel Emric)
6. Tourists and residents walk across Tromostovje bridges in downtown Ljubljana, Slovenia, August 12, 2016. (AP Photo/Darko Bandic)
7. Poppies in full bloom in a field on a hilltop near Sommepy-Tahure, France, October 14, 2014. (AP Photo/Virginia Mayo)
8. Novelist Colson Whitehead speaks to fans after discussing his Pulitzer prize-winning book "The Underground Railroad" at the English-language bookstore Shakespeare and Company in Paris, June 20, 2017. (AP Photo/Russell Contreras)
9. Fonthip Boonmak left, James Feaver, center, and Boonmak's son Jimmy Harmer, right, gathering edible sea beet leaves near southern England's Jurassic Coast, July 12, 2016. (AP Photo/Jerry Harmer)
10. Members of the British punk band The Clash circa 1983. From left, Paul Simonon, Mick Jones, Joe Strummer and Terry Chimes. (AP Photo)
11. A carving found in the rocks along sunken green paths between the villages of Symondsbury and North Chideock, in Dorset, England, July 18, 2015. (AP Photo/Jerry Harmer)

12. Climbing St. Patrick's Mountain, Ireland. (Photo courtesy of Carolyn Lessard)
13. The summit of Ben Nevis, near Fort William, Scotland, October 2013. (AP Photo/Cara Anna)
14. French national highway 116 leads from the Mediterranean into the mountains of the Pyrenees with a lot of curves. (Photo: Thomas Muncke/picture-alliance/dpa/AP Images)
15. A Catalonia-style seafood paella that is being prepared by tourists at cooking class offered by cooking school Cook and Taste in Barcelona, Spain, June 8, 2016. (AP Photo/Marjorie Miller)
16. Visitors make their way through farmland in Barbadelo, northern Spain, October 16, 2010. (AP Photo/Maya Hasson)
17. A rented BMW motorcycle sits parked on a farm road in front of an Alpine view near Graun im Vinschgau, Italy, July 3, 2015. (AP Photo/Erik Schelzig)
18. Hot air balloons rise to the sky at sunrise in Cappadocia, central Turkey, November 15, 2010. (AP Photo/Uzay Hacaoglu)
19. The Trans-Siberian railroad taking a curve on a winter day near the Mongolian capital Ulan-Bator, Date Unknown. (AP Photo)
20. Stone piles crafted by ambitious trekkers a short walk from the Abisko Mountain Lodge in the northernmost stretch of Sweden's Kungsleden trail, September 2014. (AP Photo/Cara Anna)
21. Clouds waft across the trail along a ridge above the village of Ghorepani, in central Nepal, October 23, 2014. (AP Photo/ Malcolm Foster)
22. A tiger walks at the Ranthambore National Park in Sawai Madhopur, India, April 12, 2015. (AP Photo/Satyajeet Singh Rathore)
23. A visitor poses on one of Yasuda Kan's stone sculptures at the Benesse House, one of Naoshima Island's modern art museums, December 10, 2004. (AP Photo/Kenji Hall)
24. The early morning light hitting the hills of the Kepler Track in Te Anau, New Zealand, April 6, 2014. (AP Photo/Carey J. Williams)
25. Adriano Bastos, left, of Sao Paulo, Brazil, and Bea Marie Altieri, of Clermont, Fla., pose with Mickey Mouse after receiving trophies for winning their respective divisions in the Walt Disney World Marathon in Lake Buena Vista, Fla., January 12, 2003. (AP Photo/ Phelan M. Ebenhack)

26. The first snow of the season is seen near Tioga Pass in Yosemite National Park, Calif, September 21, 2017. (AP Photo/Anna Johnson)
27. Hikers on the South Kaibab Trail in Grand Canyon National Park, Ariz., September 27, 2010. (AP Photo/Carson Walker)
28. A view of the mountains surrounding the Lamar Valley in Yellowstone National Park, August 3, 2016. (AP Photo/Matthew Brown)
29. Tony Eiguren, left, owner of the Basque Market, serving a plate of paella to a lunch customer in Boise, Idaho, August 7, 2013. (AP Photo/Todd Dvorak)
30. A fully loaded hardtail mountain bike propped up by a trail-marking post on the Maah Daah Hey Trail near Medora, North Dakota, June 19, 2017. (AP Photo/Carey J. Williams)
31. A view of Glacier National Park in Montana from the park's famous Going-to-the-Sun Road, September 4, 2017. (AP Photo/Beth J. Harpaz)
32. A mural honoring the late Prince adorns a building in the Uptown area of Minneapolis, August 28, 2016. (AP Photo/Jim Mone)
33. The Mark Twain Boyhood Home & Museum in Hannibal, Mo., September 22, 2014. (AP Photo/Beth J. Harpaz)
34. The Delta Blues Museum in Clarksdale, Miss., March 10, 2017. (AP Photo/Beth J. Harpaz)
35. The Waccamaw River and is a quiet place to cool off on sultry South Carolina summer afternoons and about 15 miles from Myrtle Beach, May 22, 2013. (AP Photo/Bruce Smith)
36. A young girl statue reads "To Kill a Mockingbird" by author Harper Lee in Monroeville, Ala., July 13, 2015. (AP Photo/Brynn Anderson)
37. A maiden from the royal court of the Krewe of Endymion Mardi Gras parade smiles towards revelers in New Orleans, February 25, 2017. (AP Photo/Gerald Herbert)
38. Fog sits in the valley of the White Mountains as leaves change colors from Milan Hill in Milan, N.H., September 28, 2014. (AP Photo/Jim Cole)
39. Alexander Hamilton's tomb in the graveyard at Trinity Church in Lower Manhattan, August 22, 2014. (AP Photo/Beth J. Harpaz)
40. John Houghton, of Vermontville, N.Y., and his sled dog team, giving a ride to a couple, in a snow fall, around Mirror Lake in Lake Placid, N.Y., January 30, 2015. (AP Photo/Mel Evans, File)

41. Local Ethiopian farmers and their camels walk past the Obelisk steles area in Axum, April 2, 2005. (AP Photo/Boris Heger).

42. The beachside pool at the Terrou-Bi hotel in Dakar, Senegal, March 18, 2016. (AP Photo/Nicole Evatt)

43. Tourists stand in front of the rock-hewn Al Khazneh, Arabic for the Treasury, in the ancient city of Petra, Jordan, March 6, 2014. (AP Photo/Mohammad Hannon)

44. With the world tallest tower, Burj Khalifa, in background, tourists and visitors cross a bridge to Souk Al Bahar in Dubai, United Arab Emirates, April 13, 2015. (AP Photo/Kamran Jebreili)

45. Inside the bubble tram atop the Canton Tower in Guangzhou, China, October 14, 2015. (AP Photo/Nicole Evatt)

46. Bicycle wheels form part of an artwork in front of a cafe in the OCT Loft district of Shenzhen, China, April 22, 2016. (AP Photo/ Kelvin Chan)

47. The sunset over a ger at the Tsagaan Sum hot springs and tourist camp in Khoton Soum, Arkhangai province, Mongolia, July 7, 2016. (AP Photo/Nicole Evatt)

48. A Thai woman arranges flowers at Wat Pho temple in Bangkok, Thailand, April 1, 2008. (AP Photo/Sakchai Lalit)

49. Special instructions on how to operate the toilet are shown on the wall at a public toilet in Tokyo Station in Tokyo, January 14. 2017. (AP Photo/Koji Sasahara)

50. Silhouettes of people line the sky as they stand on a skyway suspension bridge through a Supertree grove at the Gardens by the Bay in Singapore, August 18, 2012. (AP Photo/Wong Maye-E)

51. Kayakers head out on the water from Le Meridien resort in Bora Bora, November 4, 2015. (AP Photo/Jennifer McDermott)

52. A cook stir-fries noodles at a street food stall in George Town on the island of Penang, Malaysia, November 10, 2017. (AP Photo/ Adam Schreck)

53. A mounted police officer rides past a sculpture by Fernando Botero, in Medellin, Colombia, January 26, 2002. (AP Photo/Luis Benavides)

54. Couples dance tango during a public milonga and tango dance show in Avenida de Mayo, a central avenue in the city of Buenos Aires, December 6, 2008. (AP Photo/Natacha Pisarenko)

55. Women look for a spot to wash clothes at the Atitlan Lake, in Santiago Atitlan, Guatemala, September 10, 2011. (AP Photo/ Rodrigo Abd)

56. A visitor takes pictures during a tour of Romanian communist dictator Nicolae Ceausescu's former family home, dubbed the Palace of Spring in Bucharest, Romania, June 11, 2016. (AP Photo/ Vadim Ghirda)

57. A young tourist looks at a model representing the day the Berlin Wall fell at Miniatur Wunderland, a vast exhibition of hand-made dioramas in Hamburg, northern Germany, October 7, 2016. (AP Photo/Frank Jordans)

58. General view of the norman Cathedral of Monreale in Sicily, May 25, 2014. (Photo: Rolf aid/picture-alliance/dpa/AP Images)

59. View of the Ponte Vecchio bridgel, in Florence, May 11, 2015. (AP Photo/Andrew Medichini)

60. People gather at Lisbon's Comercio square to watch the sun set, February 5, 2016. (AP Photo/Armando Franca)

61. Replicas of boats used to transport Port Wine are seen in Douro river with downtown Porto behind in Vila Nova de Gaia, Portugal, July 7, 2011. (AP Photo/Paulo Duarte)

62. A Barbary macaque as it pauses, lower right, with the Rock of Gibraltar looming in the background on in Gibraltar, May 12, 2016. (AP Photo/Brian Witte)

63. Express boat, ships, port, La Savina, Formentera, Pityuses, Balearic Islands, Spain, Europe. (Photo: Sergi Reboredo/picture-alliance/ dpa/AP Images)

64. A woman touches the toe of the bronze statue of Scottish philosopher David Hume in Edinburgh, Scotland, February 6, 2007. (AP Photo/Martin Cleaver)

65. The Yoho River flows through Yoho National Park in Canada's stretch of the Rocky Mountains, straddling the border of British Columbia and Alberta, July 6, 2017. (AP Photo/Adam Kealoha Causey)

66. People looking at Lahaina's banyan tree, rising 60 feet and covering nearly an acre in Lahaina, Maui, Hawaii, November 19, 2016. (AP Photo/John Marshall)

67. The Seattle Seahawks "12" flag flutters atop the Space Needle and in view of downtown Seattle and Mount Rainier beyond after being raised minutes earlier atop the iconic structure, January 13, 2017. (AP Photo/Elaine Thompson)
68. A cyclist pedals up an incline, past several saguaros, in the South Mountain Park and Preserve in Phoenix, October 28, 2010. (AP Photo/Ross D. Franklin)
69. The Sunrise Amphitheater on Flagstaff Mountain in Boulder, Colo., May 13, 2017. (AP Photo/Beth J. Harpaz)
70. A visitor wearing a cowboy hat looks out onto Dealey Plaza from the Sixth Floor Museum located in the former Texas School Book Depository building in Dallas, January 25, 2013. (AP Photo/LM Otero)
71. An oarsman and sight-seeing boat floating the impounded Colorado River as bats emerge from the Congress Ave. bridge in Austin, Texas, August 11, 2009. (AP Photo/Harry Cabluck)
72. The Alp and Dell cheese store in Monroe, Wis., Sept. 25, 2016. (AP Photo/Beth J. Harpaz)
73. The exterior of the Motown Museum in Detroit, December 2, 2014. (AP Photo/Beth J. Harpaz)
74. An exhibit at the Kurt Vonnegut Museum and Library in Indianapolis displaying Kurt Vonnegut's typewriter, April 21, 2016. (AP Photo/Beth J. Harpaz)
75. A colorful mural in the Hill District of Pittsburgh honoring play-wright August Wilson and his work, February 17, 2017. (AP Photo/Beth J. Harpaz)
76. Tourist visit a statue from the movie character Rocky Balboa out-side the Philadelphia Museum of Art in Philadelphia, November 21, 2016. (AP Photo/Matt Rourke)
77. Lauren Craig, who calls herself the "glambassador" of Newark, N.J., pointing to a "Newark Vs Everybody" T-shirt on display at the Off the Hanger and ANE boutique on Linden Street in Newark, June 16, 2017. (AP Photo/Beth J. Harpaz)
78. World Trade One is seen through trees near the south pool of the 9/11 Memorial in downtown Manhattan, September 25, 2015. (AP Photo/John Minchillo)

79. The "Teammates" statue of Ted Williams, Johnny Pesky, Bobby Doerr and Dom DiMaggio circa 1946, appears at the entrance to Gate B at Fenway Park in Boston, April 13, 2012. (AP Photo/ Elise Amendola)
80. A group paddles on a whitewater rafting trip on the Kennebec River in The Forks, Maine, August 23, 2006. (AP Photo/Beth J. Harpaz)
81. Travelers walk to their gates at O'Hare International Airport in Chicago, November 29, 2015. (AP Photo/Nam Y. Huh)
82. Passengers make their way through a TSA Precheck security line inside Terminal 2 of San Francisco International Airport in San Francisco, June 29, 2016. (AP Photo/Eric Risberg)
83. Credit cards are displayed in Haverhill, Mass, June 15, 2017. (AP Photo/Elise Amendola)
84. A traveler walks past a sign advertising a Delta Air Lines credit card at Seattle-Tacoma International Airport in SeaTac, Wash., March 24, 2015. (AP Photo/Elaine Thompson)
85. A panel of cruise experts gathered on the Sojourn in a forum moderated by Beth J. Harpaz of The Associated Press, January 4, 2018.
86. Eva Santiago, a crew member on Seabourn Sojourn, on a tour of the ship in the port of Miami, January 4, 2018. (AP Photo/Beth J. Harpaz)
87. Cruise ships are docked at Port Miami, in Miami, August 21, 2017. (AP Photo/Lynne Sladky)

Be sure to check out "Get Outta Here!"
AP's travel podcast available on Apple Podcasts.

www.appodcasts.com

37105686R00221

Made in the USA
Middletown, DE
22 February 2019